The English-Italian Lexical Converter

Library of Congress Cataloging-in-Publication Data

Russo, Antonio, 1925-
  The English-Italian Lexical Converter : an easy way to learn Italian vocabulary /
Antonio Russo.
    p.cm.
  Includes bibliographical references and index.
  ISBN 1881901-37-8 (pbk. ; al. paper)
    1. Italian language—Vocabulary. 2. Italian language—Suffixes and prefixes. 3. English language—Suffixes and prefixes. 4. Latin language—Suffices and prefixes. 5. Contrastive linguistics. I. Title.
PC1445.R87 2003
458.2'421—dc21

                                            2002155391

Printed and Bound in Canada

Acknowledgments

I would like to express my most appreciation and gratitude to the following:
Dr. Robert Di Pietro - University of Delaware;
Dr. Filippo Perfetti - St. John's University;
Dr. Herman Haller - CUNY - City University of New York - Queens College;
Dr. Gaetano Cipolla - St. John's University;
Prof. Furio Colombo - Istituto Italiano di Cultura;
Prof. Gianclaudio Macchiarella - Istituto Italiano di Cultura;
Dr. Paul J. Patanè - Fordham University, New York; and
Prof. Florence Russo–Cipolla - St. John's University, New York.

For information and for orders, write to Legas at the following addresses:

P.O.Box 149	3 Wood Aster Bay	2908 Dufferin Ave
Mineola, New York	Ottawa, Ontario	Toronto, Ontario
11501, USA	K2R 1D3 Canada	M6B 3S8 Canada
E-mail cipolla@stjohns.edu		

Antonio Russo

The English-Italian
Lexical Converter

An Easy Way to Learn Italian Vocabulary

LEGAS

To the memory
of
my dear son

PHILIP

Table of Contents

Premise 9

Introduction........ 15

Abbreviations..... 19

Bibliography....... 20

Chapter I
A Comparative Table of Italian and English Prefixes. 21
Exercises 24

Chapter II
Root Assimilation Converter 27

Chapter III
Introduction........ 63
Italian Verb Conjugations with Regular Desinences 64
Verb Converter Index 72
Verb Converter... 75
Exercises 91

Chapter IV
Desinence Index. 94
Meaning of Desinences: Nouns and Adjectives......... 99
English-Italian Converter in Desinence Order.......... 103
Exercises 204

Chapter V
Adverb Converter in Desinence Order......... 207
Exercises 221

Appendices
Appendix A: Latin Words and Phrases 223
Appendix B: Rome: Cradle of Italian 225
Appendix C: Loans 231
Appendic D: Greek Borrowings 235
Appendix E: Latin Borrowings....... 241

Premise

The importance of learning vocabulary is often overlooked by the foreign language teacher, who encourages his students to master many verb forms, while putting little emphasis on the need to learn vocabulary.

One of the greatest barriers to mastering a foreign language is the structural dissimilarity between the mother tongue and the second language. This text aids the student to overcome this barrier. Students do not need to memorize endless lists of words in order to master vocabulary.

A more economical and practical approach is proposed for learning, namely the mastery of the lexical bonds that unite English to Italian by virtue of their common ties to Latin and by learning a few rules that govern the formation of words. This dictionary contains well over 30,000 English and Italian words, easily inter-translatable by means of simple lexical principles, as will be further illustrated.

The close relationship between English and Italian arises from their common root, namely and respectively their direct "borrowing" and their "derivation" from Latin. Some words borrowed from Greek are also listed. The word lists contained in this book will serve to illustrate the common ties both languages have with the model language, Latin. As students master assimilation rules, they will marvel at how simple it is to come up with Italian equivalents for English vocabulary items. The table below illustrates the common link between Latin, English and Italian:

Latin:	English:	Italian:
cre-are	cre-ate	cre-are
cre-atio	cre-ation	cre-azione
creat-ura	creat-ure	creat-ura
creativi-tas	creativi-ty	creativi-tà
creat-or	creat-or	creat-ore

from which stemmed:

creat-ive	creat-ivo	
creative-ly	creativ-amente	
creation-ism	creazion-ismo	
creation-ist	creazion-ista	

and:

procreate (procreare); procreation (procreazione); procreative (procreativo), recreate (ricreare); recreation (ricreazione); recreative (ricreativo) etc.

Over the centuries a process of Latin assimilation took place and, in many cases, English remained more faithful to Latin than Italian:
Note how Latin and English share the same root in the following examples:

LATIN:	ENGLISH:	ITALIAN:
inflex-io	inflex-ion	infless-ione
autumn-alis	autumn-al	autunn-ale
constr-uctio	constr-uction	costr-uzione

singul-aris	singul-ar	singol-are
facul-tas	facul-ty	facol-tà

Following are some examples of the phonological evolution of stressed vowels from Latin to Italian:

popolu > popolo; hora > ora ; cruce > croce;
flore > fiore; scriptu > scritto; fructu > frutto

Learning a foreign language is not an easy enterprise and it is not our intention to offer a simplistic approach to it. Memorization and study of grammatical rules and idiomatic expressions will still be required, but this volume can make learning vocabulary a lot easier by mastering a relatively few patterns of endings that have widespread application in Italian.

Words are composed of three elements that contribute to give them their meanings: a prefix, a root and a suffix or desinence. A prefix is a morpheme placed before a lexical unit (such as a root, word, another prefix etc.) to alter its meaning. A root is part of a word, consisting of one or more morphemes to which inflectional endings are added. And a suffix is a morpheme added to a root or stem primarily to indicate the function of a word. (A suffix can also indicate the gender and number of a noun, the tense of a verb etc.)

Considering that Latin is a source for a great number of English words and an even greater number of Italian words, there are literally thousands of words in the two languages that are nearly identical except for minor differences that concern the three components of a word: the prefix, the root and the suffix. This book, therefore, proposes to make a comparative study of Italian and English prefixes with the aim of providing students with the means of increasing their vocabulary exponentially. For example, knowing that the Italian prefix "in" is equivalent to putting "not" before a word and it is the same in English, can make a student produce a large number of words based on the pattern:

sane	insane	sano	insano
credible	incredible	credibile	incredibile
active	inactive	attivo	inattivo
adequate	inadequate	adeguato	inadeguato

Knowing that "in" used before the consonant "p" causes the "n" to become an "m" increases further the students' ability to produce words without knowing Italian. Thus he will know that

prudence	imprudence	prudenza	imprudenza
possible	impossible	possibile	impossibile
partial	impartial	parziale	imparziale
patient	impatient	paziente	impaziente

A similar pattern can be observed when "in" precedes the consonant "r" or "l" in which the "n" is replaced by doubling the following consonant as in

logical	illogical	logico	illogico
licit	illicit	lecito	illecito
responsible	irresponsible	responsabile	irresponsabile
rational	irrational	razionale	irrazionale

As we can see, the Italian words are very close to the English words, except for a few differences that deal with changes in the root of the word or in their ending. Owing to the fact that Latin has provided such a multitude of words to Italian and English, a substantial part of this book will be devoted to the study of the process of assimilation, that is, the process through which a Latin word evolved into English and Italian. The English adjective "rational" given above derives from the Latin "ratio," meaning reason. While the English word differs in pronunciation from the Latin "tz" sound, it retains the spelling of the word. Italian changed the spelling of the sound "tz" to a "z" which is much closer to the original Latin. Nevertheless, knowing that the "tio" combination in Latin remains practically the same in English and is written in Italian with a "z" will help students to master a great number of words sharing the root. A few examples will suffice:

abdication	abdicazione
secretion	secrezione
position	posizione
motion	mozione
restitution	restituzione
invention	invenzione
intention	intenzione
function	funzione
attention	attenzione
portion	porzione

The number of such changes is finite and therefore easily assimilated. Another example will suffice. Knowing that the Latin sound "ct" is retained in English but changes in Italian into a double "t" can help students increase their command of vocabulary.

ACT	ATT
activate, v.	attivare
active	attivo
pact	patto
tact	tatto
attracted	attratto
bacterial	batterico
distractly	distrattamente

In the section entitled Root Assimilation we have identified the most important changes that occur, listing thousand of words.

The third component of words may be seen by looking at the different endings of the Italian words in the table above. The endings or desinences are more important in Italian than they are in English. The endings provide a lot of information about the word that is vital to understanding meanings. By looking at the endings of the five words above we can tell, for example, that "attivare" is a verb of the first conjugation in the infinitive mood, meaning to "activate" The ending of "attivo" tells us that it is a masculine adjective (it could also be the first person of "attivare" in the present tense); the "o" of "patto" tells us that it is a masculine noun; as is "tatto"; the ending of "attratto" tells us that it is the past participle of the verb "attrarre" to attract; the ending of "batterico" tells us that is a masculine adjective and the "mente" of "distrattamente" tells us that it is an adverb.

Again a very important component of this volume is devoted to the study of desinences. We begin with a comparative study of noun and adjective endings and show the extreme likeness between them. Thus, if a student realizes that most English adjectives that end in "able" will form their Italian counterpart in "abile" his confidence will increase by leaps and bounds and he will be better able to coin words relying on his English knowledge: Ask him to give you the equivalent of

accusable and he will say	accusabile
adaptable* and he will say	adattabile
admirable* and he will say	ammirabile
adorable and he will say	adorabile
adoptable* and he will say	adottabile
affable and he will say	affabile
alienable and he will say	alienabile
habitable* and he will say	abitabile
honorable* and he will say	onorabile

The student will have learned in the meantime that the "pt" of "adaptable" has changed into the Italian "tt", that the "dm" of "admirable" has become "mm" and that the "h" of "habitable and "honorable" has been dropped in Italian completely. Needless to say all the English words are closer in spelling to the Latin forms from which they are derived than the Italian. We have added the dot under the vowel that receives the stress in Italian to help student pronounce correctly.

Learning the verb system represents a major undertaking, especially in Italian, which requires students to learn 48 different endings for the Indicative Mood alone against the five usually required in English. As we know, English manages to form all its tenses with a maximum of five changes to the root of the verb as in "speak, speaks, speaking, spoke, spoken" and combining these forms with have, has, will, shall, would, and should. Italian has six different endings for every tense, 48 ending for the eight tenses of the Indicative. In this text, we offer the paradigms for the three major conjugations as a reference for the students. The second and most important aspect of our text identifies the root and desinence assimilation as well. Students will quickly learn to recognize the patterns that govern verb formation from their knowledge of English. They will see that if a verb ends in "ate" in English, the Italian correspondent verb, with only a few exceptions, will end in "are," as in activate= *attivare*, generate =*generare*, etc...Verbs that end in "fy" in English will change to "ficare" in Italian as in "modify", *modificare*, rectify, *rettificare*, justify, *giustificare*. The students will also have learned that the "ju" phoneme in Italian is written "giu" in the Assimilation Converter.

The last section of the text deals with the formation of adverbs with the word "mente" which closely resembles the formation of "ly" adverbs in English.

We have designed some exercises for students that will help them master the principles presented in the different sections. In addition we have added several appendices that we think will be of invaluable help to students:

Appendix A: LATIN WORDS AND PRASES PHRASES that are commonly used in Italian and in English
Appendix B: ROME, CRADLE OF LATIN.
Appendix C: LOAN WORDS;
Appendix D: GREEK BORROWINGS.
Appendix E: ENGLISH BORROWINGS FROM LATIN.

In conclusion, we believe this book will provide Italian language students a faster and more comprehensive view of Italian vocabulary than regular grammars. It is not meant to take the place of grammars, but used as a supplement and reference work, it can be invaluable in the study of Italian. Although this text can be used by beginning students in conjunction with a traditional grammar, it is intended for students who already possess a basic understanding of the grammatical structure of Italian. Ideally those who have had one or two semesters of work in Italian would use this book to better results.

Following are some of the benefits of using this text:

• It will render continuous dictionary consultation unnecessary through mastery of a relatively few rules of assimilation;
• it will expand students' Italian vocabulary with little effort;
• it will make students realize and appreciate the importance of Latin;
• it will make students aware of the inherent lexical bond between English and Italian through their connections to Latin;
• it will encourage those students who are reluctant to register for Italian because they consider it difficult to feel more confident in doing so;
• it will build upon the solid foundation of their native language. Students quickly realize that they already have a vast knowledge of Italian by applying a few simple rules to convert from English and
• it will be very useful to graduate students who need a reading knowledge of Italian for their research, as well as for undergraduates who are taking regular college courses in intermediate levels of the language.

Conventions used in this text

Although students should already know the basic rules of pronunciation and stress, they may still encounter some difficulty in placing the stress on the proper syllable, especially when the words are composed of many syllables. The students will notice, in fact, that Latin derivation in general involves words longer than two syllables. Thus, to help the students pronounce the words correctly, we have placed a dot under the vowel to be stressed. These dots are intended as an aid to the student, but they are not written in normal usage.

As we know, most Italian words are pronounced with a stress on the second-to-last syllable as in *amore, padrone, oggetto*. In words composed of two syllables the stress will fall of the first syllable, unless there is a written accent on the last vowel, such as in "città". Since the stress falls automatically on the first syllable, we have not put a dot under two syllable words such as *mano* (hand), *vita* (life), *padre* (father), *terra* (earth), *libro* (book).

In Italian, stress on the final syllable *is written with an accent on the final vowel.* All words that end with an accented vowel will have the stress on the final vowel as in the following words:

serenità (serenity), *unità* (unity), *tassì* (taxicab), *gioventù* (youth).

In all other cases, the stress will be indicated by a dot under the vowel to be stressed as in the following:

opera (opera), *associazione* (association), *libero* (free), *psicologo* (psychologist).

INTRODUCTION

Knowledge of the linguistic relationship between Latin and its Romance derivatives is valuable and useful to the student of Romance languages. We shall briefly demonstrate the position of Latin with respect to the Romance and English languages.

Although the Romans never imposed their language on the people they conquered, Latin inevitably became the official means of communication among the various provinces and Rome, the center of the empire. Even after the Roman Empire collapsed in the fifth century AD, Latin continued to be the language of choice for official communications. At the same time, in each region of Europe the people spoke Latin with local accents and inflections even in the heyday of Roman domination. Slowly the languages underwent a process of change in which the ancient Latin had lost many of its distinguishing features. In time, they grew into different languages altogether. Thus, the so-called Romance languages (Italian, French, Spanish, Romanian and Portuguese, as well as a number of minor ones) emerged and came to take the place of Latin. While the people continued to use their new idioms for their spoken communication and refine them into full-fledged tools of literary expression, Latin did not disappear and remained, especially in Italy, an important language that played a notable role in law, literature and education. The close relationship between Latin and the languages that emerged from it becomes immediately evident when we examine some Latin words and see the changes that the same word underwent as it evolved into the various Romance languages. By the way, "Romance" has nothing to do with romance. It's simply another word for Roman. Let's look at the following table:

PARENT	ROMANCE		COGNATES	BORROWED	ENGLISH
LATIN	ITALIAN	FRENCH	SPANISH		
pacem	pace	paix	paz	-pacific	peace
tempus	tempo	temps	tiempo	-temporal	time
bene	bene	bien	bien	-benefic	well
amicus	amico	ami	amigo	-amicable	friend
manus	mano	main	mano	-manually	hand
caelum	cielo	ciel	cielo	-celestial	sky
legere	leggere	lire	leer	-legible	read, v.

Originally English, which stems mainly from Anglo-Saxon, borrowed a few words from Latin, primarily during the period of the Christianization of England (VII century). After 1066 A.D. Norman French became the language of the elite, while Anglo-Saxon was reduced to a mere "koiné". Eventually, the Anglo-Saxon language reasserted itself, but hundreds of words were borrowed again from French before English became a literary language. During the XIII and XIV centuries, more borrowing took place and Middle English was born. The borrowing trend intensified in a period spanning the Renaissance era and the XVII century and, along with the Latin-derived French words, Greek, and more importantly Latin, with all its classical and literary prestige, became the source from which to borrow more and more words. Thereafter to the present, Latin has continued to enrich the English language, giving it many features of a Romance language.

The process of evolution of Latin into Italian and into the other Romance languages was slow and involved both the learned Latin of the classical writers such as Cicero and Quintilian and the spoken language of the people. Both found a place in the new languages. A few examples will suffice to demonstrate how the new languages were enriched by both strata of Latin: the literary and the spoken. The word for horse in Italian is "cavallo". In literary Latin the word for horse was "equus" and "caballus" was the word used by the common people. Thus, in Italian we have "cavallo" derived from the spoken language and "equestre," "equitazione" "equino" from the learned "equus". A similar process can be observed in English, as the following tables demonstrate. While the Latin root is not generally used in common speech, it remains at a different level. For example, the Latin *radix*, which became the Italian *radice* and the English root, comes to be more easily recognized in such words as "radical" and "eradicate". Consider the following roots that have spawned many new words:

LATIN: ITALIAN: ENGLISH:

CENTUM   **CENTO**   **HUNDRED**
centenary (centenąrio); centigrade (centįgrade); centipede (centopiędi); centennial (centennąle); centigram/me (centigrąmmo); etc

BENE   **BENE**   **WELL**
beneficent (benęfico); benefactor (benefattǫre); beneficence (beneficęnza); benediction (benedizịǫne) etc.

FRATER   **FRATELLO**   **BROTHER**
fraternity (fraternità); fraternal (fratęrno); fratricide (fratricịdio) etc.

DULCIS   **DOLCE**   **SWEET**
dulcify (dolcificąre); dulcification (dolcificazịǫne); dulcet (dolce, gradęvole);

PISCIS   **PESCE**   **FISH**
pisciculture (piscicoltųra); pisciform (piscifǫrme); piscatorial (piscatǫrio) etc.

Consider now how English makes use of the Anglo-saxon root for a word and then borrows the Latin root to form adjectives:

PARENT LATIN	COGNATE ITALIAN	BORROWED	ENGLISH
carnem	carnąle	carnal	meat
finis	finąle	final	end
pectus	pettorąle	pectoral	chest
annum	annuąle	annual	year
ovum	ovąle	oval	egg
luna	lunąre	moon	lunar

auxilium	ausiliario	auxiliary	help
pacem	pacifico	pacific	peace
sonus	sonico	sonic	sound
lingua	linguista	linguist	tongue
dens, tis	dentista	dentist	tooth
pater	paterno	paternal	father
frater	fraterno	fraternal	brother

The following examples will show how the Latin root has remained intact in both English and Italian. The only changes involve the desinences:

LATIN	ENGLISH	ITALIAN
probabilis	probable	probabile
stabilis	stable	stabile
credibilis	credible	credibile
terribilis	terrible	terribile
naturalis	natural	naturale
personalis	personal	personale
pactum	pact	patto
factum	fact	fatto
singularis	singular	singolare
popularis	popular	popolare
matricidium	matricide	matricidio
homicidium	homicide	omicidio
perfectus	perfect	perfetto
architectus	architect	architetto
triplex	triplex	triplice
index	index	indice
metaphysica	metaphysics	metafisica
mathematica	mathematics	matematica
confusio, nis	confusion	confusione
admissio, nis	admission	ammissione
iniquitas	iniquity	iniquità
dignitas	dignity	dignità
agricultura	agriculture	agricoltura
architectura	architecture	architettura
fetus	fetus	feto
colossus	colossus	colosso
dominare, v.	dominate	dominare
interrogare, v.	interrogate	interrogare

Even from the few examples we have given above, it is obvious that knowledge of Latin helps our understanding of English. It also follows that a knowledge of English will help in understanding Italian for they both owe much of their structure directly to Latin or indirectly through French or other Romance Languages. This book will capitalize on these similarities, as it makes the point that learning Italian, for people who already know English, is a battle half won.

ABBREVIATIONS

adj.	adjective	m.	masculine
adv.	adverb	math.	mathematics
anat.	anatomy	meas.	measure
amer.	American	med.	medicine
archit.	architecture	meteorol.	meteorology
arith.	arithmetic	mil.	military
astron.	astronomy	mus.	music
biol.	biology	n.	noun
bot.	botany	p.p.	past participle
chem.	chemistry	paint.	painting
comm.	commercial	pathol.	pathology
eccl.	ecclesiastic	phil.	philosophy
electr.	electricity	phot.	photography
f.	feminine	phys.	physics
fam.	familiar	pl.	plural
fig.	figurative	pol.	politics
fr.	French	pop.	popular
G.B.	Great Britain	pref.	prefix
geol.	geology	prep.	preposition
geom.	geometry	rel.	religion
gramm.	grammar	sing.	singular
Gr.	Greek	theat.	theater
Ital.	Italian	theol.	theology
Lat.	Latin	v.	verb
		zool.	zoology

BIBLIOGRAPHY

Frederick B. Agard and Robert J. Di Pietro, *The Grammatical Structures of English and Italian*, Chicago and London: the University of Chicago Press, 1965

Rudolph C. Bambas, *The English Language - Its Origin & History*, Norman: University of Oklahoma Press, 1980.

Chambers's *Etymological English Dictionary*, Edited by A. M. MacDonald, B. A. (Oxon) New Edition, Patterson, New Jersey: Littlefield, Adams & Co., 1964,

Marcello Durante, *Dal latino all'italiano moderno: Saggio di storia linguistica e culturale*, Bologna: Zanichelli, 1985

W.Elcock, *The Romance Languages*, London: Farber & Farber, 1960

Lancelot Hobgen, *The Mother Tongue*, New York: W. W. Norton & Company Inc. 1964

Giulio C.Lepschy, *A Survey Of Structural Linguistics*, London: Andre Deutsch, Faber, 1970.

Bruno Migliorini, Ignazio Baldelli, *Breve storia della lingua italiana*, Firenze: Sansoni Editore, Nuova S.p.a. 1985.

Leonard R. Palmer, *Descriptive and Comparative Linguistics*: A Critical Introduction, Crane, New York: Russak & Company, Inc. 1972.

Eric Partridge, *Origins: A Short Etymological Dictionary of Modern English*, New York: Greenwich house, Distributed by Crown Publishers, Inc 1983.

Mario Pei, *The Story of Language*, J. B. Lippincott Company, Philadelphia & New York, 1965.

-------. *The Families of Words*, New York: Harper & Brothers, 1962

-------. *The Story of Latin and the Romance Languages*, New York: Harper & Row, Publishers, 1976.

Donald M. Ayers, *English Words from Latin and Greek Elements*, The University of Arizona Press, 1985.

Laurence Urdang, *Suffixes and Other Word-Final Elements of English*, Old Lyme, CT: Verbatim Books, 1998.

Hazon Garzanti, *Il nuovo dizionario inglese-italiano italiano inglese*, Firenze: Garzanti Editore, Terza edizione, 1991.

The Random House Dictionary of the English Language - College edition- Laurence Urdang Editor in chief, New York: Random House, 1968.

Il Nuovo Zingarelli, Vocabolario della lingua italiana di Nicola Zingarelli - Undicesima edizione, Bologna: Zanichelli, 1983

Campanini e Carboni, *Dizionario della lingua latina,* Italiano-Latino-Latino-Italiano.

Chapter I
A Comparative Table of Italian and English Prefixes

A comparative study of prefixes can provide students with a tool that would increase their knowledge of vocabulary exponentially. Prefixes constitute an extremely valuable aid to vocabulary building. English and Italian have borrowed numerous prefixes from Latin and Greek. In most cases the prefixes have become such an integral part of a word that we no longer realize their presence. For example, the English verbs "admonish" "adopt" and "abstain" derive from the Latin prefix "ad" for the first two and "ab" for the third, plus the verb "monere" "optare" and "tenere" respectively. We are not going to treat these prefixes in this section, because they have become an integral part of words. These prefixes, however, constitute an important element that is shared by the Romance languages and English. As such they can provide students with easy reference marks as they study vocabulary. The section on Root Conversion will make this abundantly clear for it will show the results of the process of assimilation by which such words as "admonere, adoptare and abstenere" became in Italian "ammonire, adottare and astenere" respectively.

The table in the following pages contains a list of the most common prefixes used in English and Italian with their original meanings and an example of a word formed with them. Familiarize yourself with these prefixes and to test your knowledge do the exercise following the table.

Abbreviations:
Gr. = Greek;
Lat. = Latin;
bc = before consonant;
bv = before vowel;
s. a. = See also.

Italian and English Prefixes

MEANING

LATIN GREEK	ENGLISH	ITALIAN	ENGLISH	ENGLISH	ITALIAN
Gr.	a (an bv)	senza, mancanza	without, not	anarchy	anarchia
Gr.	a (bc)	senza, mancanza	without, not	apathy	apatia
Lat.	a-, ad-	verso, direzione	toward	to admit	ammettere
Lat.	ante	prima	before	antecedent	antecedente
Lat.	ante [anti]	prima	before	antemeridian	antimeridiano
Gr.	anti-	contro	against	antibiotic	antibiotico
Gr.	arch- [arc]	primo	first, chief	archangel	arcangelo
Gr.	arch- [arc]	primo	first, chief	archduke	arciduca
Lat.	bi- (s.a. du)	due	two	bilingual	bilingue
Gr.	bios	vita	life	biography	biografia
Lat.	circum [circon]	intorno	around	circumference	circonferenza
Lat.	co-, con-, com-	con, comunanza	with	conjugal	coniugale
Lat.	contra	contro	against	contradiction	contraddizione
Lat.Gr.	du	due	two	duet	duetto
Lat.	ex [es] and e 1	fuori	out of, out	expectorate, v.	espettorare
Lat.	ex [es] and e 2	fuori	out of, out	emit, v.	emettere
Lat.	il		[See "IN"]		
Lat.	im		[See "IN"]		
Lat.	in "im"	dentro	into	imprisoned	imprigionato
Lat.	in "in"	in	in	induce	indurre
Lat.	in "ir"		on	irradiation	irradiazione
Lat.	in (negative): "il"	no	not	illegal	illegale
Lat.	in (negative): "im"			impossible	impossibile
Lat.	in (negative): "in"			incredible	incredibile
Lat.	in (negative): "ir"			irresponsible	irresponsabile
Lat.	inter	tra, fra	between	intercontinental	intercontinentale
Lat.	intra-, intro-	dentro	within	intramuscular	intramuscolare

Lat.	intra-, intro-	dentro	within	introduction	introduzione
Gr.	mono (s.a.uni)	singolo	single	monocle	monocolo
Lat.	omnis [onni]	tutto	all	omnipotent	onnipotente
Gr.	ortho [orto] 1	corretto, esatto	straight, right	orthography	ortografia
Gr.	philo- [filo]	amante	lover	philology	filologia
Gr.	poly- [poli]	molti	much, many	polygamy	poligamia
Lat.	pre-	prima	before	premature	prematuro
Lat.	pro	avanti, fuori	forward	prolong	prolungare
Lat.	pro	prima	before	prolusion	prolusione
Lat.	pro	in favore di	in favor of	progerman	protedesco
Lat.	re- [ri]	ripetizione	again, back, anew	renovate	rinnovare
Lat.	rect-, recti- [retti]	retto	straight	rectitude	rettitudine
Lat.	retro-	indietro	backwards	retrograde	retrogrado
Lat.	semi-	metà	half	semicircle	semicerchio
Lat.	sub-	sotto, inferiorità	under; inferiority	subaqueous	subacqueo
Lat.	sub-	sotto, inferiorità	under; inferiority	submission	sottomissione
Lat.	super-	superiorità	superiority	superman	superuomo
Lat.	trans-, tran, tra-	di là, attraverso	across, through	transatlantic	transatlantico
Lat.Gr.	tri-	tre	three	triangle	triangolo
Lat.	ultra-	al di là da, più che	beyond, exceedingly	ultramodern	ultramoderno
Lat.	uni- (s.a.mono)	one	one	unification	unificazione
Lat.	uni- (s.a.mono)	one	one	uniform	uniforme
Lat.	vice-	in vece, sostituzione	instead of, deputy	vicepresident	vicepresidente
Gr.	ambi- (s.a. amphi-)	due, ambedue	two, on both sides	ambidextrous	ambidestro
Gr.	amphi- [anfi-] (s.a. ambi-)	due, ambedue	two, on both sides	amphibious	anfibio

The table above was meant as a guide. Students are encouraged to go over each of the prefixes presented and understand how using them can increase their mastery of Italian vocabulary. Let us look at the first prefix listed: "a," meaning "not," "without". The prefix is the same in Italian and can be used to produce numerous words. If it's used with a word beginning with a consonant, it remains "a" as in "amoral" "asexual" which in Italian would be "amorale," "asessuale", making allowances for root assimilation (i.e., sexual=sessuale). If the "a" is followed by a vowel an "n" is added to the prefix as in "anarchy" which in Italian is "anarchia". Do the following exercises.

EXERCISES

Exercise 1. Given the following pattern, "cominciare" (to begin), "ricominciare" (to begin again), use the prefix with the following verbs and translate them into English:

1. Formulare   _____   _____
2. Medicare   _____   _____
3. Ascoltare   _____   _____
4. Studiare   _____   _____
5. Scrivere   _____   _____
6. Leggere   _____   _____
7. Dare   _____   _____
8. Vedere   _____   _____
9. Annunciare   _____   _____
10. Pulire   _____   _____

Exercise 2. Given that the Latin prefix "dis" indicates negation, use it to change the meaning of the following words and translate them into English:

1. Abitato   _____   _____
2. Onesto   _____   _____
3. Piacere   _____   _____
4. Occupato   _____   _____
5. Ordine   _____   _____

Exercise 3. Given that the prefix "s" in Italian means the opposite of an action or an intensification of the same, formulate new words from the following and give the meaning in English:

1. Carico   _____   _____
2. Caricare   _____   _____
3. Tonato   _____   _____
4. Padroneggiare   _____   _____
5. Parlare   _____   _____

Exercise 4. Given that the prefix "in" in Italian is equivalent to "not," change the following words into their negative and give the English meanings: Remember: if the word begins with "m" "l" or "r" the "in" will become "im," "il," and "ir," respectively:

1. Capace _____ _____
2. Logico _____ _____
3. Mobile _____ _____
4. Ragionevole _____ _____
5. Razionale _____ _____
6. Abile _____ _____
7. Utile _____ _____
8. Possibile _____ _____
9. Plausibile _____ _____
10.Giusto _____ _____

Exercise 5. The prefix "con" indicates commonality, sharing. When the word begins with a "p," the "n" of "con" changes to "m." If the word begins with "l" the "n" becomes "l" too. Give the English meaning of the new word.

1. Giungere _____ _____
2. Piangere _____ _____
3. Laborare _____ _____
4. Prendere _____ _____
5. Fondere _____ _____

Exercise 6. The prefix "ante" or "anti," not to be confused with the Greek prefix "anti" meaning against, means before. Select those words that have the meaning of "before" and those that mean "against" and give their English meaning:

1. Antipasto _____ _____
2. Anticamera _____ _____
3.Anteporre_____ _____
4. Antiacido _____ _____
5. Antinucleare_____ _____
6. Antibiotico _____ _____
7. Antiguerra _____ _____
8. Anteguerra _____ _____
9. Antefatto _____ _____
10. Anticiclone_____ _____

Exercise 7. What prefix can you put before the following words? Choose the prefix from the following list. More than one prefix can be used with the same word. (pro, de, in, a, pos(t), con, su, ri, and sotto). Give the meaning of the words you just formed:

1. Porre _____ _____ _____ _____
2. Mettere _____ _____ _____ _____

3. Giungere   _____   _____   _____   _____
4. Trarre   _____   _____   _____   _____
5. Durre (ducere) _____   _____   _____   _____

Exercise 8. Having studied the meaning of the various prefixes, give the English meaning of the following: for example, "Antipasto" means "what comes before the meal."

1. Sopravvivere   _____
2. Preposto   _____
3. Inattivo   _____
4. Oltremontano   _____
5. Disabitato   _____
6. Contraddire   _____
7. Suddetto   _____
8. Antisociale   _____
9. Analfabeta   _____
10. Antidoto   _____

Chapter II
ROOT ASSIMILATION CONVERTER

In this section we list the most important graphic changes undergone by Latin through the process known as assimilation. As already stated, the assimilation had begun probably around the third century AD and such phonemes as "pt," "ps," "ct," and "cs," (x) had already become "tt," "ss," in the pronunciation of the popular speech of Rome. The process of assimilation continued for centuries until finally the changes became codified and generally accepted into Italian. It was a slow process, as can be seen by reading some of the early "vulgar" (from Latin "vulgus," the language of the people) texts from the tenth through the thirteenth centuries where these phonemes were still written in the Latin form. In the famous poem "Cantico delle creature" (Laude creaturarum) by Saint Francis, written in 1225, we can still read words like "benedictione," "tucte," "homo," and "spetialmente," instead of their modern Italian equivalent "benedizione," "tutte," "uomo," and "specialmente".

Assimilation occurs for a number of reasons, the most important of which is probably ease of pronunciation. It is much easier for an Italian to pronounce the word "ammirazione" than its Latin equivalent "admiratio".

As stated earlier, as far as root changes are concerned, English is often closer to Latin than Italian. English root assimilation did not occur in the same way as it did for Italian. For example: the Latin verb "obtinere" retains the "phoneme "bt" in English as "obtain" while in Italian it is changed into the "tt" of "ottenere". Another example: the Latin "abstinentia" retains the "bs" phoneme in "abstinence" while Italian changed it into "astinenza".

In this section, the "Root Assimilation Converter" will give you a complete listing of the graphic changes you need to know to convert English vocabulary into Italian. By learning a relatively limited number of rules that govern the conversion you will be able to increase your knowledge of Italian exponentially, for knowing, for example, that the English phoneme "dj" as in the verb "adjust" is written in Italian as "gg" as in "aggiustare" you will have at your disposal dozens of words that make use of the phoneme such as "adjective, adjourn, adjustment". Once you learn the few changes that govern root assimilation, you can test your ability to convert English into Italian by checking the thousands of words that can be formed through the rules of conversion in the section.

Following are the most important graphic changes due to the process of assimilation:

ab+s+consonant (abs)	= as +consonant	abstinence, astinenza
ab+s+vowel(abs) = ass +vowel		absent, assente
ob+s+consonant (obs)	= os +consonant	obstacle, ostacolo
ob+s+vowel (obs)	= oss +vowel	obsession, ossessione
ad+m (adm)	= amm	admiration, ammirazione
ad+v+e/o (adv)	– avv +e/o	adversity, avversità
		advocacy, avvocatura
ct + a,e,o,u (ct)	= tt +a, e, i, o,u	benefactor, benefattore
cti + consonant (cti)	= tti + consonant	reactivate, riattivare
but:		
cti + c	= tic	practical, pratico
	action, aption, ation etc. =	azione
ex-	= es	extension, estensione
		express, espresso
		excursion, escursione
ex + ce = ecce		excellent, eccellente

Exceptions:
ex, invariable:
a) meaning previous (He was the ex president); b) meaning "extra"

h	= usually deleted	honor, onore, honesty, onestà
		theology, teologia
j	= gi	justice, giustizia, jury, giuria
mp(+t)	= nt	temptation, tentazione
ns+consonant	= s +consonant	constitution, costituzione
	("n" is dropped)	inspector, ispettore
		instructor, istruttore
Some exceptions:		to instill, instillare
		to install, installare

The following only when they mean inhalation:

inspiration = inspirazione

ph	= f	philosophy, filosofia
th	= t	athletics, atletica
y (not at end of the word)	= i	cynism, cinismo

Root Assimilation
** denote exceptions

ABAN	ABBAN
abandon, v.	abbandonare
abandoned	abbandonato
ABDO	ADDO
abdomen	addome
abdominal	addominale
ABHO	ABO
abhor, v.	aborrire, abborrire
abhorrence	aborrimento
ABJ	ABI
abject	abietto
abjection	abiezione
abjuration	abiura
abjure, v.	abiurare
ABNOR	ANOR
abnormal	anormale
abnormality	anormalità
abnormity	anormità
ABS(+vowel)	ASS(+vowel)
absence	assenza
absent	assente
absentee	assente
absenteeism	assenteismo
absolute	assoluto
absolutely	assolutamente
absolution	assoluzione
absolutism	assolutismo
absolutist	assolutista
absolutness	assolutezza
absolve, v.	assolvere
absonant	assonante
absorb, v.	assorbire
absorbent	assorbente
absorption	assorbimento
absurd	assurdo
absurdity	assurdità
ABST	AST
abstain, v.	astenere
abstain, v.	astenersi
abstention	astenzione
abstinence	astinenza
abstinent	astinente
abstract	astratto
abstract, v.	astrarre
abstraction	astrazione

abstractionism	astrazionismo
abstruse	astruso
ABUND	ABBOND
abundance	abbondanza
abundant	abbondante
ABY	ABI
abyss	abisso
abyssal	abissale
ACA	ACCA
academic	accademico
academical	accademico
academician	accademico
academy	accademia
ACOUST	ACUST
acoustic	acustico
acoustics	acustica
ACT	ATT
activate, v.	attivare
active	attivo
actively	attivamente
activism	attivismo
activist	attivista
activity	attività
actor	attore
actress	attrice
actual	attuale
actuality	attualità
actually	attualmente
actuate, v.	attuare
ADAPT	ADATT
adaptable	adattabile
adaptation	adattazione
ADHE	ADE
adherence	aderenza
adherent	aderente
adhesion	adesione
adhesive	adesivo
ADJE	AGGE
adjectival	aggettivale
adjective	aggettivo
Note:	
adjacent	adiacente
ADJOR	AGGIOR
adjourn, v.	aggiornare
adjournment	aggiornamento

ADJU	AGGIU	aesthete	estęta
adjudicate, v.	aggiudicąre	aesthetic	estętico
adjudication	aggiudicaziọne	aestheticism	esteticịsmo
adjunct	aggiụnto	aesthetics	estętica
adjunctive	aggiuntịvo	AFFIR	AFFER
adjust, v.	aggiustạre	affirmation	affermaziọne
ADM	AMM	affirmative	affermatịvo
administer, v.	amministrạre	AIR	ARIA
administration	amministraziọne	air	aria
administrate, v.	amministrạre	air-conditioner	ạria condizionạta
administrative	amministratịvo	AIR	AERO
administrator	amministratọre	airdrome	aerodrọmo
admirable	ammirạbile	airline	aerolịnea
admiral	ammirạglio	airplane	aeroplạno
admiralty	ammiraglịato	airport	aeropọrto
admiration	ammiraziọne	ALARM	ALLARM
admire, v.	ammirạre	alarm	allạrme
admissible	ammissịbile	alarm, v.	allarmạre
admission	ammissiọne	alarmism	allarmịsmo
admonition	ammoniziọne	alarmist	allarmịsta
admonitory	ammonitọrio	ALCOHOL	ALCOL
ADVA	AVA	alcoholic	alcọlico
advance, n.	avanzamẹnto	alcoholism	alcolịsmo
advance, v.	avanzạre	**alcohol	alcool
advancement	avạnzamẹnto	ALEXAN	ALESSAN
ADVE/O	AVVE/O	Alexander	Alessạndro
advent	avvẹnto	Alexandra	Alessạndra
adventure	avventụra	Alexandria	Alessạndria
adventure, v.	avventurạre	Alexandrian	alessandrịno
adventure, v.	avventurạrsi	alexandrine	alessandrịno
adventurer	avventuriẹro	ALKA	ALCA
adventuress	avventuriẹra	alkali	ạlcali
adventurous	avventurọso	alkaline	alcalịno
adverb	avvẹrbio	alkaloid	alcalọide
adversary	avversạrio	ALLI	ALLE
adversative	avversatịvo	alliance	alleạnza
adverse	avvẹrso	allied	alleạto
adversity	avversità	ALPHA	ALFA
advocacy	avvocatụra	alpha	alfa
AE	E	alphabet	alfabẹto
aedile	edịle	alphabetical	alfabẹtico
Aegean	Egẹo	AMBASSA	AMBASCIA
Aeneas	Enẹa	ambassador	ambasciatọre
Aeneid	Enẹide	ambassadress	ambasciatrịce
Aeolian	eọlio	AMNE	AMNI
Aeolus	Ẹolo	amnesty	amnistịa

amnesty, v.	amnistiare	anthropophagous	antropofago
AMOUNT	AMMONT	anthropophagy	antropofagia
amount, n.	ammontare	ANXI	ANSI
amount, v.	ammontare	anxiety	ansietà
AMPH	ANF	anxious	ansioso
amphibian	anfibio	APH	AF
amphibious	anfibio	aphasia	afasia
amphitheatre	anfiteatro	aphelion	afelio
amphitryon	anfitrione	aphides	afide
amphora	anfora	aphonia (med.)	afonia
ANACHRO	ANACRO	aphonic	afono
anachronism	anacronismo	aphony	afonia
anachronistic	anacronistico	aphorism	aforisma
ANAE	ANE	aphrodisiac	afrodisiaco
anaemia	anemia	Aphrodite	Afrodite
anaemic	anemico	APPEAR	APPAR
anaesthesia	anestesia	appear, v.	apparire
anaesthetic	anestetico	appearance	apparenza
anaesthetize, v.	anestetizzare	APPROXI	APPROSSI
anaesthetist	anestesista	approximation	approssimazione
ANCHO	ANCO	approximate	approssimativo
anchor	ancora	approximate, v.	approssimare
anchor, v.	ancorare	AQUA/E/I	ACQUA/E/I
anchorage	ancoraggio	aqua	acqua
ANECDO	ANEDDO	aquamarine	acquamarino
anecdotal	aneddotico	aquarium	acquario
anecdote	aneddoto	aqueduct	acquedotto
ANKY	ANCHI	aqueous	acqueo
ankylosis	anchilosi	aquiculture	acquicoltura
ankylostoma	anchilostoma	** aquiline	aquilino
ANNOUN	ANNUN	ARCHA	ARCA
announce, v.	annunciare	archaic	arcaico
announcement	annuncio	archaism	arcaismo
announcer	annunciatore	archaize, v.	arcaizzare
ANTHO	ANTO	archangel	arcangelo
anthologist	antologista	Note:	
anthology	antologia	arch	arco
ANTHRO	ANTRO	ARCHAEO	ARCHEO
anthropocentric	antropocentrico	archaeological	archeologico
anthropocentrism	antropocentrismo	archaeologist	archeologo
anthropoid	antropoide	archaeology	archeologia
anthropologist	antropologo	archaeozoic	archeozoico
anthropology	antropologia	ARCHI (foremost)	ARCI
anthropomorphic	antropomorfo	archibishop	arcivescovo
anthropomorphism	antropomorfismo	archibishopric	arcivescovado
anthropophagi	antropofagi	archideacon	arcidiacono

31

archiduchess	arciduchessa	ATH	AT
archiepiscopal	arcivescovile	atheism	ateismo
archipelago	arcipelago	atheist	ateo
archipriest	arciprete	atheistic	ateistico
ARCHI	ARCHI	atheistical	ateistico
architect	architetto	athenaeum	ateneo
architectonic	architettonico	athlete	atleta
architecture	architettura	athletic	atletico
architrave	architrave	athletics	atletica
archives	archivio	AUTH	AUT
archivist	archivista	authentic	autentico
archivolt	archivolto	authenticate, v.	autenticare
ARITHM	ARITM	authentication	autenticazione
arithmetic	aritmetica	authenticity	autenticità
arithmetical	aritmetico	author	autore
arithmetician	aritmetico	authoress	autrice
ARRHY	ARI	authoritarian	autoritario
arrhythmia	aritmia	authoritarianism	autoritarianismo
arrhythmic	aritmico	authority	autorità
ARTHR	ARTR	authorization	autorizzazione
arthritic	artritico	authorize, v.	autorizzare
arthritis	artrite	AXI	ASSI
arthrosis	artrosi	axial	assiale
ARTICUL	ARTICOL	axiom	assioma
articular	articolare	axiomatic	assiomatico
articulate, v.	articolare, v.	AZUR	AZZURR
articulation	articolazione	azure	azzurro
ASPH	ASF	azurine	azzurrino
asphalt	asfalto	BACCHA	BACCA
asphalt, v.	asfaltare	bacchanal	baccanale
asphodel	asfodelo	bacchanalia	baccanale
asphyxia	asfissia	bacchante	baccante
asphyxiate, v.	asfissiare	BACTE	BATTE
asphyxiation	asfissia	bacterial	batterico
ASSIGN	ASSEGNA	bactericide	battericida
assign, v.	assegnare	bacteriological	batteriologico
assignation	assegnazione	bacteriologist	batteriologo
assignee	assegnatario	bacteriology	batteriologia
ASTHM	ASM	bacterium	batterio
asthma	asma	BALLIST	BALIST
asthmatic	asmatico	ballistic	balistico
ASY	ASI	ballistics	balistica
asylum	asilo	ballistite	balistite
asymmetrical	asimmetrico	BALUST	BALAUST
asymmetry	asimmetria	baluster	balaustro
asynchronous	asincrono	balustrade	balaustrata

balustrated	balaustrato	calculation	calcolo
BANK	BANC	calculator	calcolatore
bank	banca	calculus	calcolo
bankable	bancabile	CALUMN	CALUNN
banker	banchiere	calumniate, v.	calunniare
bank-note	banconota	calumny	calunnia
BAPT	BATT	CAME	CAMME
baptism	battesimo	camel	cammello
baptismal	battesimale	cameo	cammeo
Baptist	Battista	CAMOUFLA	CAMUFFA
baptistery	battistero	camouflage	camuffamento
baptize, v.	battezzare	camouflage, v.	camuffare
BEAST	BEST	CAMPHOR	CANFOR
beast	bestia	camphor	canfora
beastly	bestialmente	camphorated	canforato
BLOC/K	BLOCC	camphoric	canforato
bloc	blocco	CAPT	CATT
block	blocco	captivity	cattività
block, v.	bloccare	capture	cattura
blockade	bloccata	capture, v.	catturare
blockade, v.	bloccare		
blond	biondo	CAPTA	CAPITA
blonde	bionda	captain	capitano
BOYCO	BOICO	captain,v	capitanare
boycott	boicottaggio	CARESS	CAREZZ
boycott, v.	boicottare	caress	carezza
BRILLIAN	BRILLAN	caress, v.	carezzare
brilliant	brillante	caressingly	carezzevolmente
brilliantine	brillantina	CARNIV	CARNEV
BUREAU	BURO	carnival	carnevale
bureaucracy	burocrazia	CAROUS	CAROS
bureaucrat	burocrate	carousel	carosello
bureaucratic	burocratico	CATHEDR	CATTEDR
CABIN	GABIN	cathedral	cattedrale
cabinet	gabinetto	CATHOL	CATTOL
CABLE	CABLO	catholic	cattolico
cablegram	cablogramma	Catholicism	cattolicesimo
CACOPH	CACOF	catholicity	cattolicità
cacophonous	cacofonico	CEREMO	CERIMO
CADA	CATA	ceremonial	cerimoniale
cadastral	catastale	ceremonious	cerimonioso
CAE	CE	ceremony	cerimonia
Caesar	Cesare	CHA	CA
caesura	cesura	chalcedony	calcedonio
CALCUL	CALCOL	chalcography	calcografia
calculate, v.	calcolare	chalice	calice

chamber	camera	chloroform	cloroformio
chameleon	camaleonte	chloroform, v.	cloroformizzare
champion	campione	chlorophyll	clorofilla
championship	campionato	CHO	CIO
chancellery	cancelleria	chocolate	cioccolato
chancellor	cancelliere	CHO	CO
chandelier	candeliere	cholera	colera
channel	canale	cholesterol	colesterolo
chaos	caos	choral	corale
chaotic	caotico	chord	corda
chaotically	caoticamente	choreographer	coreografo
chapel	cappella	choreography	coreografia
chaplain	cappellano	chorus	coro
chapter	capitolo	CHRO	CRO
character	carattere	chromatic	cromatico
characteristic	caratteristico	chromatography	cromatografia
characterize, v.	caratterizzare	chrome	cromo
charisma	carisma	chromium	cromo
charitable	caritatevole	chromosome	cromosoma
charity	carità	chronic	cronico
chast	casto	chronicle	cronaca
chastity	castità	chronicler	cronista
**charade	sciarada	chronograph	cronografo
chaperon	chaperon	chronological	cronologico
CHARL	CIARL	chronology	cronologia
charlatan	ciarlatano	chronometer	cronometro
charlatanism	ciarlataneria	CHRY	CRI
CHAUVIN	SCIOVIN	chrysalid	crisalide
chauvinism	sciovinismo	chrysanthemum	crisantemo
chauvinist	sciovinista	Chryst	Cristo
chauvinistic	sciovinistico	Chrystian	Cristiano
CHEMI	CHIMI	Chrystianity	Cristianità
chemical	chimico	CI	SI
chemist	chimico	cigar	sigaro
chemistry	chimica	cigarette	sigaretta
CHI	CI	CIRCUM	CIRCON
chicory	cicoria	circumcise, v.	circoncidere
China	Cina	circumcision	circoncisione
chinchilla	cincilla	circumference	circonferenza
Chinese	cinese	circumflex	circonflesso
**chimpanzee	scimpanzè	circumlocution	circonlocuzione
CHIR	CHIR	**circumnavigate, v.	circumnavigare
chirograph	chirografo	CIRCUMS	CIRCOS
chiromancy	chiromanzia	circumscribe	circoscrivere
CHLOR	CLOR	circumscription	circoscrizione
chlorine	cloro	circumspect	circospetto

circumstance	circostanza	**command	commando
circumstantial	circostanziale	COMMER	COMMER
CIT	CITT	commerce	commercio
citadel	cittadella	commercial	commerciale
citizen	cittadino	COMMUN	COMUN
citizenship	cittadinanza	communicable	comunicabile
city	città	communicate, v.	comunicare
CLAIRV	CHIAROV	communication	comunicazione
clairvoyant	chiaroveggente	communicative	comunicativo
clairvoynce	chiaroveggenza	communion	comunione
CLARIF	CHIARIF	communism	comunismo
clarification	chiarificazione	communist	comunista
clarify, v.	chiarire	community	comunità
COAST	COST	COMPREHEN	COMPREN
coast	costa	comprehend, v.	comprendere
coast, v.	costeggiare	comprehensible	comprensibile
coastal	costiero	comprehension	comprensione
COEX	COES	CONCUR	CONCORR
coexist, v.	coesistere	concur, v.	concorrere
coexistence	coesistenza	concurrent	concorrente
coexistent	coesistente	CONDEMN	CONDANN
COHE	COE	condemn, v.	condannare
coherence	coerenza	condemnation	condanna
coherent	coerente	CONFIRM	CONFERM
cohesion	coesione	confirm, v.	confermare
COLLAPS	COLLASS	confirmation	confermazione
collapse	collasso	CONJECT	CONGETT
collapse, v.	collassare	conjecture	congettura
COMBAT	COMBATT	conjecture, v.	congetturare
combat	combattimento	CONJOIN	CONGIUN
combat, v.	combattere	conjoin, v.	congiungere
combatant	combattente	conjoint	congiunto
COMED	COMMED	CONJUG	CONIUG
comedian	commediante	conjugal	coniugale
comedienne	commediante	conjugate, v.	coniugare
comedy	commedia	conjugation	coniugazione
COMF	CONF	CONJUR	CONGIUR
comfort	conforto	conjuration	congiurazione
comfort, v.	confortare	conjure, v.	congiurare
comfortable	confortabile	CONQUE	CONQUI
comforter	confortatore	conquer, v.	conquistare
COMMAND	COMAND	conqueror	conquistatore
command, v.	comandare	conquest	conquista
commandant	comandante	CONS	COS
commander	comandante	conscience	coscienza
commandment	comandamento	conscientious	coscienzioso

35

conscript	coscritto	council	consiglio
conscript, v.	coscrivere	councillor	consigliere
conspicous	cospicuo	counsel	consiglio
conspiracy	cospirazione	counsel, v.	consigliare
conspire, v.	cospirare	counsellor	consigliere
constancy	costanza	COUNT	CONT
constant	costante	count	conte
constellation	costellazione	count	conto
consternation	costernazione	count, v.	contare
constipate, v.	costipare	COUNTER	CONTR
constipation	costipazione	counterattack	contrattacco
constituent	costituente	counterattack, v.	contrattaccare
constitute, v.	costituire	counterespionage	controspionaggio
constitution	costituzione	counterfeit	contraffatto
constitutional	costituzionale	counterfeit, v.	contraffare
constitutionalism	costituzionalismo	countermarch	contromarcia
construct, v.	costruire	countermove	contromossa
constructive	costruttivo	counterpoint	contrappunto
**conscious	conscio	counterreformation	controriforma
CONSECRA	CONSACRA	counterrevolution	controrivoluzione
consecrate	consacrato	COURAG	CORAGG
consecrate, v.	consacrare	courage	coraggio
consecration	consacrazione	courageous	coraggioso
CONSEQUE	CONSEGUE	COURT	CORT
consequence	conseguenza	court	corte
consequent	conseguente	court, v.	corteggiare
CONSIGN	CONSEGNA	courteous	cortese
consign, v.	consegnare	courtesan	cortigiana
consignee	consegnatario	courtesy	cortesia
CONSUL	CONSOL	courtship	corte
consul	console	court-martial	corte marziale
consular	consolare	CRUCI	CROCI
CONTEXT	CONTEST	crucifix	crocifisso
context	contesto	crucifixion	crocifissione
contextual	contestuale	crucify, v.	crocifiggere
CONTRAB	CONTRABB	Exception:	
contraband	contrabbando	crucial	cruciale
contrabass	contrabbasso	CRUST	CROST
CORRESPOND	CORRISPOND	crust	crosta
correspond, v.	corrispondere	crustacean	crostaceo
correspondence	corrispondenza	CRYSTA	CRISTA
correspondent	corrispondente	crystal	cristallo
CORRU	CORRO	crystalline	cristallino
corrupt	corrotto	crystallization	cristallizzazione
corrupt, v.	corrompere	crystallize, v.	cristallizzare
COUNCI/COUNSE	CONSI	CULP	COLP

culpable	colpęvole	deaconess	diaconęssa
culpability	colpevolęzza	deaconry	diaconạto
culprit	colpęvole	DEBAT	DIBATT
CULTIV	COLTIV	debate	dibạttito
cultivate, v.	coltivạre	debate, v.	dibạttere
cultivation	coltivaziọne	DECLAR	DICHIAR
CURR	CORR	declaration	dichiaraziọne
current	corręnte	declare, v.	dichiarạre
currently	correntemęnte	DEFAM	DIFFAM
CY	CI	defamate, v.	diffamạre
cynic	cịnico	defamation	diffamaziọne
cynism	cinịsmo	DEFEAT	DISFATT
Cypriot	cipriọta	defeat	disfạtta
Cyprus	Cipro	defeatism	disfattịsmo
Cyrenaica	Cirenạica	defeatist	disfattịsta
cyst	ciste	DEFECT	DIFETT
cystitis	cistịte	defect	difętto
** cymbal	cęmbalo	defective	difettịvo
CYCL	CICL	DEFENS	DIFES
cycle	ciclo	defense	difęsa
cyclic	cịclico	defensive	difensịvo
cyclone	ciclọne	DEMAND	DOMAND
cyclonic	ciclọnico	demand	domạnda
Cyclopean	ciclọpico	demand, v.	domandạre
Cyclops	Ciclọpe	DEMOBILIZ	SMOBILIT
cyclostyle	ciclostịle	demobilization	smobilitaziọne
cyclotron	ciclotrọne	demobilize, v.	smobilitạre
CZA	ZA	DEMONSTR	DIMOSTR
czar	zar	demonstrate, v.	dimostrạre
czarina	zarịna	demonstration	dimostraziọne
CZEC	CEC	demonstrative	dimostratịvo
Czech	ceco	demonstrator	dimostratọre
Czechoslovak	cecoslovạcco	DEPARTMEN	DIPARTIMEN
Czechoslovakia	Cecoslovạcchia	department	dipartimẹnto
DAMN	DANN	departmental	dipartimentạle
damn, v.	dannạre	DEPEND	DIPEND
damnation	dannaziọne	depend, v.	dipęndere
DANCE	DANZA	dependant	dipendęnte
dance	dạnza	dependent	dipendęnte
dance, v.	danzạre	DEPOPUL	DEPOPOL
danccr	danzatọre	depopulate, v.	depopolạre
DARWIN	DARVIN	depopulation	depopolaziọne
Darwinian	darviniạno	DESCEND	DISCEND
Darwinism	darvinịsmo	descend, v.	discęndere
DEACON	DIACON	descendant	discendęnte
deacon	diạcono	DESER	DISER

desert, v.	disertare	doctrinal	dottrinale
desertion	diserzione	doctrine	dottrina
desertor	disertore	DRAMA	DRAMMA
DESIGN	DISEGN	drama	dramma
design	disegno	dramatic	drammatico
design, v.	disegnare	dramatical	drammatico
designer	disegnatore	ENCY	ENCI
DESIGN	DESIGN	encyclical	enciclico
designate	designato	encyclopedia	enciclopedia
designate, v.	designare	ENTHUS	ENTUS
designation	designazione	enthusiasm	entusiasmo
DESP	DISP	enthusiast	entusiasta
despair	disperazione	enthusiastic	entusiastico
despair, v.	disperare	ETH	ET
desperate	disperato	ether	etere
desperation	disperazione	ethereal	etereo
despite	dispetto	ethic	etico
despotic	dispotico	ethical	etico
despotism	dispotismo	ethics	etica
DESTR0/U	DISTRU	ethnic	etnico
destroy, v.	distruggere	ETHNO	ETNO
destroyer	distruttore	ethnographic	etnografico
destruction	distruzione	ethnography	etnografia
destructive	distruttivo	ethnologist	etnologo
DETAIL	DETTAGLI	ethnology	etnologia
detail	dettaglio	ETYMO	ETIMO
detail, v.	dettagliare	etymological	etimologico
detailed	dettagliato	etymologist	etimologista
DEXT	DEST	etymology	etimologia
dexterity	desterità	etymon	etimo
dexterous	destro	EULO	ELO
dextrorse	destrorso	eulogist	elogiatore
DICTA	DETTA	eulogize, v.	elogiare
dictate, v.	dettare	eulogy	elogio
dictation	dettato	EX	ES
DICTA	DITTA	exacerbate, v.	esacerbare
dictator	dittatore	exact	esatto
dictatorial	dittatoriale	exaction	esazione
DICTIO	DIZIO	exactly	esattamente
diction	dizione	exactor	esattore
dictionary	dìzionario	exalt, v.	esaltare
DOCTO	DOTTO	exaltation	esaltazione
doctor	dottore	exalted	esaltato
doctorate	dottorato	exam	esame
DOCTRIN	DOTTRIN	examination	esame
doctrinaire	dottrinario	examine, v.	esaminare

examinee	esaminando	exsiccate, v.	essiccare
examiner	esaminatore	exsiccation	essiccazione
example	esempio	extemporaneous	estemporaneo
exanimate	esanime	extend, v.	estendere
exasperate, v.	esasperare	extension	estensione
expatriate	espatriato	extensive	estensivo
expatriate, v.	espatriare	extenuate, v.	estenuare
expatriation	espatrio	extenuation	estenuazione
expectorant	espettorante	exterior	esteriore
expectorate, v.	espettorare	exteriority	esteriorità
expedient	espediente	exteriorize, v.	esternare
expel, v.	espellere	external	esterno
experience	esperienza	externalize, v.	esternare
experience, v.	esperimentare	exterritorial	estraterritoriale
experiment	esperimento	extinct	estinto
experiment, v.	esperimentare	excitation	eccitazione
expert	esperto	excite, v.	eccitare
expiable	espiabile	excited	eccitato
expiate, v.	espiare	excitement	eccitamento
expiation	espiazione	EXH	ES
expiration	espirazione	exhalation	esalazione
explicate, v.	esplicare	exhale, v.	esalare
explication	esplicazione	exhaust, v.	esaurire
explicit	esplicito	exhausted	esausto
explode, v.	esplodere	exhaustion	esaurimento
exploration	esplorazione	exhaustive	esauriente
explore, v.	esplorare	exhibit, v.	esibire
explorer	esploratore	exhibition	esibizione
explosion	esplosione	exhibitionist	esibizionista
explosive	esplosivo	exhilarate, v.	esilarare
exponent	esponente	exhort, v.	esortare
export, v.	esportare	exhortation	esortazione
exportation	esportazione	exhumation	esumazione
expose, v.	esporre	exhume, v.	esumare
exposition	esposizione	EXTERMIN	STERMIN
express	espresso	exterminate, v.	sterminare
expression	espressione	extermination	sterminio
expressionism	espressionismo	F	
expressionist	espressionista	FABR	FABBR
expressive	espressivo	fabricate, v.	fabbricare
expropriate, v.	espropriare	fabrication	fabbricazione
expropriation	espropriazione	FACT	FATT
expulsion	espulsione	fact	fatto
expunction	espunzione	factor	fattore
expurgate, v.	espurgare	FACTIO	FAZIO
expurgation	espurgazione	faction	fazione

factious	fazioso	H	
FACUL	FACOL	HABIT	ABIT
facultative	facoltativo	habit	abito
faculty	facoltà	habitable	abitabile
FAVOUR	FAVOR	habitant	abitante
favour	favore	habitation	abitazione
favour, v.	favorire	habitual	abituale
favourable	favorevole	habituate, v.	abituare
favoured	favorito	habitude	abitudine
fracture	frattura	** habitat	habitat
fracture, v.	fratturare	HAEM	EM
FRUCTI/U	FRUTTI/U	haematic	ematico
fructiferous	fruttifero	haematite	ematite
fructify, v.	fruttificare	haemoglobin	emoglobina
fructuous	fruttuoso	haemoptysis	emottisi
FUNCTION	FUNZION	haemorrhage	emorragia
function	funzione	haemorrhoids	emorroidi
function, v.	funzionare	haemostatic	emostatico
functional	funzionale	haemotoma	ematoma
functionary	funzionario	HAGIO	AGIO
FUNDAM	FONDAM	hagiographer	agiografo
fundament	fondamento	hagiography	agiografia
fundamental	fondamentale	HAL	AL
fundamentally	fondamentalmente	halberd	alabarda
G		halberdier	alabardiere
GALLAN	GALAN	halleluiah	alleluia
gallant	galante	hallucinate, v.	allucinare
gallantry	galanteria	hallucination	allucinazione
GANGR	CANCR	HAR	AR
gangrene	cancrena	harmonic	armonico
gangrenous	cancrenoso	harmonica	armonica
GAS	GASS	harmonious	armonioso
gaseous	gassoso	harmonium	armonium
gasification	gas(s)ificazione	harmonize, v.	armonizzare
gasify, v.	gassificare	HER	ER
gasify, v.	gas(s)ificare	herb	erba
GAZE	GAZZE	herbaceous	erbaceo
gazelle	gazzella	herbalist	erborista
gazette	gazzetta	herbarium	erbario
GIANT	GIGANT	herbivorous	erbivoro
giant	gigante	herborist	erborista
giantess	gigantessa	Herculean	erculeo
giantism	gigantismo	Hercules	Ercole
GYNAECOLO	GINECOLO	hereditary	ereditario
gynaecological	ginecologico	heredity	ereditarietà
gynaecology	ginecologia	heresy	eresia
gynaecologyst	ginecologo		

40

heretic	erętico
heretical	erętico
heritage	eredità
herm	erma
Herman	Ermạnno
hermaphrodite	ermafrodịto
hermaphroditism	ermafroditịsmo
hermeneutics	ermenęutica
hermetic	ermętico
hermit	eremịta
hernia	ęrnia
hernial	ernạrio
hero	erǫe
Herod	Erǫde
Herodotus	Erǫdoto
heroic	erǫico
heroine	erǫina
heroin (chim.)	erǫina
herpes	ęrpete
HESI	ESI
Hesiod	Esịodo
hesitance	esitaziǫne
hesitant	esitạnte
HET	ET
heteroclite	eterǫclito
heterodox	eterodǫsso
heterodoxy	eterodossịa
heterogeneity	eterogeneità
heterogeneous	eterogęneo
HEXA	ESA
hexagon	esạgono
hexagonal	esagonạle
hexameter	esạmetro
HIB	IB
hibernate, v.	ibernạre
hibernation	ibernaziǫne
hibiscus	ibịsco
HOM	OM
homicide	omicịda
homicide	omicịdio
hominid	omịnide
homogeneity	omogeneità
homogeneous	omogęneo
homogenize, v.	omogeneizzạre
homologate, v.	omologạre
homologation	omologaziǫne
homologous	omǫlogo
homonym	omǫnimo
homonymous	omǫnimo
homosexual	omosessuạle
homosexuality	omosessualità
HON	ON
honest	onęsto
honestly	onestamęnte
honesty	onestà
honor	onǫre
honorable	onorạbile
honorarium	onorạrio
honorary	onorịfico
honorific	onirịfico
honour	onǫre
honourable	onorạbile
HOR	OR
Horace	Orạzio
Horatio	Orạzio
horizon	orizzǫnte
horizontal	orizzontạle
hormone	ormǫne
horoscope	orǫscopo
horrible	orrịbile
horrid	ǫrrido
horripilation	orripilaziǫne
horror	orrǫre
horticulture	orticoltụra
HOS	OS
hosanna	osạnna
hospice	ospịzio
hospitable	ospitạle
hospitality	ospitalità
hospitalization	ospedalizzaziǫne
host	ǫstia
host	oste
hostile	ostịle
hostility	ostilità
HUM	UM
human	umạno
hydropic	idrǫpico
hydropsy	idropisịa
hydrosphere	idrosfęra
hydrostatics	idrostạtica
hydroxide	idrǫssido
hydro-electric	idroelęttrico

HYG	IG	idyllic	idillico
hygiene	igiene	ILLEGI	ILLEGGI
hygienic	igienico	illegibility	illeggibilità
hygienist	igienista	illegible	illeggibile
hygrometer	igrometro	ILLEGIT	ILLEGITT
hygroscope	igroscopio	illegitimacy	illegittimità
hygroscopic	igroscopico	illegitimate	illegittimo
HYM	IM	IMAG	IMMAG
Hymalaia	Imalaia	image	immagine
Hymalayan	imalaiano	imaginable	immaginabile
hymen (anat.)	imene	imaginary	immaginario
**hymn	inno	imagination	immaginazione
HYP	IP	imaginative	immaginativo
hyperbola	iperbole	imagine, v.	immaginare
hyperbole	iperbole	IMBECIL	IMBECILL
hyperbolic	iperbolico	imbecile	imbecille
hypercritical	ipercritico	imbecility	imbecillità
hypermetric	ipermetro	INADEQUA	INADEGUA
hypermetrical	ipermetro	inadequacy	inadeguatezza
hypermetropia	ipermetropia	inadequate	inadeguato
hypersensitive	ipersensibile	INADMI	INAMMI
hypertension	ipertensione	inadmissibility	inammissibilità
hyperthyroid (med.)	ipertiroideo	anadmissible	inammissibile
hypertrophy	ipertrofia	INCALCUL	INCALCOL
hypnosis	ipnosi	incalculability	incalcolabilità
hypnotic	ipnotico	incalculable	incalcolabile
hypnotism	ipnotismo	INCINER	INCENER
hypnotist	ipnotista	incinerate, v.	incenerire
hypnotize, v.	ipnotizzare	incineration	incenerazione
hypocondria	ipocondria	INCOHER	INCOER
hypocondriac	ipocondriaco	incoherence	incoerenza
hypocrisy	ipocrisia	incoherent	incoerente
hypocrite	ipocrita	INCOMMUN	INCOMUN
hypocritical	ipocrita	incommunicability	incomunicabilità
hypodermic	ipodermico	incommunicable	incomunicabile
hypordermoclysis	ipodermoclisi	INCOMPREHEN	INCOMPREN
hypostasis	ipostasi	incomprehensibility	incomprensibilità
hypostatic	ipostatico	incomprehensible	incomprensibile
hypotension	ipotensione	incomprehension	incomprensione
hypotenuse	ipotenusa	INDEMNI	INDENNI
hypotesis	ipotesi	indemnify, v.	indennizzare
hypotetic	ipotetico	indemnity	indennità
hypothesize, v.	ipotizzare	INDEP	INDIP
I		independent	indipendente
IDYLL	IDILL	independence	indipendenza
idyll	idillio	INDESTRU	INDISTRU

indestructibility	indistruttibilità	INSECU	INSIC
indestructible	indistruttibile	insecure	insicuro
INDOCTRI	INDOTTRI	insecurity	insicurezza
indoctrinate, v.	indottrinare	INSP	ISP
indoctrination	indottrinamento	inspect, v.	ispezionare
INELIGI	INELIGGI	inspector	ispettore
ineligibility	ineleggibilità	inspectorate	ispettorato
ineligible	ineleggibile	inspire, v.	ispirare
INEQUA	INEGUA	Exception when meaning "inhalation":	
inequable	ineguale	inspiration	inspirazione
inequality	inegualità	inspire, v.	inspirare
Note:		INST	IST
inequity	iniquità	instance	istanza
INEX	INES	instant	istante
inhalation	inalazione	instantaneous	istantaneo
inhale, v.	inalare	instigate, v.	istigare
inhaler	inalatore	instigation	istigazione
INHE/I/O/U	INE/I/O/U	instigator	istigatore
inherence	inerenza	instinct	istinto
inherent	inerente	instinctive	istintivo
inhibit, v.	inibire	institute	istituto
inhibition	inibizione	institute, v.	istituire
inhibitory	inibitorio	institution	istituzione
inhospitable	inospitabile	institutional	istituzionale
inhospitality	inospitalità	instruct, v.	istruire
inhuman	inumano	instruction	istruzione
inhumanity	inumanità	instructive	istruttivo
inhume, v.	inumare	instructor	istruttore
INJE	INIE	INST	INST
inject, v.	iniettare	instability	instabilità
injection	iniezione	install, v.	installare
injector	iniettore	installation	installazione
INJU	INGIU	instill, v.	instillare
injunction	ingiunzione	INSUL	ISOL
injure, v.	ingiuriare	insulate, v.	isolare
injured	ingiuriato	insulator	isolatore
injurious	ingiurioso	INSUR	INSOR
injury	ingiuria	insurmountability	insormontabilità
injustice	ingiustizia	insurmountable	insormontabile
INOBS	INOSS	INTELLECT	INTELLETT
inobservance	inosservanza	intellect	intelletto
inobservant	inosservante	intellectual	intellettuale
INSECT	INSETT	intellectualism	intellettualismo
insect	insetto	intellectualist	intellettualista
insecticide	insetticida	intellectuality	intellettualità
insectology	insettologia	intellectualize, v.	intellettualizzare

INTOLER	INTOLLER	jungle	giungla
intolerable	intollerabile	jurisprudence	giurisprudenza
intolerance	intolleranza	juror	giurato
intolerant	intollerante	jury	giuria
IRRESPONSIB	IRRESPONSAB	justice	giustizia
irresponsibility	irresponsabilità	KI	CHI
irresponsible	irresponsabile	kilo	chilo
IRREVER	IRRIVER	kilocycle	chilociclo
irreverence	irriverenza	kilogram	chilogrammo
irreverent	irriverente	kilowatt	chilowatt
J		kimono	chimono
JA	GIA	** kinetic	cinetico
Jacob	Giacobbe	KO	CO
jade	giada	Koran	Corano
Jaguar	giaguaro	Korea	Corea
Jamaica	Giamaica	Korean	coreano
Jamaican	Giamaicano	LABOU	LAVO
Japan	Giappone	labour	lavoro
Japanese	giapponese	labour, v.	lavorare
Jason	Giasone	LACHRY	LACRI
Java	Giava	lachrymal	lacrimale
** jazz	jazz	lachrymation	lacrimazione
JE	GE	lachrymatory	lacrimogeno
Jesuit	gesuita	lachrymose	lacrimoso
Jesus	Gesù	LACT	LATT
JO	GIO	lactation	lattazione
jocose	giocoso	lacteal	latteo
jocund	giocondo	lactiferous	lattifero
John	Giovanni	lactose	lattosio
Jonah	Giona	LARYN	LARIN
Jordan	Giordano	laryngeal	laringeo
joy	gioia	laryngitis	laringite
JOIN	GIUN	larynx	laringe
join	giuntura	LEAGUE	LEGA
join, v.	giungere	league	lega
JOURN	GIORN	league, v.	legare
journal	giornale	league (meas.)	lega
journalism	giornalismo	LEBAN	LIBAN
journalist	giornalista	Lebanese	libanese
journalistic	giornalistico	Lebanon	Libano
JU	GIU	LEG	LEGG
jeep	jeep	legend	leggenda
jubilate, v.	giubilare	legendary	leggendario
jubilation	giubilazione	legible	leggibile
judo	judo	LEGIT	LEGITT
june	giugno	legitimacy	legittimità

44

legitimate, v.	legittimare	Lycurgus	Licurgo
legitimation	legittimazione	lymph	linfa
LEPR	LEBBR	lymphatic	linfatico
leprosarium	lebbrosario	lynch, v.	linciare
leprosy	lebbra	lynx	lince
leprous	lebbroso	lyre (mus.)	lira
LETH	LET	lyric	lirico
lethal	letale	lyrical	lirico
lethargic	letargico	lyricism	lirismo
lethargy	letargo	lyrist	lirista
Lethe	Lete	lysol	lisolo
LEXIC	LESSIC	M	
lexical	lessicale	MACAR	MACCHER
lexicographer	lessicografo	macaroni	maccheroni
lexicographic	lessicografico	macaronic	maccheronico
lexicographical	lessicogrfico	MACHIN	MACCHIN
lexicography	lessicografia	machine	macchina
lexicologic	lessicologico	machinery	macchinario
lexicological	lessicologico	machinist	macchinista
lexicologist	lessicologo	MAINTAIN	MANTEN
lexicology	lessicologia	maintain, v.	mantenere
lexicon	lessico	maintainance	mantenimento
LINOTYP	LINOTIP	MANIPUL	MANIPOL
linotypist	linotipista	manipulate, v.	manipolare
LION	LEON	manipulation	manipolazione
lion	leone	MANNER	MANIER
lioness	leonessa	manner	maniera
LITER	LETTER	mannerism	manierismo
literal	letterale	mannerist	manierista
literally	letteralmente	MANOEUVR	MANOVR
literate	letterato	manoeuvre	manovra
literature	letteratura	manoeuvre, v.	manovrare
LITHO	LITO	MASCUL	MASCHIL
lithograph	litografia	masculin	maschile
lithograph, v.	litografare	**masculinity	mascolinità
lithographer	litografo	MATHEM	MATEM
lithology	litologia	mathematic	matematico
lithosphere	litosfera	mathematician	matematico
LUX	LUSS	mathematics	matematica
luxate, v.	lussare	MAXIM	MASSIM
luxation	lussazione	maxim	massima
luxe	lusso	maximum	massimo
luxury	lusso	MEASUR	MISUR
LY	LI	measurable	misurabile
Lybia	Libia	measure	misura
Lybian	libico	measure, v.	misurare

45

MECHAN	MECCAN	MULTIPL	MOLTIPL
mechanic	meccanico	multiplication	moltiplicazione
mechanical	meccanico	multiplier	moltiplicatore
mechanics	meccanica	multiply, v.	moltiplicare
mechanism	meccanismo	MURM	MORM
mechanize, v.	meccanizzare	murmur	mormoro
MEDAL/LL	MEDAGLI	murmur, v.	mormorare
medal	medaglia	MUSCA/O	MOSCA/O
medallion	medaglione	muscat	moscato
medallist	medaglista	Muscovite	moscovita
MELANCHOL	MALINCON	MUSCUL	MUSCOL
melancholia	malinconia	muscular	muscolare
melancholic	malinconico	musculature	muscolatura
melancholy	malinconia	MUSS	MUSU
MELODRAM	MELODRAMM	Mussulman	musulmano
melodrama	melodramma	MY	MI
melodramatic	melodrammatico	myopia	miopia
MENSTR	MESTR	myopic	miope
menstrual	mestruale	myriad	miriade
menstruation	mestruazione	myrr	mirra
METAMORPH	METAMORF	myrtle	mirto
metamorphic	metamorfico	mystic	mistico
metamorphosis	metamorfosi	mysticism	misticismo
METAPH	METAF	mystification	mistificazione
metaphor	metafora	mystify, v.	mistificare
metaphoric	metaforico	myth	mito
metaphysical	metafisico	mythic	mitico
metaphysician	metafisico	mythical	mitico
metaphysics	metafisica	mythological	mitologico
MEX	MESS	mythology	mitologia
Mexican	messicano	N	
Mexico	Messico	NEURA	NEVRA
MILL	MIL	neuralgia	nevralgia
milliard	miliardo	neuralgic	nevralgico
million	milione	NEW	NUOVA
millionaire	milionario	New Guinea	Nuova Guinea
millionairess	milionaria	New Yorker	nuovaiorchese
MODEL	MODELL	New Zeland	Nuova Zelanda
model	modello	NIHI	NICHI
model, v.	modellare	nihilism	nichilismo
MOLECUL	MOLECOL	nihilist	nichilista
molecular	molecolare	NOCTUR	NOTTUR
molecule	molecola	nocturn	notturno
MOUNT	MONT	nocturnal	notturno
mount	monte	NORW	NORV
mount, v.	montare	Norway	Norvegia

Norwegian	norvegęse	obscure, v.	oscurạre
NUMBER	NUMER	obscurity	oscurità
number	nụmero	obstacle	ostạcolo
number, v.	numerạre, contạre	obstetric	ostẹtrico
NYMPH	NINF	obstetrician	ostẹtrico
nymph	ninfa	obstetrics	ostetrịcia
nymphomania	ninfomanịa	obstinacy	ostinazịọne
nymphomaniac	ninfọmane	obstinate	ostinạto
O		obstination	ostinazịọne
OBJE	OGGE	obstruct, v.	ostruịre
object	oggẹtto	obstruction	ostruzịọne
objectify, v.	oggettivạre	obstructionism	ostruzionịsmo
objective	oggettịvo	obstructionist	ostruzionịsta
objectivity	oggettività	OBT	OTT
OBED	UBBID	obtain, v.	ottenẹre
obedience	ubbidịęnza	obtainable	ottenịbile
obedient	ubbidịęnte	obtuse	ottụso
OBJE	OBIE	obtuseness	ottusità
objection	obiezịọne	OBV	OVV
object, v.	obiettạre	obviate, v.	ovviạre
objector	obiettọre	obvious	ọvvio
OBLIG	OBBLIG	OCT	OTT
obligate, v.	obbligạre	octagon	ottagọno
obligation	obbligazịọne	octagonal	ottagonạle
obligatory	obbligatọrio	octane	ottạno
oblige, v.	obbligạre	octet	ottẹtto
OBS+VOWEL	OSS+VOWEL	october	ottọbre
obsequious	ossequịọso	octogenarian	ottogenạrio
obsequiousness	ossequiosità	octonarian	ottonạrio
observable	osservạbile	octuple	ọttuplo
observance	osservạnza	OE	E
observant	osservạnte	oedema (med.)	edẹma
observation	osservazịọne	Oedipus	Edịpo
observatory	osservatọrio	oenologist	enọlogo
observe, v.	osservạre	oesophagus	esọfago
observer	osservatọre	oestregen	estrọgeno
obsess, v.	ossessionạre	OFFI	OFFI
obsession	ossessịọne	officiant	officịạnte
obsessive	ossessịvo	officiate, v.	officịạre
** obsequies	ossẹquie	OFFI	UFFI
OBS+CONSONANT	OS+CONSONANTE	office	uffịcio
obscene	oscẹno	officer	ufficịạle
obscenity	oscenità	official	ufficịạle
obscurantism	oscurantịsmo	officially	ufficialmẹnte
obscurantist	oscurantịsta	officious	ufficịọso
obscuration	oscuramẹnto	OLYMP	OLIMP
obscure	oscụro		

47

Olympiad	Olimpiade	PARACHU	PARACADU
Olympian	olimpico	parachute	paracadute
Olympic	olimpico	parachute, v.	paracadutare
Olympus	Olimpo	parachutist	paracadutista
OMNI	ONNI	PARADOX	PARADOSS
omnipotence	onnipotenza	paradox	paradosso
omnipotent	onnipotente	paradoxical	paradossale
omnipresence	onnipresenza	PARASI	PARASSI
omniscience	onniscienza	parasite	parassita
omniscient	onnisciente	parasitic	parassitico
omnivorous	onnivoro	parasitical	parassitico
OPHTHA	OFTA	PARIS	PARIG
ophthalmic	oftalmico	Paris	Parigi
ophthalmology	oftalmologia	Parisian	parigino
OPIUM	OPPIO	** Paris	Paride
opium	oppio	** parisyllabic	parisillabo
opiumism	oppiomania	PARLIAMEN	PARLAMEN
OPT	OTT	parliament	parlamento
optative	ottativo	parliamentarian	parlamentare
optic	ottico	parliamentary	parlamentare
optical	ottico	PAROXY	PAROSSI
optician	ottico	paroxysm	parossismo
optimism	ottimismo	paroxysmal	parossistico
optimist	ottimista	PARTIA	PARZIA
optimize, v.	ottimare	partial	parziale
**opt, v.	optare	partiality	parzialità
**optimum	optimum	PARTICIPA	PARTECIPA
OPTIO	OPZIO	participant	partecipante
option	opzione	participate, v.	partecipare
optional	opzionale	participation	partecipazione
OUTRA	OLTRA	PARTICUL	PARTICOL
outrage	oltraggio	particular	particolare
outrage, v.	oltraggiare	particularity	particolarità
OX	OSS	particularize, v.	particolareggiare
oxalic	ossalico	particularly	particolarmente
oxidation	ossidazione	PASTEUR	PASTOR
oxide	ossido	pasteurization	pastorizzazione
oxidize, v.	ossidare	pasteurize, v.	pastorizzare
oxigen	ossigeno	PATHO	PATO
oxygenate, v.	ossigenare	pathologic	patologico
P		pathological	patologico
PAED	PED	pathologist	patologo
paederast	pederasta	pathology	patologia
paediatric	pediatrico	PATIEN	PAZIEN
paediatrician	pediatra	patience	pazienza
paediatrics	pediatria	patient	paziente

patiently	pazientemente	philosophy	filosofia
PATRIOTI	PATRIOTTI	phlebitis	flebite
patriotic	patriottico	phlebotomy	flebotomia
patriotism	patriottismo	phlegm	flemma
PREFECTIO	PERFEZIO	phlegmatic	flemmatico
perfection	perfezione	phobia	fobia
perfectionism	perfezionismo	phocomelia	focomelia
perfectionist	perfezionista	Phoebus	Febo
PERFU	PROFU	Phoenician	fenicio
perfume	profumo	phoenix	fenice
perfumer	profumiere	phon	fon
perfumery	profumeria	phonation	fonazione
PH	F	phoneme	fonema
phantasm	fantasma	phonetic	fonetico
phantasmagoria	fantasmagoria	phonetics	fonetica
phantasy	fantasia	phonic	fonico
phantom	fantasma	phonogram	fonogramma
Pharaoh	faraone	phonograph	fonografo
pharinx	faringe	phonology	fonologia
pharmaceutical	farmaceutico	phosphate	fosfato
pharmacist	farmacista	phosphite	fosfito
pharmacology	farmacologia	phosphorescence	fosforescenza
pharmacy	farmacia	phosphorescent	fosforescente
phase	fase	phosphorus	fosforo
phenomenal	fenomenale	photo	foto
phenomenon	fenomeno	photoelectric	fotoelettrico
phial	fiala	photogenic	fotogenico
Philadelphia	Filadelfia	photograph	fotografia
philanthrope	filantropo	photograph, v.	fotografare
philanthropic	filantropico	photographer	fotografo
philanthropist	filantropo	photographic	fotografico
philanthropy	filantropia	photomontage	fotomontaggio
philarmonic	filarmonico	photon	fotone
philatelist	filatelico	photostat	fotostatico
philately	filatelia	phrase	frase
Philip	Filippo	phraseology	fraseologia
philippic	filippica	phrenic	frenico
Philippine	filippino	phrenologist	frenologo
Philistinism	filiteismo	Phrygian	frigio
philological	filologico	phylloxera	fillossera
philologist	filologo	physical	fisico
philology	filologia	physicist	fisico
philosopher	filosofo	physics	fisica
philosophic	filosofico	physiognomist	fisionomista
philosophical	filosofico	physiognomy	fisionomia
philosophize, v.	filosofare	physiological	fisiologico

physiology	fisiologia	population	popolazione
physiotherapy	fisioterapia	populous	popoloso
physique	fisico	PORTUG	PORTOG
** phthisis	tisi	Portugal	Portogallo
PILGRIM	PELLEGR	Portuguese	portoghese
pilgrim	pellegrino	PRACTI	PRATI
pilgrimage	pellegrinaggio	practicability	praticabilità
PIROUE	PIROE	practicable	praticabile
pirouette	piroetta	practical	pratico
pirouette, v.	piroettare	practicality	praticalità
PLANT	PIANT	practically	praticamente
plant	pianta	practice	pratica
plant, v.	piantare	practise, v.	praticare
plantation	piantagione	PRAET	PRET
planter	piantatore	praetor	pretore
POLY	POLI	praetorian	pretoriano
polychrome	policromo	PRECIO	PREZIO
polyclinic	policlinico	preciosity	preziosità
polygamist	poligamo	precious	prezioso
polygamous	poligamo	preciousness	preziosità
polygamy	poligamia	PREHISTOR	PREISTOR
polyglot	poliglotta	prehistoric	preistorico
polygon	poligono	prehistory	preistoria
polyhedral	poliedrico	PREJUD	PREGIUD
polyhedron	poliedro	prejudice	pregiudizio
polymer	polimero	prejudice, v.	pregiudicare
polymerization	polimerizzazione	prejudicial	pregiudizievole
polymorphism	polimorfismo	PROGNOST	PRONOST
Polynesia	Polinesia	prognostic	pronostico
Polynesian	polinesiano	prognosticate, v.	pronosticare
polynomial	polimonio	prognostication	pronostico
polyp	polipo	PROHIB	PROIB
Polypheme	Polifemo	prohibit, v.	proibire
polyphonic	polifonico	prohibition	proibizione
polyphony	polifonia	prohibitionism	proibizionismo
polypus	polipo	prohibitive	proibitivo
polysyllabic	polisillabo	PROJE	PROGE
polysyllable	polisillabo	project	progetto
polythene	politene	project, v.	progettare
polyvinyl	polivinile	PROJE	PROIE
POPUL	POPOL	projectile	proiettile
popular	popolare	projection	proiezione
popularity	popolarità	projector	proiettore
popularization	popolarizzazione	PROMPT	PRONT
popularize, v.	popolarizzare	prompt	pronto
populate, v.	popolare	promptness	prontezza

PROSEC	PROCESS	publication	pubblicazione
prosecute, v.	processare	publicist	pubblicista
prosecution	processo	publicity	pubblicità
PROTECT	PROTETT	publicize, v.	pubblicizzare
protective	protettivo	publish, v.	pubblicare
protector	protettore	PULMON	POLMON
protectorate	protettorato	pulmonary	polmonare
protectress	protettrice	pulmonic	polmonare
PROTECTIO	PROTEZIO	PULP	POLP
protection	protezione	pulp	polpa
protectionism	protezionismo	pulpy	polposo
protectionist	protezionista	PULVER	POLVER
PROXI	PROSSI	pulverization	polverizzazione
proximity	prossimità	pulverize, v.	polverizzare
proximo	prossimo	PUNCT	PUNT
PSAL	SAL	punctual	puntuale
psalm	salmo	punctuality	puntualità
psalmist	salmista	punctuate, v.	punteggiare
psalmodist	salmista	punctuation	punteggiatura
psalmody	salmodia	puncture	puntura
psaltery	salterio	PY	PI
PSY	PSI	pygmy	pigmeo
psyche	psiche	pyjamas	pigiama
psychiatric	psichiatrico	pylon	pilone
psychiatrist	psichiatra	pylorus	piloro
psychiatry	psichiatria	pyorrhoea	piorrea
psychic	psichico	pyramid	piramide
psychical	psichico	pyramidal	piramidale
psychoanalysis	psicanalisi	pyre	pira
psychoanalyst	psicanalista	Pyrenees	Pirenei
psychologic	psicologico	pyrites	pirite
psychological	psicologico	pyrolysis	pirolisi
psychologist	psicologo	pyromaniac	piromane
psychology	psicologia	pyrope	piropo
psychopath	psicopatico	pyrotechny	pirotecnica
psychopathic	psicopatico	pyrotethnic	pirotecnico
psychopathology	psicopatologia	pyrotethnics	pirotecnica
psychosis	psicosi	Pythagoras	Pitagora
psychotechnics	psicotecnica	Pythagorean	pitagorico
psychotherapy	psicoterapia	python	pitone
psychotic	psicopatico	pyx	pisside
PTO	TO	Q	
Ptolemaic	tolemaico	QUIXO	CHISCIO
Ptolemy	Tolomeo	Quixote	Chisciotte
PUBLI	PUBBLI	Quixotic	donchisciottesco
public	pubblico	quixotry	donchisciottismo

R

RABI	RABBI
rabidiness	rabbia
RACI	RAZZI
racial	razziale
racialism	razzismo
racialist	razzista
racism	razzismo
racist	razzista
RADIOACTI	RADIOATTI
radioactive	radioattivo
radioactivity	radioattività
RATIO	RAZIO
ratiocinate, v.	raziocinare
ratiocination	raziocinio
ration	razione
rational	razionale
rationalism	razionalismo
rationalist	razionalista
rationality	razionalità
rationalization	razionalizzazione
rationalize, v.	razionalizzare
REACT	REATT
reactive	reattivo
reactivity	reattività
reactor	reattore
REACTIO	REAZIO
reaction	reazione
reactionary	reazionario
REARM	RIARM
rearm, v.	riarmare
rearmament	riarmamento
REBEL	RIBELL
rebel,v	ribellare,v
rebellion	ribellione
rebellious	ribelle
RECE	RICE
receive, v.	ricevere
receiver	ricevente
receptacle	ricettacolo
reception	ricezione
receptive	ricettivo
RECO	RICO
recognition	riconoscimento
recognizable	riconoscibile
recognize, v.	riconoscere
recompense	ricompensa
recompense, v.	ricompensare
reconcile, v.	riconciliare
reconciliation	riconciliazione
reconsider, v.	riconsiderare
RECOMMEND	RACCOMAND
recommend, v.	raccomandare
recommendation	raccomandazione
RECONST	RICOST
reconstitute, v.	ricostituire
reconstruct, v.	ricostruire
reconstruction	ricostruzione
RECREA	RICREA
recreate, v.	ricreare
recreation	ricreazione
recreational	ricreativo
RECT	RETT
rectal	rettale
rectangle	rettangolo
rectangular	rettangolare
rectification	rettificazione
rectifier	rettificatore
rectify, v.	rettificare
rectilineal	rettilineo
rectilinear	rettilineo
rectitude	rettitudine
rector	rettore
rectum	retto
RECUP	RICUP
recuperate, v.	ricuperare
recuperation	ricuperazione
RECUR	RICORR
recur, v.	ricorrere
recurrence	ricorrenza
recurrent	ricorrente
REDUND	RIDOND
redundance	ridondanza
redundancy	ridondanza
redundant	ridondante
REF	RIF
refer, v.	riferire
reflect, v.	riflettere
reflection	riflessione
reflective	riflessivo
reflector	riflettore
reflex	riflesso

reflexive	riflessivo	remedy	rimedio
reflux	riflusso	remedy, v.	rimediare
reform	riforma	remit, v.	rimettere
reform, v.	riformare	remonstrance	rimostranza
reformation	riforma	remorse	rimorso
reformatory	riformatorio	remount, v.	rimontare
reformed	riformato	remove, v.	rimuovere
reformer	riformatore	remunerate, v.	rimunerare
REFRA	RIFRA	remuneration	rimunerazione
refract, v.	rifrangere	remunerative	rimunerativo
refraction	rifrazione	RENOV	RINNOV
refractor	rifrattore	renovate, v.	rinnovare
refractory	refrattario	renovation	rinnovazione
refrangible	rifrangibile	renovator	rinnovatore
REFUGE	RIFUGI	REPAR	RIPAR
refuge	rifugio	reparation	riparazione
refugee	rifugiato	repartition	ripartizione
REGENERA	RIGENERA	REPATRIA	RIMPATRIA
regenerate, v.	rigenerare	repatriate, v.	rimpatriare
regeneration	rigenerazione	repatriation	rimpatrio
REGIME	REGGIME	REPEAT	RIPET
regiment	reggimento	repeat, v.	ripetere
regimental	reggimentale	repeatedly	ripetutamente
REGULA	REGOLA	repeater	ripetitore
regular	regolare	** repetition	ripetizione
regularity	regolarità	REPOS	RIPOS
regularize, v.	regolarizzare	repose	riposo
regulate, v.	regolare	repose, v.	riposare
regulation	regolamento	REPRESENT	RAPPRESENT
regulator	regolatore	represent, v.	rappresentare
REGURGI	RIGURGI	representation	rappresentazione
regurgitare, v.	rigurgitare	representative	rappresentativo
regurgitation	rigurgito	REPROD	RIPROD
REHA	RIA	reproduce, v.	riprodurre
rehabilitate, v.	riabilitare	reproduction	riproduzione
rehabilitation	riabilitazione	REPUBL	REPUBBL
RELAX	RILASS	republic	repubblica
relax,v	rilassare,v	republican	repubblicano
relaxation	rilassamento	** republish, v.	ripubblicare
relaxing	rilassante	REPUD	RIPUD
RELUCT	RILUTT	repudiate, v.	ripudiare
reluctance	riluttanza	repudiation	ripudio
reluctant	riluttante	REPUGN	RIPUGN
REM	RIM	repugnance	ripugnanza
remand, v.	rimandare	repugnant	ripugnante
remediable	rimediabile	REPULS	RIPULS

53

repulse	ripulsa	REUN	RIUN
repulsive	ripulsivo	reunion	riunione
** repulsion	repulsione	reunite, v.	riunire
RES	RIS	REV	RIV
respond, v.	rispondere	reveal, v.	rivelare
respondent	rispondente	revelation	rivelazione
restaurant	ristorante	revendication	rivendicazione
restoration	ristaurazione	reverberate, v.	riverberare
result	risultato	reverberation	riverbero
result, v.	risultare	revere, v.	riverire
resultant	risultante	reverence	riverenza
resurge, v.	risorgere	reverent	riverente
resurgence	risurrezione	revive, v.	rivivere
resurgent	risorgente	revivify, v.	rivivificare
resurrect, v.	risorgere	revolt	rivolta
resurrection	risurrezione	revolution	rivoluzione
resuscitate, v.	risuscitare	revolutionary	rivoluzionario
resuscitation	risuscitamento	revulutionize, v.	rivoluzionare
RESO	RISO	** reverend	reverendo
resoluble	risolubile	RH	R
resolute	risoluto	rhabdomancy	rabdomanzia
resolutness	risolutezza	rhapsode	rapsodo
resonance	risonanza	rhapsodic	rapsodico
resonant	risonante	rhapsodical	rapsodico
resonator	risonatore	rhapsodist	rapsodista
resound, v.	risonare	rhapsody	rapsodia
resource	risorsa	rheostat	reostato
RESPECT	RISPETT	rhesus (zool.)	reso
respect	rispetto	rhetoric	retorica
respect, v.	rispettare	rhetorical	retorico
respectability	rispettabilità	rheumatic	reumatico
respectable	rispettabile	rheumatism	reumatismo
respectful	rispettoso	rhino	rinoceronte
respective	rispettivo	rhinoceros	rinoceronte
respectively	rispettivamente	rhizome (bot.)	rizoma
RET	RIT	Rhodes	Rodi
retain, v.	ritenere	Rhodesian	rodesiano
retard	ritardo	rhododendron	rododendro
retard, v.	ritardare	rhombic	rombico
retardation	ritardo	rhomboid	romboide
retention	ritenzione	rhombus	rombo
retire, v.	ritirare	rhomb (geom.)	rombo
retired	ritirato	rhotacism	rotacismo
retirement	ritiro	RHY	RI
** reticular	reticolare	rhyme	rima
** reticulate	reticolato	rhyme, v.	rimare

rhythm	ritmo
rhythmic	ritmico
rhythmical	ritmico
RISK	RISCHI
risk	rischio
risk, v.	rischiare
risky	rischioso
ROMANC	ROMANZ
romance	romanzo
romance, v.	romanzare
RUIN	ROV
ruin	rovina
ruin, v.	rovinare
ruinous	rovinoso
SABBAT	SABAT
sabbatical	sabatico
SACCHA	SACCA
saccharin	saccarina
saccharine	saccarina
saccharoid	saccaroide
saccharose	saccarosio
SACRIST	SAGREST
sacrist	sagrestano
sacristan	sagrestano
sacristy	sagrestia
SANCT	SANT
sanctification	santificazione
sanctify, v.	santificare
sanctity	santità
sanctuary	santuario
SATISF	SODDISF
satisfaction	soddisfazione
satisfactory	soddisfacente
satisfied	soddisfatto
satisfy, v.	soddisfare
satisfying	soddisfacente
SAX	SASS
Saxon	Sassone
saxophone	sassofono
SCAPUL	SCAPOL
scapula	scapola
scapular	scapolare
SCARC	SCARS
scarce	scarso
scarcity	scarsezza
SCHIS	SCIS
schism	scisma
schismatic	scismatico
schist	scisto
SCHOL	SCOL
scholastic	scolastico
scholasticism	scolastica
** school	scuola
SECRET	SEGRET
secret	segreto
secretarial	segretariale
secretariat	segretariato
secretary	segretario
SECT	SETT
sect	setta
sectarian	settario
sectary	settario
sector	settore
SECTIO	SEZIO
section	sezione
section, v.	sezionare
SECUL	SECOL
secular	secolare
secularize, v.	secolarizzare
SEISM	SISM
seismic	sismico
seismograph	sismografo
seismographic	sismografico
seismography	sismografia
seismologic	sismologico
seismological	sismologico
seismologist	sismologo
seismology	sismologia
SELECT	SELETT/SELEZ
select	seletto
select, v.	selezionare
selection	selezione
selective	selettivo
SEPT	SETT
september	settembre
septenary	settenario
septennial	settennale
septic	settico
septicaemia	setticemia
SEPUL	SEPOL
sepulchral	sepolcrale
sepulchre	sepolcro

SERGEAN	SERGEN	solicitation	sollecitazione
sergeant	sergente	solicitude	sollecitudine
sergeant-major	sergente	SOMN	SONN
maggiore		somnambulism	sonnambulismo
SEX	SESS	somnambulist	sonnambulo
sex	sessso	somnolence	sonnolenza
sexagenarian	sessagenario	somnolent	sonnolento
sexual	sessuale	SOPHIS	SOFIS
sexuality	sessualità	sophism	sofismo
SEXT	SEST	sophist	sofista
sextant	sestante	sophistic	sofistico
sextet	sestetto	sophistical	sofistico
sextuple	sestuplo	sophisticate, v.	sofisticare
SIGN	SEGN	sophisticated	sofisticato
sign	segno	sophistication	sofisticazione
signal	segnale	sophistry	sofisma
signalize, v.	segnalare	SOVEREIGN	SOVRAN
SIMPL	SEMPL	sovereign	sovrano
simple	semplice	sovereignty	sovranità
simplicity	semplicità	SPACE/I	SPAZI
simplify, v.	semplificare	space	spazio
simply	semplicemente	space, v.	spaziare
SINGUL	SINGOL	spacious	spazioso
singular	singolare	SPECT	SPETT
singularity	singolarità	spectacle	spettacolo
SKELET	SCHLETR	spectacular	spettacolare
skeleton	scheletro	spectator	spettatore
skeletonize, v.	scheletrire	spectral	spettrale
SKEPT	SCETT	spectre	spettro
skeptic	scettico	spectrograph	spettrografo
skeptical	scettico	spectrographic	spettrografico
skepticism	scetticismo	spectrometer	spettrometro
SNOBB	SNOB	spectroscope	spettroscopio
snobbery	snobismo	spectroscopic	spettroscopico
snobbish	snobistico	spectroscopy	spettroscopia
SOBER	SOBRI	spectrum	spettro
sober	sobrio	SPH	SF
soberness	sobrietà	sphere	sfera
SOJOURN	SOGGIORN	spheric	sferico
sojourn	soggiorno	spheroid	sferoide
sojourn, v.	soggiornare	sphincter	sfintere
SOLEMN	SOLENN	Sphinx	Sfinge
solemn	solenne	SQUAL	SQUALL
solemnity	solennità	squalid	squallido
solemnize, v.	solennizzare	squalor	squallore
SOLICI	SOLLECI	STIMUL	STIMOL

stimulant	stimolante	suffering	sofferenza
stimulate, v.	stimolare	suffocate, v.	soffocare
stimulation	stimolazione	SUGAR	ZUCCHER
stimulus	stimolo	sugar	zucchero
STRANGUL	STRANGOL	sugar, v.	zuccherare
strangulate, v.	strangolare	SULPH	SOLF
strangulation	strangolamento	sulphate	solfato
STROPH	STROF	sulphite	solfito
strophe	strofa	sulphurate, v.	solforare
strophic	strofico	sulphuretted	solforato
STRUCT	STRUTT	sulphuric	solforico
structural	strutturale	SULPH	SULF
structure	struttura	sulphonamide	sulfamidico
SUBSI	SUSSI	sulphureous	sulfureo
subsidiary	sussidiario	SULPH	ZOLF
subsidize, v.	sussidiare	sulphur	zolfo
subsidy	sussidio	SUM	SOMM
subsist, v.	sussistere	sum	somma
subsistence	sussistenza	sum, v.	sommare
SUBST	SOST	summarily	sommariamente
substance	sostanza	summary	sommario
substantial	sostanzioso	summation	somma
substantiality	sostanzialità	SUPPR	SOPPR
substantially	sostanzialmente	suppress, v.	sopprimere
substantiate, v.	sostanziare	suppression	soppressione
substantive	sostantivo	SURPRI	SORPRE
substitute	sostituto	surprise	sorpresa
substitute, v.	sostituire	surprise, v.	sorprendere
substitution	sostituzione	surprising	sorprendente
substratum	sostrato	SURVIV	SOPRAVVIV
SUBT	SOTT	survival	sopravvivenza
subterfuge	sotterfugio	survive, v.	sopravvivere
subterranean	sotterraneo	SUSCEPT	SUSCETT
subtitle	sottotitolo	susceptibility	suscettibilità
subtract, v.	sottrarre	susceptible	suscettibile
subtraction	sottrazione	SUSPE	SOSPE
SUBVER	SOVVER	suspect	sospetto
subversion	sovversione	suspect, v.	sospettare
subversive	sovversivo	suspend, v.	sospendere
subvert, v.	sovvertire	suspension	sospensione
SUCCO/U	SOCCO	suspensory	sospensorio
succour	soccorso	SUST	SOST
succour, v.	soccorrere	sustain, v.	sostenere
succumb, v.	soccombere	sustenance	sostentamento
SUFF	SOFF	SY	SI
suffer, v.	soffrire	sybarite	sibarita

sybaritic	sibaritico	synonym	sinonimo
Sybil	Sibilla	synonymity	sinonimia
sybilline	sibillino	synonymous	sinonimo
sycamore	sicomoro	synonymy	sinonimia
syllabary	sillabario	synopsis	sinossi
syllabic	sillabico	synoptic	sinottico
syllabification	sillabazione	synovia	sinovia
syllable	sillaba	synovitis	sinovite
syllable, v.	sillabare	syntactic	sintattico
syllibicate, v.	sillabare	syntax	sintassi
syllogism	sillogismo	synthetize, v.	sintetizzare
syllogize, v.	sillogizzare	syphilis	sifilide
sylphid	silfide	syphilitic	sifilitico
sylvan	silvano	Syracuse	Siracusa
Sylvia	Silvia	Syria	Siria
symbiosis	simbiosi	Syrian	siriano
symbol	simbolo	syringe	Siringa
symbolic	simbolico	systaltic	sistaltico
symbolical	simbolico	system	sistema
symbolism	simbolismo	systematic	sistematico
symbolist	simbolista	systematization	sistemazione
symbolize, v.	simboleggiare	systole	sistole
symmetric	simmetrico	SYRUP	SCIROPP
symmetrical	simmetrico	syrup	sciroppo
symmetry	simmetria	syrupy	sciropposo
symphisis	sinfisi	T	
symphonic	sinfonico	TACT	TATT
symphony	sinfonia	tactical	tattico
symposium	simposio	tactician	tattico
symptom	sintomo	tactics	tattica
symptomatic	sintomatico	tactual	tattile
symptomatical	sintomatico	TAX	TASS
synagogue	sinagoga	tax	tassa
synchronism	sincronismo	tax, v.	tassare
synchronization	sincronizzazione	taxability	tassabilità
synchronize, v.	sincronizzare	taxable	tassabile
synchronous	sincrono	taxation	tassazione
synchrotron	sincrotrone	taxi	tassì
syncopate, v.	sincopare	taxidermist	tassidermista
syncope	sincope	taxidermy	tassidermia
syncretism	sincretismo	taximeter	tassametro
syndicalism	sindacalismo	TECHN	TECN
syndicalist	sindacalista	technical	tecnico
syndicate	sindacato	technician	tecnico
syndrome	sindrome	technique	tecnica
synod	sinodo	technological	tecnologico

technology	tecnologia	thermodynamics	termodinamica
TECT	TETT	thermometer	termometro
tectonic	tettonico	thermonuclear	termonucleare
tectonics	tettonica	thermos	t(h)emos
TELEGRAPH	TELEGRAF	thermostat	termostato
telegraphic	telegrafico	thermostatic	termostatico
telegraphist	telegrafista	thesis	tesi
telegraphy	telegrafia	Thomas	Tommaso
TELEPH	TELEF	Thomism	tomismo
telephone	telefono	thorax	torace
telephone, v.	telefonare	Thrace	Tracia
telephonist	telefonista	Thracian	Tracio
TEMPT	TENT	thrombosis	trombosi
tempt, v.	tentare	throne	trono
temptation	tentazione	TION	See "TION" in
tempter	tentatore	Desinences	
TEXT	TEST	TOBACC	TABACC
text	testo	tobacco	tabacco
textual	testuale	tobacconist	tabaccaio
** textile	tessile	TOLER	TOLLER
TH	T	tolerable	tollerabile
theatre	teatro	tolerance	tolleranza
theatrical	teatrale	tolerant	tollerante
theatricality	teatralità	tolerate, v.	tollerare
theism	teismo	toleration	tolleranza
theist	teista	TOURI	TURI
thematic	tematico	tourism	turismo
theme	tema	tourist	turista
theocracy	teocrazia	TOURN	TORN
theodolite	teodolite	tournament	torneo
Theodore	Teodoro	tourney	torneo
theologian	teologo	TOXI	TOSSI
theological	teologico	toxic	tossico
theology	teologia	toxicity	tossicità
theorem	teorema	TRACT	TRATT
theoretical	teorico	tractability	trattabilità
theorist	teorico	tractable	trattabile
theorize, v.	teorizzare	tractate	trattato
theory	teoria	tractor	trattore
theosophy	teosofia	** traction	trazione
therapeutic/al	terapeutico	TRAIT	TRADIT
therapy	terapia	traitor	traditore
Theresa	Teresa	traitress	traditrice
thermal	termico	TRANS	TRAS
thermal	termale	transcription	trascrizione
thermionics (fis.)	termoionica	transfer	trasferimento

59

transfer, v.	trasferire	treat, v.	trattare
transferable	trasferibile	treatment	trattamento
transference	trasferimento	treaty	trattato
transfiguration	trasfigurazione	TRIUMPH	TRIONF
transfigure, v.	trasfigurare	triumph	trionfo
transfix, v.	trafiggere	triumph, v.	trionfare
transform, v.	trasformare	triumphal	trionfale
transformation	trasformazione	triumphant	trionfante
transformer	trasformatore	TURBID	TORBID
transfuse, v.	trasfondere	turbid	torbido
transfusion	trasfusione	turbidity	torbidità
transgress, v.	trasgredire	TURBULEN	TURBOLEN
transgression	trasgressione	turbulence	turbolenza
transliterate, v.	traslitterare	turbulent	turbolento
translucence	traslucidità	TY	TI
translucent	traslucido	tympanum	timpano
transmigrate, v.	trasmigrare	type	tipo
transmigration	trasmigrazione	typhoid	tifoideo
transmission	trasmissione	typhoon	tifone
transmit, v.	trasmettere	typhus	tifo
transmute, v.	trasmutare	typical	tipico
transparence	trasparenza	typographer	tipografo
transparency	trasparenza	typography	tipografia
transparent	trasparente	typology	tipologia
transport	trasporto	tyrannical	tirannico
transport, v.	trasportare	tyrannicide	tirannicida
transportable	trasportabile	tyrannize, v.	tiranneggiare
transportation	trasportazione	tyrannous	tirannico
transposal	trasposizione	tyranny	tirannia
transpose, v.	trasporre	tyrant	tiranno
transposition	trasposizione	Tyrol	Tirolo
transribe, v.	trascrivere	Tyrolean	tirolese
** translate, v.	tradurre	Tyrrhene	Tirreno
** translation	traduzione	U	O
** translator	traduttore	umbilical	ombelicale
TRANSCEND	TRASCEND	umbra	ombra
transcend, v.	trascendere	umbrageous	ombroso
transcendent	trascendente	umbrella	ombrello
transcendentalism	trascendentalismo	UKRA	UCRA
transcendentalist	trascendentalista	Ukraine	Ucraina
TRANSV	TRAV	Ukranian	ucraino
transversal	trasversale	UN	IN
transverse	trasverso	unable	inabile
transvestite	travestito	unappealable	inappellabile
transvestitism	travestitismo	unapt	inetto
TREAT	TRATT	uncertain	incerto

uncertainty	incertezza	valvular	valvolare
uncivil	incivile	VARIOL	VAIOL
unconceivable	inconcepibile	variola	vaiolo
unconditional	incondizionato	variolar	vaioloso
unconditioned	incondizionato	VEHEM	VEEM
unconscious	inconscio	vehemence	veemenza
uncontainable	incontenibile	vehement	veemente
uncultured	incolto	VEIL	VEL
undecided	indeciso	veil	velo
undecipherable	indecifrabile	veil, v.	velare
undeclinable	indeclinabile	VEIN	VEN
unedited	inedito	vein	vena
unequal	ineguale	vein, v.	venare
unhospitable	inospitale	veined	venato
unjust	ingiusto	VENTUR	AVVENTUR
unjustness	ingiustizia	venture	avventura
unnatural	innaturale	venture, v.	avventurare
UN	IM	venturer	avventuriero
unpardonable	imperdonabile	VERGIL	VIRGIL
unpopular	impopolare	Vergil	Virgilio
unpopularity	impopolarità	Vergilian	virgiliano
unproductive	improduttivo	VESIC	VESCIC
unpunished	impunito	vesica	vescica
** unquiet	inquieto	vesicle	vescicola
UNR	IRR	vesicular	vescicolare
unreal	irreale	VESTIBUL	VESTIBOL
unreality	irrealtà	vestibular	vestibolare
unreconciliable	irreconciliabile	vestibule	vestibolo
unrepeatable	irripetibile	VICT	VITT
unresponsible	irresponsabile	victim	vittima
UNS/UNT	INS/INT	Victor	Vittorio
unstable	instabile	Victoria	Vittoria
untouchable	intoccabile	Victorian	vittoriano
untranslatable	intraducibile	victorious	vittorioso
UXOR	UXOR/USSOR	** victress	vincitrice
uxoricide	uxoricida	VINDICA	RIVENDICA
uxoricide	ussoricida	vindicate, v.	rivendicare
V		vindication	rivendicazione
VAINGLOR	VANAGLOR	vindicator	rivendicatore
vainglorious	vanaglorioso	** vindictive	vendicativo
vainglory	vanagloria	VIRGIN	VERGIN
VALID	CONVALID	virgin	vergine
validate, v.	convalidare	virginal	verginale
validation	convalidazione	virginity	verginità
VALV	VALVO	VITR	VETR
valve	valvola	vitreosity	vetrosità

vitrifaction	vetrificazįone	zealous	zelạnte
vitriol	vetriǫlo	zealousness	zelo
vitriolize, v.	vetrioleggiạre	ZION	SION
VITR	VITR	Zion	Sion
vitrify, v.	vitrificạre	Zionism	sionįsmo
vitreous	vịtreo	Zionist	sionįsta
VOLCAN	VULCAN	ZOOPH	ZOOF
volcanic	vulcạnico	zoophile	zoǫfilo
volcanicity	vulcanįsmo	zoophilous	zoǫfilo
volcano	vulcạno	zoophily	zoofilįa
VOLUNT	VOLONT	zoophobia	zoofobįa
voluntariness	volontarietà		
voluntary	volontạrio		
volunteer	volontạrio		
VOLUPT	VOLUTT		
voluptuary	voluttuǫso		
voluptuous	voluttuǫso		
voluptuousness	voluttà		
VOODOO	VUDU		
voodoo	vuduįsmo		
voodooism	vuduįsmo		
VULG	VOLG		
vulgar	volgạre		
vulgarism	volgarįsmo		
vulgarity	volgarità		
vulgarization	volgarizzazįone		
vulgarize, v.	volgarizzạre		
** Vulgate	Volgạta		
WZ			
X	S		
Xanthippe	Santįppe		
Xenophon	Senofǫnte		
xylograph	silografįa		
xylography	silografįa		
xylophone	silǫfono		
xylophonist	silofonįsta		
Note:			
Xanthippe	moglie bisbętica		
Y	I		
yucca (bot.)	iµcca		
Yugoslav	iugoslạvo		
** Yugoslavia	Jugoslạvia		
ZEAL	ZEL		
zeal	zelo		
Zealand	Zelạnda		
Zealander	zelandęse		

Chapter III
VERB CONVERTER

In this section we list verbs alphabetically by endings. As you know, Italian has three conjugations: the First Conjugation verbs end with "are" in the infinitive; the Second Conjugation verbs end with "ere, and the Thirst Conjugation end with "ire". We begin with the verbs of the First Conjugation. The verbs are broken down alphabetically since they are so numerous. As you can see, the equivalent of the "are" verbs in English end with "ate". Thus you will have "associate" = *associare*, "narrate" = *narrare*, etc... The verbs of the second and third conjugations follow a more complex pattern. Nevertheless, they can be grouped according to their endings: for example, verbs like "offend" in English will have a second conjugation ending as in *offendere*; verbs like "precede" *precedere* will also belong to the second conjugation; and verbs like "contradict," "abolish," "transfer," *contraddire*, *abolire*, and *trasferire* will belong to the third conjugation. Naturally, there are many irregular verbs, but even for these, patterns of similarities can be established. In many cases we are dealing with verbs that are formed by adding prefixes to them like the verb "pose" from which many other verbs can be formed like "compose," "suppose," "oppose". The same process will apply in Italian where given the verb *porre* you can form *comporre*, *supporre*, *opporre*, etc...Similar patterns exist for verbs ending with "act," and "uce" which become in Italian *arre* and *urre*.

To find the Italian equivalent of an English verb, look up the English ending and find the Italian equivalent. For example, to find the equivalent of "pretend" look for the ending "end"= *endere*, and you will find *pretendere*.

Learning how to convert infinitives is only a part of the conversion. As you know, verbs must be conjugated to express time and person. The endings attached to the root of the verb will tell you the subject and sometimes also the gender, and the time frame of the action. Thus, the ending "erei" of the verb "amerei" tells us that it is the first person of the Conditional Present tense, meaning "I would love". The "asse" ending of "pensasse" tells us that it is the third person of the Subjunctive Imperfect tense, meaning "that he/she might think". Learning the endings of the various tenses is an essential component of learning Italian. This text assumes that you are already familiar with the various tenses in Italian. Reviewing them here will help you to assimilate the material contained in this book.

Prima Coniugazione--First Conjugation

AMARE   TO LOVE

Indicativo	**Indicative**	**Indicativo**	**Indicative**
Presente	*Present*	*Passato Prossimo*	*Present Perfect*
amo	I love	ho amato	I have loved
ami	You love	hai amato	You have loved
ama	He/she loves	ha amato	He/she has loved
amiamo	We love	abbiamo amato	We have loved
amate	You love	avete amato	You have loved
amano	They love	hanno amato	They have loved

Futuro	*Future*	*Futuro anteriore*	*Future Perfect*
amerò	I will love	avrò amato	I will have loved
amerai	You will love	avrai amato	You will have loved
amerà	He/she will love	avrà amato	He/she will have loved
ameremo	We will love	avremo amato	We will have loved
amerete	You will love	avrete amato	You will have loved
ameranno	They will love	avranno amato	They will have loved

Imperfetto	*Past Descriptive*	*Piuccheperfetto*	*Past Perfect*
amavo	I used to love	avevo amato	I had loved
amavi	You used to love	avevi amato	You had loved
amava	He/she used to love	aveva amato	He/she had loved
amavamo	We used to love	avevamo amato	We had loved
amavate	You used to love	avevate amato	You had loved
amavano	They used to love	avevano amato	They had loved

Passato Remoto	*Past Absolute*	*Trapassato remoto*	*Past Perfect*
amai	I loved	ebbi amato	I had loved
amasti	You loved	avesti amato	You had loved
amò	He/she loved	ebbe amato	He/she had loved
amammo	We loved	avemmo amato	We had loved
amaste	You loved	aveste amato	You had loved
amarono	They loved	ebbero amato	They had loved

Condizionale	**Conditional**	**Condizionale**	**Conditional**
Presente	*Present*	*Passato*	*Perfect*
amerei	I would love	avrei amato	I would have loved
ameresti	You would love	avresti amato	You would have loved
amerebbe	He/she would love	avrebbe amato	He/she would have loved
ameremmo	We would love	avremmo amato	We would have loved
amereste	You would love	avreste amato	You would have loved
amerebbero	They would love	avrebbero amato	They would have loved

Congiuntivo	Subjunctive	Congiuntivo	Subjunctive
Presente	*Present*	*Passato*	*Present Perfect*
che ami	that I may love	che abbia amato	I may have loved
che ami	that you may love	che abbia amato	You may have loved
che ami	that he/she may love	che abbia amato	He/she may have loved
che amiamo	that we may love	che abbiamo amato	We may have loved
che amiate	that you may love	che abbiate amato	You may have loved
che amino	that they may love	che abbiano amato	They may have loved
Imperfecto	*Imperfect*	*Piuccheperfetto*	*Past Perfect*
che amassi	that I might love	che avessi amato	I might have loved
che amassi	that you might love	che avessi amato	You might have loved
che amasse	that he/she might love	che avesse amato	He/she might have loved
che amassimo	that we might love	che avessimo amato	We might have loved
che amaste	that you might love	che aveste amato	You might have loved
che amassero	that they might love	che avessero amato	They might have loved

Imperativo	Imperative	Participio	Participle
ama	love	*Passato*	*Past*
ami	love	amato	loved
amiamo	let us love		
amate	love		
amino	love	Infinitivo	Infinitive
		Presente	*Present*
Gerundio	Gerund	amare	to love
Presente	*Present*	*Passato*	*Past*
amando	loving	avere amato	to have loved
Passato	*Past*		
avendo amato	having loved		

Seconda Coniugazione--Second Conjugation

VENDERE   TO SELL

Indicativo	Indicative	Indicativo	Indicative
Presente	*Present*	*Passato Prossimo*	*Present Perfect*
vendo	I sell	ho venduto	I have sold
vendi	You sell	hai venduto	You have sold
vende	He/she sells	ha venduto	He/she has sold
vendiamo	We sell	abbiamo venduto	We have sold
vendete	You sell	avete venduto	You have sold
vendono	They sell	hanno venduto	They have sold

Futuro	Future	*Futuro Anteriore*	*Future Perfect*
venderò	I will sell	avrò venduto	I will have sold
venderai	You will sell	avrai venduto	You will have sold
venderà	He/she will sell	avrà venduto	He/she will have sold
venderemo	We will sell	avremo venduto	We will have sold
venderete	You will sell	avrete venduto	You will have sold
venderanno	They will sell	avranno venduto	They will have sold

Imperfetto	*Past Descriptive*	*Piuccheperfetto*	*Past Perfect*
vendevo	I used to sell	avevo venduto	I had sold
vendevi	You used to sell	avevi venduto	You had sold
vendeva	He/she used to sell	aveva venduto	He/she had sold
vendevamo	We used to sell	avevamo venduto	We had sold
vendevate	You used to sell	avevate venduto	You had sold
vendevano	They used to sell	avevano venduto	They had sold

Passato Remoto	*Past Absolute*	*Trapassato Remoto*	*Past Perfect*
vendei	I sold	ebbi venduto	I had sold
vendesti	You sold	avesti venduto	You had sold
vendette	He/she sold	ebbe venduto	He/she had sold
vendemmo	We sold	avemmo venduto	We had sold
vendeste	You sold	aveste venduto	You had sold
vendettero	They sold	ebbero venduto	They had sold

Condizionale	**Conditional**	**Condizionale**	**Conditional**
Presente	*Present*	*Passato*	*Perfect*
venderei	I would sell	avrei venduto	I would have sold
venderesti	You would sell	avresti venduto	You would have sold
venderebbe	He/she would sell	avrebbe venduto	He/she would have sold
venderemmo	We would sell	avremmo venduto	We would have sold
vendereste	You would sell	avreste venduto	You would have sold
venderebbero	They would sell	avrebbero venduto	They would have sold

Congiuntivo	**Subjunctive**	**Congiuntivo**	**Subjunctive**
Presente	*Present*	*Passato*	*Present Perfect*
che venda	that I may sell	che abbia venduto	I may have sold
che venda	that you may sell	che abbia venduto	You may have sold
che venda	thathe/she may sell	che abbia venduto	He/she may have sold
che vendiamo	that we may sell	che abbiamo venduto	We may have sold
che vendiate	that you may sell	che abbiate venduto	You may have sold
che vendano	that they may sell	che abbiano venduto	They may have sold

Imperfetto	*Past Descriptive*
che vendessi	that I might sell
che vendessi	that you might sell
che vendesse	that he/she might sell
che vendessimo	that we might sell
che vendeste	that you might sell
che vendessero	that they might sell

Piuccheperfetto	*Past Perfect*
avessi venduto	I might have sold
avessi venduto	You might have sold
avesse venduto	He/she might have sold
avessimo venduto	We might have sold
aveste venduto	You might have sold
avessero venduto	They might have sold

Imperativo — **Imperative**

vendi	sell
venda	sell
vendiamo	let us sell
vendete	sell
vendano	sell

Participio — **Participle**

Passato	*Past*
venduto	sold

Gerundio — **Gerund**

Presente	*Present*
vendendo	selling
Passato	*Past*
avendo venduto	having sold

Infinitivo — **Infinitive**

Presente	*Present*
vendere	to sell
Passato	*Past*
avere venduto	to have sold

Terza Coniugazione--Third Conjugation

DORMIRE   TO SLEEP

Indicativo	Indicative	Indicativo	Indicative
Presente	*Present*	*Trapassato Remoto*	*Past Perfect*
dormo	I sleep	ebbi dormito	I had slept
dormi	You sleep	avesti dormito	You had slept
dorme	He/she sleeps	ebbe dormito	He/she had slept
dormiamo	We sleep	avemmo dormito	We had slept
dormite	You sleep	aveste dormito	You had slept
dormono	They sleep	ebbero dormito	They had slept

Futuro	*Future*	*Passato Prossimo*	*Present Perfect*
dormirò	I will sleep	ho dormito	I have sold
dormirai	You will sleep	hai dormito	You have sold
dormirà	He/she will sleep	ha dormito	He/she has slept
dormiremo	We will sleep	abbiamo dormito	We have slept
dormirete	You will sleep	avete dormito	You have slept
dormiranno	They will sleep	hanno dormito	They have slept

Imperfetto	*Past Descriptive*	*Futuro Anteriore*	*Future Perfect*
dormivo	I used to sleep	avrò dormito	I will have slept
dormivi	You used to sleep	avrai dormito	You will have slept
dormiva	He/she used to sleep	avrà dormito	He/she will have slept
dormvamo	We used to sleep	avremo dormito	We will have slept
dormivate	You used to sleep	avrete dormito	You will have slept
dormivano	They used to sleep	avranno dormito	They will have slept

Passato remoto	*Past Absolute*	*Piuccheperfetto*	*Past Perfect*
dormii	I slept	avevo dormito	I had slept
dormisti	You slept	avevi dormito	You had slept
dormì	He/she slept	aveva dormito	He/she had slept
dormimmo	We slept	avevamo dormito	We had slept
dormiste	You slept	avevate dormito	You had slept
dormirono	They slept	avevano dormito	They had slept

Condizionale	Conditional	Condizionale	Conditional
Presente	*Present*	*Passato*	*Conditional Perfect*
dormirei	I would sleep	avrei dormito	I would have slept
dormiresti	You would sleep	avresti dormito	You would have slept
dormirebbe	He/she would sleep	avrebbe dormito	He/she would have slept
dormiremmo	We would sleep	avremmo dormito	We would have slept
dormireste	You would sleep	avreste dormito	You would have slept
dormirebbero	They would sleep	avrebbero dormito	They would have slept

Congiuntivo	Subjunctive	Congiuntivo	Subjunctive
Presente	*Present*	*Passato*	*Present Perfect*
che dorma	that you may sleep	che abbia dormito	I may have slept
che dorma	that I may sleep	- abbia dormito	You may have slept
che dorma	thathe/she may sleep	- abbia dormito	He/she may have slept
che dormiamo	that we may sleep	- abbiamo dormito	We may have slept
che dormiate	that you may sleep	- abbiate dormito	You may have slept
che dormano	that they may sleep	- abbiano dormito	They may have sold

Imperfetto	*Past Descriptive*	*Piuccheperfetto*	*Past Perfect*
che dormissi	that I might sleep	avessi dormito	I might have slept
che dormissi	that you might sleep	avessi dormito	You might have slept
che dormisse	that he/she might sleep	avesse dormito	He/she might have slept
che dormissimo	that we might sleep	avessimo dormito	We might have slept
che dormiste	that you might sleep	aveste dormito	You might have slept
che dormissero	that they might sleep	avessero dormito	They might have slept

Imperativo	Imperative	Gerundio	Gerund
dormi	sleep	*Presente*	*Present*
dorma	sleep	dormendo	sleeping
dormiamo	let us sleep	*Passato*	*Past*
dormite	sleep	avendo dormito	having slept
dormano	sleep		

		Infinitivo	Infinitive
		Presente	*Present*
Participio	Participle	dormire	to sleep
Passato	*Past*	*Passato*	*Past*
dormito	slept	avere dormito	to have slept

Terza Coniugazione--Third Conjugation-

FINIRE   TO FINISH

Indicativo	Indicative	Indicativo	Indicative
Presente	*Present*	*Passato Prossimo*	*Present Perfect*
finisco	I finish	ho finito	I have finished
finisci	You finish	hai finito	You have finished
finisce	He/she finishes	ha finito	He/she has finished
finiamo	We finish	abbiamo finito	We have finished
finite	You finish	avete finito	You have finished
finiscono	They finish	hanno finito	They have finished
Futuro	*Future*	*Futuro Anteriore*	*Future Perfect*
finirò	I will finish	avrò finito	I will have finished
finirai	You will finish	avrai finito	You will have finished
finirà	He/she will finish	avrà finito	He/she will have finished
finiremo	We will finish	avremo finito	We will have finished
finirete	You will finish	avrete finito	You will have finished
finiranno	They will finish	avranno finito	They will have finished
Imperfetto	*Past Descriptive*	*Piuccheperfetto*	*Past Perfect*
finivo	I used to finish	avevo finito	I had finished
finivi	You used to finish	avevi finito	You had finished
finiva	He/she used to finish	aveva finito	He/she had finished
finivamo	We used to finish	avevamo finito	We had finished
finivate	You used to finish	avevate finito	You had finished
finivano	They used to finish	avevano finito	They had finished
Passato remoto	*Past Absolute*	*Trapassato Remoto*	*Past Perfect*
finii	I finished	ebbi finito	I had finished
finisti	You finished	avesti finito	You had finished
finì	He/she finished	ebbe finito	He/she had finished
finimmo	We finished	avemmo finito	We had finished
finiste	You finished	aveste finito	You had finished
finirono	They finished	ebbero finito	They had finished

Condizionale	Conditional	Condizionale	Conditional
Presente	*Present*	*Passato*	*Conditional Perfect*
finirei	I would finish	avrei finito	I would have finished
finiresti	You would finish	avresti finito	You would have finished
finirebbe	He/she would finish	avrebbe finito	He/she would have finished
finiremmo	We would finish	avremmo finito	We would have finished
finireste	You would finish	avreste finito	You would have finished
finirebbero	They would finish	avrebbero finito	They would have finished

Congiuntivo	Subjunctive	Congiuntivo	Subjunctive
Presente	*Present*	*Passato*	*Present Perfect*
che finisca	that I may finish	che abbia finito	I may have finished
che finisca	that you may finish	che abbia finito	You may have finished
che finisca	thathe/she may finish	che abbia finito	He/she may have finished
che finiamo	that we may finish	che abbiamo finito	We may have finished
che finiate	that you may finish	che abbiate finito	You may have finished
che finiscano	that they may finish	che abbiano finito	They may have finished

Imperfetto	*Past Descriptive*	*Piuccheperfetto*	*Past Perfect*
che finissi	that I might finish	avessi finito	I might have finished
che finissi	that you might finish	avessi finito	You might have finished
che finisse	that he/she might finish	avesse finito	He/she might have finished
che finissimo	that we might finish	avessimo finito	We might have finished
che finiste	that you might finish	aveste finito	You might have finished
che finissero	that they might finish	avessero finito	They might have finished

Imperativo	**Imperative**	**Participio**	**Participle**
finisci	finish	*Passato*	*Past*
finisca	finish	finito	finished
finiamo	let us finish		
finite	finish		
finiscano	finish	**Infinitivo**	**Infinitive**
		Presente	*Present*
		finire	to finish
Gerundio	**Gerund**	*Passato*	*Past*
Presente	*Present*	avere finito	to have finished
finendo	finishing		
Passato	*Past*		
avendo finito	having finished		

VERB CONVERTER INDEX

-act	-arre
-arm	-armare
-ate	-are
-cede	-cedere
-cept	-cepire
-cile	-ciliare
-cite	-citare
-claim	-clamare
-cline	-clinare
-cur	-correre
-dict	-dire
-duce	-durre
-duct	-durre
-ect	-eggere
-ect	-ettare
-ect	-ezionare
-empt	-entare
-end	-endere
-ense	-ensare
-ent	-entare
-ess	-are
-est	-estare
-exist	see-sist-sistere
-fect	see-ect-ettare
-fend	see-end-endere
-fer	-ferire
-fest	see-est-estare
-figure	-figurare
-firm	-fermare
-flect	-flettere
-flict	-fliggere
-form	-formare
-fuse	-fondere
-fy	-ficare
-gest	-gerire
-grade	-gradare
-gress	-gredire
-habit	-abitare
-hibit	-ibire
-ide	-idere
-ify	see-fy-ficare
-ign	-ignare
-ile	-are

-ile	-iare
-ine	-inare
-ion	-ionare
-ire	-irare
-ish	-ire
-it	-itare
-ite	-itare
-ive	-ivare
-ize	-izzare
-ject	see-ect-ettare
-lude	-ludere
-lyze	see-ize-izzare
-mand	-mandare
-mend	see-end-endere
-merge	-mergere
-mit	-mettere
-mit	-mitare
-mute	-mutare
-note	-notare
-nounce	-nunciare
-ore	-orare
-pend	see-end-endere
-pense	see-ense-ensare
-ple	-plicare
-plore	-plorare
-pone	-porre
-port	-portare
-pose	-porre
-prehend,	see-end-endere
-press	-primere
-prove	-provare
-rest	see-est-estare
-rupt	-rompere
-scend	see-end-endere
-scind	-scindere
-scribe	-scrivere
-sect	-secare
-sent	-sentire
-sert	-serire
-serve	-servare
-side	-siedere
-sign	-segnare
-sist/-exist	-sisterc
-solve	-solvere
-spire	-spirare
-spond	-spondere

73

-strict	-stringere
-struct	-struire
-suade	-ere
-sume	-sumere
-tain	-tenere
-tend	see-end-endere
-tract	see-act-atto
-trude	-trudere
-ult	-ultare
-ume	-umare
-unite	-unire
-ure	-urare
-use	-usare
-ute	-uire
-ute	-utare
-vade	-vadere
-vene	-venire
-verge	-vergere
-vert	-vertire
-vest	-vestire
-vive	-vivere
-voke	-vocare
-volve	-volvere
-yse	see-ize-izzare
-yze	see-ize-izzare

VERB CONVERTER

-ACT	-ARRE	agitate	agitare
-tract	See-ACT	alienate	alienare
abstract*	astrarre	alleviate	alleviare
attract	attrarre	altercate	altercare
contract	contrarre	alternate	alternare
detract	detrarre	ambulate	ambulare
distract	distrarre	amalgamate	amalgamare
extract*	estrarre	amputate	amputare
protract	protrarre	animate	animare
retract*	ritrarre	annihilate*	annichilare
subtract*	sottrarre	annotate	annotare
Exceptions:		antedate*	antidatare
contact	contattare	anticipate	anticipare
react	reagire	appreciate	apprezzare
refract	rifrangere	appropriate	appropriare
transact	trattare	approximate*	approssimare
-ARM	-ARMARE	arbitrate	arbitrare
arm	armare, armarsi	arrogate	arrogare
alarm*	allarmare	articulate*	articolare
disarm	disarmare	asphyxiate*	asfissiare
rearm*	riarmare	aspirate	aspirare
-ATE	-ARE	assassinate	assassinare
		asseverate	asseverare
		assimilate	assimilare
		associate	associare

Generally all verbs ending in –ate change to "-are" (1st conjugation)

abbreviate	abbreviare	attenuate	attenuare
abdicate	abdicare	auscultate	auscultare
abnegate	abnegare	authenticate*	autenticare
abominate	abominare	B	
abrogate	abrogare	bifurcate*	biforcare
accelerate	accelerare	C	
accentuate	accentuare	calculate	calcolare
accommodate	accomodare	calibrate	calibrare
accumulate	accumulare	calumniate*	calunniare
acerbate	acerbare	capitulate*	capitolare
activate*	attivare	captivate*	accattivare
actuate	attuare	captivate*	accattivarsi
adjudicate*	giudicare	captivate*	cattivare
administrate*	amministrare	carburate	carburare
adulterate	adulterare	castigate	castigare
adumbrate	adombrare	castrate	castrare
agglomerate	agglomerare	celebrate	celebrare
agglutinate	agglutinare	centuplicate	centuplicare
aggravate	aggravare	circulate	circolare
aggregate	aggregare		

circumnavigate	circumnavigare	decelerate	decelerare
coagulate	coagulare	decimate	decimare
cogitate	cogitare	deconsecrate*	sconsacrare
collaborate	collaborare	decorate	decorare
collate	collare	dedicate	dedicare
collocate	collocare	defecate	defecare
commemorate	commemorare	degenerate	degenerare
commiserate	commiserare	delegate	delegare
communicate	comunicare	deliberate	deliberare
compensate	compensare	delineate	delineare
complicate	complicare	demonstrate*	dimostrare
concatenate	concatenare	denominate	denominare
concentrate	concentrare	depilate	depilare
conciliate	conciliare	depopulate*	depopolare
confabulate	confabulare	deprecate	deprecare
confederate	confederare	depreciate*	deprezzare
confiscate	confiscare	depredate	depredare
conglomerate	conglomerare	depurate	depurare
congratulate	congratulare	derogate	derogare
congregate	congregare	desiccate*	essiccare
conjugate*	coniugare	designate	designare
consecrate*	consacrare	desolate	desolare
consolidate	consolidare	deteriorate	deteriorare
constipate*	costipare	determinate	determinare
consummate*	consumare	detonate	detonare
contaminate	contaminare	detoxicate*	disintossicare
contemplate	contemplare	devastate	devastare
cooperate	cooperare	deviate	deviare
coordinate	coordinare	diagnosticate	diagnosticare
copulate	copulare	dictate*	dettare
correlate	correlare	differentiate	differenziare
corroborate	corroborare	dilapidate	dilapidare
corrugate	corrugare	dilate	dilatare
create	creare	disarticulate*	disarticolare
cremate	cremare	discriminate	discriminare
crepitate	crepitare	disculpate*	discolpare
culminate	culminare	disintegrate	disintegrare
cultivate	coltivare	dislocate*	dislogare
cumulate*	accumulare	disorientate	disorientare
D		disseminate	disseminare
date	datare	dissimulate	dissimulare
debate*	dibattere	dissipate	dissipare
debilitate	debilitare	dissociate	dissociare
decaffeinate*	decaffinare	distillate	distillare
decaffeinate*	decaffeinizzare	dominate	dominare
decapitate	decapitare	donate	donare

duplicate	duplicare	fornicate	fornicare
E		frustrate	frustrare
educate	educare	fulminate	fulminare
ejaculate*	eiaculare	G	
elaborate	elaborare	gelatinate*	gelatinizzare
elevate	elevare	geminate	geminare
eliminate	eliminare	generate	generare
emanate	emanare	germinate	germinare
emancipate	emancipare	gesticulate*	gesticolare
emigrate	emigrare	grate	grattare
emulate	emulare	gravitate	gravitare
enucleate	enucleare	H	
enumerate	enumerare	habituate*	abituare
enunciate	enunciare	hallucinate*	allucinare
equilibrate	equilibrare	hesitate*	esitare
equivocate	equivocare	hibernate*	ibernare
eradicate*	sradicare, estirpare	homologate*	omologare
evacuate	evacuare	humiliate*	umiliare
evaporate	evaporare	hydrogenate*	idrogenare
exacerbate*	esacerbare	I	
exaggerate*	esagerare	illuminate	illuminare
exasperate*	esasperare	illustrate	illustrare
excogitate*	escogitare	immigrate	immigrare
excoriate*	escoriare	immolate	immolare
exculpate*	discolpare	impersonate	impersonare
exhilarate*	esilarare	implicate	implicare
exonerate*	esonerare	imprecate	imprecare
expatriate*	espatriare	impregnate	impregnare
expectorate*	espettorare	inaugurate	inaugurare
expiate*	espiare	incarcerate	incarcerare
explicate*	esplicare	incarnate	incarnare
expropriate*	espropriare	incoronate	incoronare
expurgate*	espurgare	incorporate	incorporare
exsiccate*	essiccare	incriminate	incriminare
extenuate*	estenuare	incubate	incubare
exterminate*	sterminare	inculcate	inculcare
extirpate*	estirpare	inculpate*	incolpare
extrapolate*	estrapolare	incurvate	incurvare
F		indicate	indicare
fabricate*	fabbricare	individuate	individuare
facilitate	facilitare	infatuate	infatuare
fecundate*	fecondare	infiltrate	infiltrare
federate	federare	ingratiate*	ingraziare
felicitate	felicitare	ingurgitate	ingurgitare
flagellate	flagellare	initiate*	iniziare
formulate	formulare	innervate	innervare

innovate	innovare	moderate	moderare
inoculate	inoculare	modulate	modulare
insalivate	insalivare	motivate	motivare
inseminate	inseminare	mutilate	mutilare
insinuate	insinuare	**N**	
instigate*	istigare	narrate	narrare
insufflate	insufflare	nauseate	nauseare
insulate*	isolare	navigate	navigare
intercalate	intercalare	necessitate	necessitare
interpellate	interpellare	negate	negare
interpolate	interpolare	negotiate*	negoziare
interrogate	interrogare	nominate	nominare
inundate*	inondare	**O**	
invaginate	invaginare	obfuscate*	offuscare
invalidate	invalidare	obligate*	obbligare
investigate	investigare	obviate*	ovviare
irradiate	irradiare	officiate	officiare
irrigate	irrigare	operate	operare
irritate	irritare	orchestrate	orchestrare
iterate	iterare	orientate	orientare
J		originate	originare
jubilate	giubilare	ornate	ornare
L		oscillate	oscillare
lacerate	lacerare	osculate	osculare
laminate	laminare	oxygenate*	ossigenare
legate	legare	**P**	
legislate*	legiferare	palpitate	palpitare
legitimate*	legittimare	participate	partecipare
levitate	levitare	penetrate	penetrare
liberate	liberare	perforate	perforare
liquidate	liquidare	permeate	permeare
litigate	litigare	perorate	perorare
lubricate	lubricare	perpetrate	perpetrare
luxate*	lussare	perpetuate	perpetuare
M		placate	placare
macerate	macerare	pontificate	pontificare
machinate*	macchinare	populate*	popolare
maculate	maculare	postdate	postdatare
manipulate*	manipolare	postulate	postulare
masticate	masticare	potentiate*	potenziare
masturbate	masturbare	precipitate	precipitare
mediate	mediare	predestinate	predestinare
medicate	medicare	predominate	predominare
meditate	meditare	prefabricate*	prefabbricare
migrate	migrare	premeditate	premeditare
mitigate	mitigare	preponderate	preponderare

procrastinate	procrastinare	segregate	segregare
procreate	procreare	separate	separare
prognosticate*	pronosticare	sequestrate	sequestrare
proliferate	proliferare	simulate	simulare
promulgate	promulgare	situate	situare
propagate	propagare	sophisticate	sofisticare
propitiate*	propiziare	speculate	speculare
proportionate*	proporzionare	stimulate	stimolare
prostrate	prostrare	stipulate	stipulare
pullulate	pullulare	strangulate*	strangolare
pulsate	pulsare	subjugate*	soggiogare
punctuate*	punteggiare	subordinare	subordinare
Q		substantiate*	sostanziare
quadruplicate	quadruplicare	suffocate*	soffocare
quintuplicate	quintuplicare	sulphurate*	solforare
R		supplicate	supplicare
ratiocinate*	raziocinare	suppurate	suppurare
reanimate	rianimare	syncopate*	sincopare
recalcitrate	recalcitrare	T	
reciprocate	reciprocare	tergiversate	tergiversare
recreate*	ricreare	terminate	terminare
recriminate	recriminare	titillate	titillare
recuperate*	ricuperare	tolerate*	tollerare
reintegrate*	reintegrare	transliterate*	traslitterare
refrigerate	refrigerare	transmigrate*	trasmigrare
regenerate*	rigenerare	triplicate	triplicare
regulate*	regolare	triturate	triturare
regurgitate*	rigurgitare	truncate	troncare
rehabilitate*	riabilitare	U	
reincarnate	reincarnare	ulcerate	ulcerare
reiterate	reiterare	ululate	ululare
relegate	relegare	V	
remunerate	rimunerare	vaccinate	vaccinare
renovate*	rinnovare	vacillate	vacillare
repatriate*	rimpatriare	validate	convalidare
repudiate*	ripudiare	variegate	variegare
resuscitate*	risuscitare	vaticinate	vaticinare
reverberate*	riverberare	vegetate	vegetare
rotate	rotare	venerate	venerare
ruminate	ruminare	ventilate	ventilare
S		vibrate	vibrare
salivate	salivare	vindicate*	rivendicare
satiate*	saziare	violate	violare
saturate	saturare	vitiate*	viziare
scintillate	scintillare	vociferate	vociferare
sedate	sedare	*Some exceptions*:	

appropriate	appropriarsi	interdict	interdire
incinerate	incenerire	maledict	maledire
indurate	indurire	predict	predire
intimidate	intimidire	-DUCT	-DURRE
translate	tradurre	conduct	condurre
-CEDE	-CEDERE	deduct	dedurre
accede	accedere	-ECT	-EGGERE
cede	cedere	correct	correggere
concede	concedere	elect	eleggere
intercede	intercedere	protect	proteggere
precede	precedere	*Exceptions*:	
recede	recedere	connect	connettere
retrocede	retrocedere	direct	dirigere
-CEPT	-CEPIRE	erect	erigere
concept	concepire	intersect	intersecare
percept	percepire	resurrect	risorgere
but:		-ECT	-ETTARE
intercept	intercettare	-fect	
-CILE	-CILIARE	-ject	
domicile	domiciliare	collect	collettare
reconcile*	riconciliare	disinfect	disinfettare
-CITE	-CITARE	infect	infettare
cite	citare	inject*	iniettare
excite	eccitare	object*	obiettare
incite	incitare	project*	progettare
recite	recitare	project*	proiettare
-CLAIM	-CLAMARE	respect*	rispettare
acclaim	acclamare	suspect*	sospettare
claim	reclamare	*Exceptions*:	
declaim	declamare	effect	effettuare
exclaim*	esclamare	interject	interporre
proclaim	proclamare	-ECT	-EZIONARE
-CLINE	-CLINARE	defect	defezionare
decline	declinare	inspect*	ispezionare
incline	inclinare	perfect	perfezionare
but:		select	selezionare
disincline	distogliere	vivisect	vivisezionare
-CUR	-CORRERE	*Note:*	
concur	concorrere	defect	disertare
incur	incorrere	-EMPT	-ENTARE
recur*	ricorrere	attempt	tentare
but:		exempt*	esentare
occur*	accadere	tempt	tentare
recline	reclinare	-END	-ENDERE
-DICT	-DIRE	-fend	
contradict*	contraddire	-mend	

80

-pend		orient	orientare
-prehend		ornament	ornamentare
-scend		present	presentare
-tend		represent*	rappresentare
ascend	ascendere	segment	segmentare
comprehend*	comprendere	torment	tormentare
condescend*	condiscendere	*but:*	
defend*	difendere	prevent	prevenire
depend*	dipendere	-ESS	-ARE
descend*	discendere	confess	confessare
extend*	estendere	profess	professare
intend	intendere	*Exceptions:*	
offend	offendere	caress	accarezzare
pretend	pretendere	obsess	ossessionare
reprehend*	riprendere	possess	possedere
subtend*	sottendere (math.)	repress	reprimere
suspend*	sospendere	-EST	-ESTARE
tend	tendere	arrest	arrestare
transcend*	trascendere	attest	attestare
vend	vendere	contest	contestare
vilipend	vilipendere	detest	detestare
Exceptions:		disinfest	disinfestare
amend	emendare	infest	infestare
emend	emendare	manifest	manifestare
apprehend	arrestare	molest	molestare
recommend	raccomandare	protest	protestare
-ENSE	-ENSARE	*Exceptions:*	
-pense	See-ENSE	interest	interessare
condense	condensare	invest	investire
dispense	dispensare	-exist	See-SIST
incense	incensare	-FER	-FERIRE
recompense	ricompensare	confer	conferire
-ENT	-ENTARE	defer*	differire
aliment	alimentare	differ	differire
augment*	aumentare	infer	inferire
cement	cementare	prefer	preferire
comment	commentare	refer*	riferire
complement	complementare	transfer*	trasferire
compliment	complimentare	*Exceptions:*	
content	contentare	offer	offrire
document	documentare	suffer	soffrire
experiment*	esperimentare	-FIGURE	-FIGURARE
ferment	fermentare	configure	configurare
frequent	frequentare	prefigure	prefigurare
invent	inventare	transfigure	trasfigurare
lament	lamentare	-FIRM	-FERMARE

affirm	affermare	falsify	falsificare
confirm	confermare	fortify	fortificare
-FLECT	-FLETTERE	fructify*	fruttificare
deflect	deflettere	gasify	gassificare
genuflect	genuflettere	gasify	gasificare
inflect	inflettere	glorify	glorificare
reflect*	riflettere	identify	identificare
-FLICT	-FLIGGERE	intensify	intensificare
afflict	affliggere	justify*	giustificare
inflict	infliggere	modify	modificare
-FORM	-FORMARE	mortify	mortificare
conform	conformare	mummify	mummificare
deform	deformare	mystify*	mistificare
form	formare	notify	notificare
inform	informare	nullify	nullificare
reform*	riformare	ossify	ossificare
transform*	trasformare	pacify	pacificare
Exceptions:		personify	personificare
chloroform	cloroformizzare	petrify*	pietrificare
perform	operare	purify	purificare
FUSE	-FONDERE	qualify	qualificare
confuse	confondere	ramify	ramificare
diffuse	diffondere	ratify	ratificare
effuse	effondere	rectify*	rettificare
fuse	fondere	revivify*	rivivificare
infuse	infondere	sanctify*	santificare
transfuse*	trasfondere	saponify	saponificare
but:		scarify	scarificare
defuse	disinnestare	signify	significare
refuse	rifiutare	simplify	semplificare
-FY	-FICARE	solidify	solidificare
acidify	acidificare	specify	specificare
amplify	amplificare	stratify	stratificare
beatify	beatificare	syllabify*	sillabare
calcify	calcificare	syllabify*	sillabifare
certify	certificare	unify	unificare
classify	classificare	verify	verificare
codify	codificare	versify	versificare
decalcify	decalcificare	vitrify	vitrificare
deify	deificare	vivify	vivificare
diversify	diversificare	*Some exceptions*:	
dulcify*	dolcificare	clarify	chiarire
edify	edificare	crucify	crocifiggere
electrify*	elettrificare	dignify	nobilitare
esterify	esterificare	emulsify	emulsionare
exemplify*	esemplificare	indemnify	indennizzare

liquefy	liquefare	-IGN	-IGNARE
magnify	ingrandire	malign	malignare
objectify	oggettivare	reign*	regnare
putrefy	putrefare	*but:*	
rarefy	rarefare	align	allineare
stupify	istupidire	-ILE	-ARE
stupify	stupidire	compile	compilare
tumefy	tumefare	profile	profilare
-GEST	-GERIRE	-ILE	-IARE
digest	digerire	domicile	domiciliare
ingest	ingerire	exile*	esiliare
suggest	suggerire	reconcile*	riconciliare
Exception:		-INE	-INARE
congest	congestionare	calcine	calcinare
-GRADE	-GRADARE	combine	combinare
degrade	degradare	confine	confinare
retrograde	retrogradare	decline	declinare
but:		destine	destinare
grade	graduare	determine	determinare
retrograde	retrocedere	discipline	disciplinare
-GRESS	-GREDIRE	examine*	esaminare
regress	regredire	guillotine	ghigliottinare
progress	progredire	illumine	illuminare
transgress	trasgredire	imagine*	immaginare
Exception:		incline	inclinare
retrogress	retrocedere	mine	minare
-HABIT	-ABITARE	opine	opinare
cohabit*	coabitare	predestine	predestinare
inhabit*	abitare	predetermine	predeterminare
-HIBIT	-IBIRE	recline	reclinare
exhibit*	esibire	*Exceptions:*	
inhibit*	inibire	define	definire
prohibit*	proibire	interline	interlineare
-IDE	-IDERE	-ION	-IONARE
coincide	coincidere	commission	commissionare
decide	decidere	condition*	condizionare
deride	deridere	confection*	confezionare
divide	dividere	function*	funzionare
elide	elidere	mention*	menzionare
subdivide*	suddividere	proportion*	proporzionare
Note:		section*	sezionare
confide	confidare	-IRE	-IRARE
guide	guidare	admire*	ammirare
preside	presiedere	aspire	aspirare
		conspire*	cospirare
-IFY	See-FY	expire*	spirare

inspire*	ispirare
respire	respirare
retire*	ritirare
Exceptions:	
acquire	acquistare
desire	desiderare
require	richiedere

Third Conjugation Verbs

-ISH	-IRE
abolish	abolire
admonish*	ammonire
brandish	brandire
demolish	demolire
diminish**	diminuire
establish*	stabilire
finish	finire
furnish*	fornire
impoverish	impoverire
languish	languire
perish	perire
punish	punire
vanish*	svanire

First Conjugation Verbs:

fish	pescare
publish	pubblicare
republish	ripubblicare
varnish	verniciare

Second Conjugation Verbs:

distinguish	distinguere
extinguish	estinguere
-IT	-ITARE
debit*	addebbitare
deposit	depositare
discredit	discreditare
merit	meritare
visit	visitare
but:	
intuit	intuire
-ITE	-ITARE
cite	citare

excite*	eccitare
incite	incitare
invite	invitare
recite	recitare
Exception:	
extradite	estradare
-IVE	-IVARE
arrive	arrivare
deprive	deprivare
derive	derivare
Other:	
perceive	percepire
receive	ricevere
-IZE	-IZZARE
A	
allegorize	allegorizzare
alphabetize	alfabetizzare
Americanize	americanizzare
anaesthetize*	anestetizzare
analyze*	analizzare
anathemize*	anatemizzare
anatomize	anatomizzare
anglicize	anglicizzare
archaize*	arcaizzare
aromatize	aromatizzare
atomize	atomizzare
authorize*	autorizzare
B	
barbarize	barbarizzare
brutalize	brutalizzare
C	
canonize	canonizzare
capitalize	capitalizzare
carbonize	carbonizzare
catechize	catechizzare
cauterize	cauterizzare
centralize	centralizzare
characterize*	caratterizzare
christianize*	cristianizzare
cicatrize	cicatrizzare
civilize	civilizzare
colonize	colonizzare
commercialize	commercializzare
crystallize*	cristallizzare
D	
demagnetize*	demagnetizzare

demilitarize	demilitarizzare
democratize	democratizzare
demoralize	demoralizzare
denationalize	denazionalizzare
devitalize	devitalizzare
disorganize	disorganizzare
dogmatize	dogmatizzare
dramatize*	drammatizzare
E	
economize	economizzare
equalize	equalizzare
etymologize*	etimologizzare
Europeanize	europeizzare
evangelize	evangelizzare
exorcize*	esorcizzare
F	
familiarize	familiarizzare
fertilize	fertilizzare
formalize	formalizzare
fossilize	fossilizzare
fraternize	fraternizzare
G	
galvanize	galvanizzare
generalize	generalizzare
Germanize	germanizzare
H	
harmonize*	armonizzare
hellenize*	ellenizzare
homogenize*	omogeneizzare
humanize*	umanizzare
hypnotize*	ipnotizzare
hypothesize*	ipotizzare
I	
idealize	idealizzare
immunize	immunizzare
individualize	individualizzare
industrialize	industrializzare
intellectualize*	intellettualizzare
internationalize	internazionalizzare
Italianize	italianizzare
J	
judaize*	giudaizzare
L	
laicize	laicizzare
Latinize	latinizzare
legalize	legalizzare

localize	localizzare
M	
macadamize	macadamizzare
magnetize	magnetizzare
materialize	materializzare
mechanize*	meccanizzare
memorize	memorizzare
mesmerize	mesmerizzare
metallize	metallizzare
methodize*	metodizzare
militarize	militarizzare
mineralize	mineralizzare
minimize	minimizzare
modernize	modernizzare
monetize	monetizzare
monopolize	monopolizzare
moralize	moralizzare
motorize	motorizzare
municipalize	municipalizzare
N	
narcotize	narcotizzare
nasalize	nasalizzare
nationalize	nazionalizzare
naturalize	naturalizzare
neutralize	neutralizzare
normalize	normalizzare
O	
Occidentalize	occidentalizzare
organize	organizzare
Orientalize	orientalizzare
ostracize	ostracizzare
P	
pasteurize*	pastorizzare
penalize	penalizzare
personalize	personalizzare
pluralize	pluralizzare
poetize	poetizzare
polarize	polarizzare
polemize	polemizzare
popularize*	popolarizzare
pressurize	pressurizzare
publicize*	pubblicizzare
pulverize*	polverizzare
R	
rationalize	razionalizzare
realize	realizzare

regularize*	regolarizzare	baptize	battezzare
reorganize*	riorganizzare	caponize	capponare
Romanize	romanizzare	carburize	carburare
S		criticize	criticare
scandalize	scandalizzare	decentralize	decentrare
schematize	schematizzare	dehumanize	disumanare
secularize*	secolarizzarc	demobilize	smobilitare
sensitize*	sensibilizzare	denaturize	denaturare
solemnize*	solennizzare	deodorize	deodorare
sovietize	sovietizzare	epitomize	epitomare
specialize	specializzare	eternilize	eternare
stabilize	stabilizzare	eulogize	elogiare
standardize	standardizzare	exteriorize	esternare
sterilize	sterilizzare	externalize	esternare
stigmatize	stigmatizzare	fractionize	frazionare
stylize*	stilizzare	hybridize	ibridare
syllogize*	sillogizzare	idolatrize	idolatrare
sympathize*	simpatizzare	idolize	idolatrare
synchronize*	sincronizzare	immortalize	immortalare
synthetize*	sintetizzare	mobilize	mobilitare
systematize*	sistematizzare	optimize	ottimare
T		oxidize	ossidare
terrorize	terrorizzare	patronize	patrocinare
theorize*	teorizzare	philosophize	filosofare
totalize	totalizzare	plagiarize	plagiare
tranquillize	tranquillizzare	platinize	platinare
U		poeticize	poetare
universalize	universalizzare	recognize	riconoscere
urbanize	urbanizzare	revulutionize	rivoluzionare
utilize	utilizzare	satirize	satireggiare
V		scrutinize	scrutare
valorize	valorizzare	signalize	segnalare
vaporize	vaporizzare	skeletonize	scheletrire
victimize*	vittimizzare	subsidize	sussidiare
visualize	visualizzare	symbolize	simboleggiare
vitaminize	vitaminizzare	temporize	temporeggiare
vocalize	vocalizzare	tyrannize	tiranneggiare
volatilize	volatizzare	vitriolize	vetrioleggiare
vulcanize	vulcanizzare	-LUDE	-LUDERE
vulgarize*	volgarizzare	allude	alludere
Some exceptions:		collude	colludere
acclimatize	acclimare	conclude	concludere
amortize	ammortare	delude*	illudere
anagram(matize)	anagrammare	elude	eludere
apostrophize	apostrofare	exclude*	escludere
bastardize	imbastardire	illude	illudere

86

include	includere	implore	implorare
occlude	occludere	*Exception*:	
preclude	precludere	restore	restaurare
prelude	preludere	-PLE	-PLICARE
-MAND	-MANDARE	centuple	centuplicare
command*	comandare	quadruple	quadruplicare
demand*	domandare	quintuple	quintuplicare
remand*	rimandare	triple	triplicare
-MERGE	-MERGERE	-PLORE	-PLORARE
emerge	emergere	implore	implorare
immerge	immergere	explore*	esplorare
submerge*	sommergere	deplore	deplorare
submerge*	immergere	-PONE	-PORRE
but:		postpone*	posporre
merge	incorporare	depone/depose	deporre
-MIT	-METTERE	-PORT	-PORTARE
admit*	ammettere	comport	comportare
commit	commettere	deport	deportare
emit	emettere	export*	esportare
manumit*	manomettere	import	importare
omit	omettere	reimport	reimportare
permit	permettere	transport*	trasportare
remit	rimettere	-POSE	-PORRE
transmit*	trasmettere	appose	apporre
-MIT	-MITARE	compose	comporre
delimit	delimitare	decompose	decomporre
limit	limitare	depose	deporre
vomit	vomitare	dispose	disporre
-MUTE	-MUTARE	expose*	esporre
commute	commutare	impose	imporre
permute	permutare	indispose	indisporre
transmute*	trasmutare	interpose	interporre
-NOTE	-NOTARE	oppose	opporre
connote	connotare	pose	porre
denote	detonare	predispose	predisporre
note	notare	presuppose	presupporre
-NOUNCE	-NUNCIARE	propose	proporre
announce	annunciare	recompose*	ricomporre
denounce	denunciare	suppose	supporre
pronounce	pronunciare	transpose*	trasporre
renounce	rinunciare	*Exception*:	
-ORE	-ORARE	repose	riposare
adore	adorare	-PRESS	-PRIMERE
deplore	deplorare	compress	comprimere
explore*	esplorare	decompress	decomprimere
ignore	ignorare	depress	deprimere

express*	esprimere
impress	imprimere
oppress	opprimere
repress	reprimere
suppress*	sopprimere
Exceptions:	
press	premere
impress	impressionare
-PROVE	-PROVARE
approve	approvare
disapprove	disapprovare
disprove*	invalidare
prove	provare
reprove*	riprovare
but:	
improve	migliorare
-RUPT	-ROMPERE
corrupt*	corrompere
interrupt*	interrompere
irrupt	irrompere
but:	
erupt	eruttare
-SCIND	-SCINDERE
prescind	prescindere
rescind	rescindere
-SCRIBE	-SCRIVERE
circumscribe*	circoscrivere
describe	descrivere
prescribe	prescrivere
proscribe	proscrivere
transcribe*	trascrivere
but:	
inscribe	incidere
inscribe	scolpire
-SECT	-SECARE
bisect	bisecare
intersect	intersecare
but:	
vivisect	vivisezionare
-SENT	-SENTIRE
assent	assentire
consent	consentire
dissent	dissentire
-SERT	-SERIRE
assert	asserire
insert	inserire

but:	
desert	disertare
-SERVE	-SERVARE
conserve	conservare
observe*	osservare
preserve	preservare
reserve*	riservare
but:	
serve	servire
-SIDE	-SIEDERE
preside	presiedere
reside*	risiedere
but:	
subside	calare; cedere
-SIGN	-SEGNARE
assign	assegnare
consign	consegnare
design*	disegnare
-SIST/-EXIST	-SISTERE
assist	assistere
coexist*	coesistere
consist	consistere
desist	desistere
exist*	esistere
insist	insistere
persist	persistere
pre-exist*	preesistere
resist	resistere
subsist*	sussistere
-SOLVE	-SOLVERE
absolve*	assolvere
dissolve	dissolvere
resolve*	risolvere
solve	solvere
-SPIRE	-SPIRARE
aspire	aspirare
conspire*	cospirare
expire*	spirare
inspire*	ispirare
transpire*	traspirare
but:	
expire*	morire
expire*	scadere
-SPOND	-SPONDERE
correspond*	corrispondere
respond*	rispondere

Exception:		reproduce*	riprodurre
despond	scoraggiarsi	seduce	sedurre
-STRICT	-STRINGERE	*Note:*	
restrict	restringere	educe	trarre, estrarre
constrict*	costringere	*Exception:*	
-STRUCT	-STRUIRE	translate	tradurre
construct*	costruire	-ULT	ULTARE
instruct*	istruire	catapult	catapultare
obstruct*	ostruire	consult	consultare
reconstruct*	ricostruire	exult*	esultare
but:		insult	insultare
destruct*	distruggere	occult	occultare
-SUADE	-ERE	result*	risultare
dissuade	dissuadere	*Exceptions:*	
persuade	persuadere	assault	assalire
-SUME	-SUMERE	-UME	-UMARE
assume	assumere	exhume*	esumare
presume	presumere	fume	fumare
reassume*	riassumere	inhume*	inumare
but:		-UNITE	-UNIRE
consume	consumare	disunite	disunire
resume	riprendere	reunite*	riunire
-TAIN	-TENERE	unite	unire
abstain*	astenere	-URE	-URARE
contain	contenere	abjure*	abiurare
detain	detenere	adventure*	avventurare
entertain*	intrattenere	assure	assicurare
maintain*	mantenere	capture*	catturare
obtain*	ottenere	censure	censurare
retain*	ritenere	configure	configurare
sustain*	sostenere	conjecture*	congetturare
sustain*	mantenere	conjure*	congiurare
-TRUDE	-TRUDERE	cure	curare
extrude*	estrudere	denature	denaturare
intrude	intrudere	fracture*	fratturare
also:		mature	maturare
extrude	spingere fuori	measure*	misurare
protrude	sporgere	obscure*	oscurare
-DUCE	-DURRE	procure	procurare
adduce	addurre	suture	suturare
conduce	condurre	tonsure	tonsurare
deduce	dedurre	torture	torturare
induce	indurre	transfigure*	trasfigurare
introduce	introdurre	venture*	avventurare
produce	produrre	*Exceptions:*	
reduce*	ridurre	injure	ingiuriare

puncture	pungere
rupture	rompere
sculpture	scolpire
-USE	-USARE
abuse	abusare
accuse	accusare
cause	causare
excuse*	scusare
use	usare
-UTE	-UIRE
attribute	attribuire
constitute*	costituire
contribute	contribuire
dilute	diluire
distribute	distribuire
execute*	eseguire
institute*	istituire
prostitute	prostituire
reconstitute*	ricostituire
restitute	restituire
substitute*	sostituire
-UTE	-UTARE
commute	commutare
compute	computare
confute	confutare
depute	deputare
dispute	disputare
impute	imputare
parachute*	paracadutare
permute	permutare
repute	reputare
salute	salutare
transmute*	trasmutare
but:	
compute	calcolare
persecute	perseguitare
-VADE	-VADERE
evade	evadere
invade	invadere
pervade	pervadere
-VENE	-VENIRE
contravene*	contravvenire

convene	convenire
but:	
convene	convocare
intervene	intervenire
-VERGE	-VERGERE
converge	convergere
diverge	divergere
Exception:	
verge	volgere
-VERT	-VERTIRE
convert	convertire
divert	divertire
introvert	introvertire
invert	invertire
pervert	pervertire
subvert	sovvertire
but:	
divert	deviare
introvert	introvertere (zoo.)
-VEST	-VESTIRE
divest	svestire
invest	investire
-VIVE	-VIVERE
revive*	rivivere
survive*	sopravvivere
-VOKE	-VOCARE
convoke	convocare
evoke	evocare
invoke	invocare
provoke	provocare
re-evoke*	rievocare
revoke	revocare
-VOLVE	-VOLVERE
devolve	devolvere
evolve	evolvere
involve	involvere
Exception:	
revolve	girare

Exercises

Exercise 1. You have learned that English verbs ending in "ate" will change the ending to "are" in Italian. Convert the verbs in parenthesis into Italian.

1. Botticelli ha voluto _____ il testo della *Divina Commedia*. (illustrate)
2. Nel *Decameron* ogni giovane deve _____ dieci novelle. (narrate)
3. Non bisogna _____davanti alle buone occasioni. (hesitate*)
4. Il contadino pensava di _____ solo una parte del suo terreno. (cultivate*)
5. Prima di agire bisognerebbe _____.(meditate)

Exercise 2. English verbs that end in "fy" add "ficare" to the root of the verb in Italian. Convert the verbs in the parenthesis into Italian.

1. Prima di preparare altri programmi bisognava _____ la zona. (pacify)
2. L'acqua era inquinata. Bisognava _____ l'acqua. (purify)
3. Il trattato di pace da _____ era favorevole alla nazione vincente. (ratify)
4. Le forze etniche erano in conflitto. Bisognava _____tutti prima della guerra. (unify)
5. Il governo decise di _____ la base militare. (fortify)

Exercise 3. Given that verbs in "ize" in English change to "izzare" in Italian and that the past participle of "izzare" is "izzato/a", convert the words in the parenthesis.

1. L'Europa è stata _____ negli ultimi trent'anni. (Americanized)
2. I paesi _____ aiutano i paesi del terzo mondo. (civilized)
3. Il divorzio è stato _____ in Italia. (legalized)
4. Il medico ha _____la signora per farle ricordare una memoria soppressa. (hypnotized*)
5. In tempi difficili abbiamo dovuto _____ nelle spese. *(economize)*

Exercise 4. Given the patterns: act=*arre*; uce=*urre*; ose=*orre*, give the Italian equivalent of the verbs in the parenthesis.

1. Per fare fronte alla fame, bisognava _____ più frumento. (produce)
2. Per _____ investimenti bisogna offrire un ottimo guadagno. (attract)
3. Il presidente voleva _____la pace, ma finì per fare la guerra. (propose)
4. Puccini non ha potuto _____ la parte finale dell'opera *Turandot*. (compose)
5. Si dice che sia l'uomo a _____ e Dio a _____. (propose, dispose)

Exercise 5. Given that the English verb ending "ish" becomes "ire" in Italian, give the Italian equivalent of the words in the parenthesis.

1. Il senatore voleva _____ la pena di morte. (abolish)
2. Prima di andare a letto lo studente doveva _____ i compiti. (finish)

*denotes root change.

91

3. Per _____ i parametri del negoziato era necessario consultare le unioni. (establish*)
4. Per _____ l'omicida il giudice lo condannò a vita. (punish)
5. Hanno dovuto _____ la casa dopo il terremoto. (demolish)

Exercise 6. As you saw on p. 81, verbs ending in *ent* in English change to *entare* in Italian. Change the verbs in parenthesis into their Italian equivalent.

1. Non voglio _____ su questa tua azione. (comment)
2. Nella vita a volte un uomo si deve _____ di quello che ha. (content)
3. Veramente questo vino non mi piace, ma ho voluto _____ .(experiment)
4. Non c'è bisogno di _____ altre scuse. Ormai ti conosco. (invent)
5. Per favore, non mi _____ con queste lagnanze inutili. (torment)

Exercise 7. A good number of verbs that end in *mit* in English change into *mettere* in Italian. Convert the verbs in parenthesis into their Italian equivalent.

1. E' impossibile _____ tanta libertà d'azione in un mondo come il nostro. (permit)
2. La telefonista non ha potuto _____ il messaggio al destinatario. (transmit)
3. Devi _____ una cosa. Luigi è veramente antipatico. (admit*)
4. Non bisogna mai _____ un'azione di cui bisognerà pentirsi dopo. (commit)
5. La Banca d'Italia ha dovuto _____ una nuova banconota (emit)

Exercise 8. Verbs that finish in *end* change into *endere* in Italian. Change the English verbs into their Italian equivalents.

1. La commissione è stata costretta a _____ il lavoro. (suspend*)
2. Nessuno può _____ di sapere tutto. (pretend)
3. Tu sei sempre pronto a _____ ad ogni occasione. (offend)
4. Gli Americani sono pronti a _____ i loro interessi nel mondo. (defend)
5. Tu non vuoi _____ come stanno veramente le cose. (comprehend*)

*denotes root change.

Chapter IV
ENGLISH-ITALIAN CONVERTER IN DESINENCE ORDER

In this section, English adjectives and nouns are presented by their endings in alphabetical order together with their Italian equivalent. It is not surprising, ny now, that with a relatively few exceptions, so many English adjectives and nouns can be converted into their Italian equivalent with such little effort. In the next few pages, we provided a table containing the meaning of most English endings. Students should familiarize themselves with them because their vocabulary will increase dramatically. Be aware, however, that some of the endings may have different meanings, depending on the words used. The corresponding Italian endings will have basically the same meanings. For example, the English ending "able" comes from the Latin "abilis" and it indicates capability, worthiness, or fitness for something. The Italian counterpart is "abile" and it has the same meaning. Owing to the different development of the language, Italian may have several different endings for one English ending. Thus, the English "able" will be either "abile" in Italian, if the verb from which the adjective is derived ends in "are", or "ibile" if the Italian verb ends in either "ere" or "ire". A few will change in "evole". Naturally, there will be some exceptions, indicated at the end of the list.

An asterisk indicates root assimilation and the dot under the vowel, as indicated before, indicates stress in the Italian pronunciation.

The desinence converter contains over 20,000 English and Italian words that share many common and easily assimilated elements. Knowledge of these words, needless to say, does not constitute mastery of the Italian language. Words, after all, are like bricks. They are one of the building materials with which linguistic ability is constructed. The study of words must be combined with the study of the mortar that holds everything together: grammar. Students who approach learning a foreign language with apprehension should find comfort in the fact that foreign words are not so foreign after all, at least as far as Italian and the other Romance languages are concerned.

To look up a word, identify the ending and look for it in the index. For example, to look up the word "agrarian" look for the ending "arian" and you will find "arian-ario, p. 116". Go to page 116 and you will find "agrarian" together with a list of words ending with "arian" and their Italian equivalent.

As for previous chapters, you will find some exercises to test your comprehension of this material at the end of the Desinence Converter.

DESINENCE INDEX

-ABLE	-ABILE, p. 103	APTION See-TION	
-ABLE	-IBILE, p. 104		
-ABLE	-EVOLE, p. 105	-AR	-ARE, p. 115
-AC	-ΛCO, p. 105	-ular	
-ACT	-ATTO, p. 105	-ARCH	-ARCA, p. 116
-ACY	-ACIA, p. 105	-ARCHY	-ARCHIA, p. 116
-ACY	-ATEZZA, p. 105	-ARD	-ARDO, p. 116
-ACY	-ATO, p. 105	-ARIAN	-ARIANO, p. 116
-ACY	-ATURA, p. 105	-ARIAN	-ARIO, p. 116
-ACY	-AZIA, p. 105	-ARIOUS	see-OUS
-ACY	-AZIONE, p. 105	-ARY	-ARE, p. 116
-ACY	-ITÀ, p. 105	-ARY	-ARIO, p. 117
-AD	-ADE, p. 106	-ASM	-ASMA, p. 118
-ADE	-ADA, p. 106	-plasm	
-ADE	-ATA, p. 106	-ASM	-ASMO, p. 118
-AGE	-AGGIO, p. 106	-ASTER	See-STER
-AGOGUE	-AGOGO, p. 107	-AT	-ATO, p. 118
-AIN	-ANO, p. 107	-stat	
-AIRE	-ARIO, p. 107	-ATE	-ATA, p. 118
-AL	-ALE, p. 107	-ATE	-ATO, p. 118
-ial		-AX	-ACE, p. 120
-ennial		-BER	-BRE, p. 120
-social		-BLE	-BILE, p. 120
See also-fugal		(preceded by e/o/u)	(preceduta da e/o/u)
See also-ical		-CENTER	-CENTRO, p. 120
-AL	-ALLO, p. 111	-CENTRE	-CENTRO, p. 120
-AL	-ALO, p. 111	-CEPHALIC	-CEFALO, p. 120
-AL	-ARIO, p. 111	-CEPHALY	-CEFALIA, p. 120
-AL	-ICO, p. 111	-CIDAL	-CIDA, p. 120
-physical		-CIDE	-CIDA/CIDIO, p. 120
-AL	-IMO, p. 111	-CLE	-COLA, p. 121
-AL	-IVO, p. 111	-CLE	-COLO, p. 121
-AL	-O, p. 111	-acle,-icle	
-AL	-ORIO, p. 111	-COPY	See-SCOPY
-AL	-OSO, p. 111	-CORN	-CORNO, p. 121
-AL	-VARIOUS, p. 111	-COSM	-COSMO, p. 121
-AN	-ANO, p. 112	-CRACY	-CRAZIA, p. 121
See also-IAN-IANO		-CRAT	-CRATE
-ANCE	-AMENTO, p. 113		/-CRATICO, p. 121
-ANCE /-ANCY	-ANZA, p. 113	-CRATIC	-See -IC
-ANCE	-AZIONE, p. 113	-CRE/-CHRE	-CRO, p. 122
-ANCE	-ENZA, p. 113	-CYCLE	-CICLO, p. 122
-ANCY	-ANZIA, p. 113	-DERM	-DERMA, p. 122
-ANGLE	-ANGOLO, p. 113	-DOX	-DOSSO, p. 122
-ANT	-ANTE, p. 114	-DOXY	-DOSSIA, p. 122
-ANT	-ENTE, p. 115	-DROME	-DROMO, p. 122
-ANTHROPE	-ANTROPO, p. 115	-DUCT	-DOTTO, p. 122
-ANTHROPY-	-ANTROPIA, p. 116	-EAL	-EO, p. 122

-EAN	-EO, p. 122	-iform
-ECT	-ETTO, p. 122	-FUGAL	-FUGO, p. 132
-spect		-FUGE	-FUGIO, p. 132
-ECTOMY	-ETOMIA/	-GAMOUS	SEE-OUS
	-ECTOMIA, p. 123	-GAMY	-GAMIA, p. 132
-EE	-ATARIO, p. 123	-GEN	-GENO, p. 132
-EM	-EMA, p. 123	-GON	-GONO, p. 132
-ENCE	-ENZA, p. 123	-GRADE	-GRADO, p. 132
-escence		-GRAM	-GRAMMA, p. 132
-valence		Denoting "written" or "drawn"
-ENCY	-ENZA, p. 125	-GRAM	-GRAMMO, p. 132
-END	-ENDO, p. 125	Denoting metric system
-ENSE	-ENSO, p. 125	-GRAPH	-GRAFIA, p. 132
-ENSE	-ESA, p. 125	-GRAPH	-GRAFO, p. 132
-ENT	-ENTE, p. 125	-GRAPHER	-GRAFISTA, p. 133
-ENT	-ENTO, p. 128	-GRAPHER	-GRAFO, p. 133
-lent		-GRAPHIC	SEE-IC
-ment		-GRAPHICAL	-GRAFICO, p. 133
-ulent		-GRAPHY	-GRAFIA, p. 133
-EPT	-ETTO, p. 129	-IA	-IA, p. 134
-ER	-ORE, p. 129	-aesthesia
-ERN	-ERNA, p. 129	-algia
-ERSE	-ERSO, p. 129	-anemia
-ERY	-ERIA, p. 129	-asia
-ERY	-ERIO, p. 129	-emia
-ERY	-ERO, p. 129	-leukemia
-ESE	-ESE, p. 129	-lexia
-ESQUE	-ESCO, p. 129	-mania
-ESS	-ERA, p. 129	-mnesia
-ESS	-ESSA, p. 130	-noia
-ESS	-ESSO, p. 130	-opia
-gress		-orexia
-ESS	-EZZA, p. 130	-phoria
-ESS	-ITÀ, p. 130	-(r)rhytmia
-ET	-ETA/-ETTA, p. 130	-somnia
-ET	-ETO, p. 130	-thanasia
-ET	-ETTO, p. 130	-IAD	-IADE, p. 136
-ETTE	-ETTA, p. 131	-IAL	See-AL
-ETUDE	SEE –TUDE	-IAN	-ESE, p. 136
-EX	-ESSO, p. 131	-IAN	-IANO, p. 136
-EX	-ICE, p. 131	-IAN	-ICO, p. 136
-plex		-IATRY	-IATRA, p. 136
-FEROUS	SEE-OUS	-latry
-FIC	SEE-IC	-IBLE	-IBILE, p. 137
-FICE	-FICIO, p. 131	-IC	-ICA, p. 138
-FICENT	-FICO, p. 131	-IC	-ICO, p. 138
-FIX	-FISSO, p. 131	-anthropic
-FLECTION	-FLESSIONE, p. 131	-astic
-FLEX/FLUX	-FLESSO/	-atic
	-FLUSSO, p. 131	-centric
-FOIL	-FOGLIO, p. 131	-cosmic
-FORM	-FORME, p. 132	-cratic

-demic	
-etic	
-fic	
-genic	
-glyphic	
-graphic	
-iatric	
-istic	
-itic	
-logic	
-metric	
-morphic	
-otic	
-pathic	
-pedic	
-periodic	
-phonic	
-plegic	
-psychic	
-scopic	
-seismic	
-sonic	
-sophic	
-spheric	
-static	
-technic	
-thoracic	
-tic	
-tomic	
-utic	
-ICAL	-ALE, p. 145
-ICAL	-ICALE, p. 145
-ICAL	-ICO, p. 146
-ICE	-ICIO, p. 147
-ICE	-IZIA, p. 147
-ICE	-IZIO, p. 147
-ICIAN	-ICO, p. 147
-ICIAN	-ISTA, p. 147
-ICLE	See-CLE
-ICS	-IA, p. 147
-iatrics	-iatria
-ICS	-ICA, p. 148
-physics	
-statics	
-therapeutics	
-ID	-IDE, p. 148
-ID	-IDO, p. 148
-acid	
-IER	-IERE, p. 149
-ILE/YLE	-ILE, p. 149
-atile	
-febrile	

-fertile	
-mobile	
-ILLA	-IGLIA, p. 150
-IN	-INA, p. 150
-IN	-INE, p. 150
-IN	-INO, p. 150
-INA	-INA, p. 150
-INE	-INA, p. 151
-INE	-INO, p. 151
-ION	-IONE, p. 152
-flexion	
-pulsion	
-sion	
-vision	
-IQUE	-ICA, p. 154
-ISK	-ISCO, p. 154
-ISM	-ESIMO, p. 154
-ISM,-YSM	-ISMA, p. 154
-ISM/-YSM	-ISMO, p. 154
-theism	
-IST	-ICO, p. 157
-IST/YST	-ISTA, p. 157
-gamist	
-linguist	
-theist	
-IT	-ITO, p. 159
-ITE	-ITA, p. 159
-site	
-ITE	-ITE, p. 159
-ITE/YTE	-ITO, p. 159
-ITIS	-ITE, p. 159
-ITUDE	See-TUDE
-IVE	-IVA, p. 160
-IVE	-IVO, p. 160
-ative	
-itive	
-tive	
-utive	
-IX /-YX	-ICE, p. 163
-IZER	-IZZATORE, p. 164
-LEGE	-LEGIO, p. 164
-LINGUAL	-LINGUE, p. 164
-LITRE	-LITRO, p. 164
-LOGIC	SEE-IC
-LOGICAL	-LOGICO, p. 164-
LOGIST	-LOGISTA, p. 164
-LOGIST	-LOGO, p. 164
-LOGUE	-LOGO, p. 165
-LOGY	-LOGIA, p. 165
-MA	-MA, p. 166
-coma	
-drama	

-emma	
-oma	
-orama	
-rama	
-MANIAC	-MANE, p. 166
-ME	-ME, p. 167
-ME	-MO, p. 167
-MESTER	-MESTRE, p. 167
-METER	-METRO, p. 167
-METRE	-METRO, p. 167
-METRY	-METRIA, p. 167
-MONY/-IMONY	-MONIA /
	-IMONIA, p. 167
-NAUT	-NAUTA, p. 167
-NOMY	-NOMIA, p. 167
-gnomy	
-ODE	-ODE, p. 167
-ODE	-ODO, p. 167
-OID/-OIDS	-OIDE/-OIDI, p. 167
-ON	-ONE, p. 168
-ON	-ONTE, p. 169
-ONE	-ONE, p. 169
-ONE	-ONO, p. 169
-tone	
-ONYM	-ONIMO, p. 169
-OR	-ORE, p. 169
-ator	
-color	
-ior	
-motor	
-tor	
-ORY	-IVO, p. 171
-ORY	-ORIA, p. 171
-ORY	-ORIO, p. 172
-OSE	-OSO, p. 172
-icose	
-ulose	
-OT	-OTA, p. 172
-OUS	
-acious	-ACE , p. 173
-arious	-ARIO, p. 173
-cephalous	-CEFALO, p. 173
-eous	-EO, p. 173
-ferous	-FERO, p. 174
-gamous	-GAMO, p. 174
-ious	-IOSO, p. 174
-ous	-OSO, p. 175
-parous	-PARO, p. 176
-ulous	-ULO, p. 176
-ulous	-OLOSO, p. 176
-uous	-UO, p. 176
-uous	-UOSO, p. 176

-vorous	-VORO, p. 177
-PATHY	-PATIA, p. 177
-PED	-PEDE, p. 177
-PEDE	-PIEDI, p. 177
-PHILE	-FILO, p. 177
-PHILIA	-FILIA, p. 177
-PHOBIA	-FOBIA, p. 177
-PHOBIC	-FOBO, p. 177
-PHONE	-FONO, p. 177
-PHONY	-FONIA, p. 177
-PLANE	-PLANO, p. 177
-PLE	-PLO, p. 177
-POLIS	-POLI, p. 178
-PORT	-PORTO, p. 178
-REME	-REME, p. 178
-RRHEA	-RREA, p. 178
-RY	-RIA, p. 178
-SAUR/TAUR	-SAURO/
	TAURO, p. 178
-SAURUS	-SAURO, p. 178
-SCOPE	-SCOPIO, p. 178
-SCOPY	-SCOPIA, p. 178
copy	
-SIS	-SI, p. 178
-asis	
-esis	
-gnosis	
-iasis	
-lysis	
-neurosis	
-osis	
-phasis	
-synthesis	
-thesis	
-SOPHY	-SOFIA, p. 179
-SPERM	-SPERMA, p. 179
-SPHERE	-SFERA, p. 179
-STER	-STRO, p. 179
-aster	
-STICE	-STIZIO, p. 180
-STOLE	-STOLE, p. 180
-STROPHE	-STROFE, p. 180
-SYLLABLE	-SILLABO, p. 180
-THROPHY	-TROPIA, p. 180
-THERAPY	-TERAPIA, p. 180
-TION	-ZIONE, p. 180

The nouns with desinence in-tion are
numerous. They are assimilated as follows:

-ACTION	-AZIONE, p. 180
-APTION	p. 181

-ATION	p. 181	-ULE	-ULO, p. 198
-IZATION	-IZZAZIONE, p. 187	-cule	
-ECTION	-EZIONE, p. 188	-ULT	-ULTO, p. 198
EPTION		-UM	-O, p. 198
-ETION		-arium	
		-cranium	
-ICTION	-IZIONE, p. 189	-ellum	
-IPTION		-ennium	
-ITION		-ium	
		-orium	
-OCTION	-OZIONE, p. 190-	-podium	
OPTION		-sternum	
-OTION		-UND	-ONDO, p. 199
-UCTION	-UZIONE, p. 190	-bund	
-UPTION		-cund	
-UTION		-UNE	-UNA, p. 199
		-UNE	-UNO, p. 199
-TION	-ZIONE, p. 190	-URE	-URA, p. 199
preceded by consonant:		-ature	
-TOMY	-TOMIA, p. 191-	-cure	
TRESS	-TRICE, p. 191	-facture	
-ress		-ture	
-TRIX	-TRICE, p. 191	-URE	-URO, p. 200
-rix		-URN	-URNO, p. 200
-TUDE	-TUDINE, p. 191	-US	-O, p. 200
-itude		-USE	-USA, p. 202
-etude		-USE	-USO, p. 202
-TY	-TÀ, p. 192	-UTE	-UTO, p. 202
-acity		-VORE	-VORO, p. 202
-ality		-VOROUS	-VORO, p. 202
-aneity		-Y	-IA, p. 202
-arity		-asy	
-bility		-eny	
-city		-epsy	
-eity		-ergy	
-ety		-ery	
-icity		-nomy	
-idity		-ry	
-ility		-sy	
-ity		-urgy	
-TY	-EZZA, p. 197		
-TYPE	-TIPO, p. 197		

MEANING OF DESINENCES: NOUNS AND ADJECTIVES

Lat.	-ABLE	able to be
Gr.	-AC	pertaining to
Lat.	-ACIOUS	tending to
Lat.	-ACY	quality of being or having
Lat./Gr.	-AGOGUE	leader
Lat.	-AL	pertaining to
Lat/Gr.	-AL	pertaining to
Lat.	-AL	similar to, pertaining
Lat.	-AN	pertaining to
Lat/Gr.	-AN,-IAN	concerned with
Lat/Gr.	-AN,-IAN	pertaining to
Lat.	-ANCE,-ANCY	quality of
Lat.	-ANT	present participle
Gr.	-ANTHROPE	human
Lat.	-AR	pertaining to
Gr.	-ARCH	the ruler
Gr.	-ARCHY	rule by
Lat.	-ARY	pertaining to
Gr.	-ASIS	action, process
Gr.	-ASM	result, condition
Lat.	-AT	state, action
Lat.	-ATE	possessing, office of
Lat.	-ATION	state, action
Gr.	-CEPHALY	head
Lat.	-CIDE	to kill
Gr.	-CRACY	rule by
Gr.	-CRAT	he who practices rule
Lat.	-CULE	little
Lat/Gr.	-DERM	skin
Gr.	-ECTOMY	surgical removal
Lat.	-ENCE,-ENY	quality of
Fr.-Ital.	-ESQUE (-ESC)	style or manner
Lat.	-ET	small
Lat.	-EVOLE	able to be
Lat.	-FEROUS	to bear, to carry
Gr.	-GRAM	written thing
Gr.	-GRAPH	writing
Gr.	-GRAPH	writing
Gr.	-GRAPHER	person who writes
Gr.	-GRAPHY	writing
Gr.	-IA	quality of
Gr.	-IASIS	a diseased state or condition
Lat.	-IBILE	able to be

Lat.	-IBLE	able to be
Gr.	-IC	pertaining to
Lat.	-IC	pertaining to
Gr.	-ICIAN	specialist in
Lat.	-ID	tending to
Lat.-Fr.	-IER	a person connected with
Lat.	-(I)FIC	making, causing
Lat.	-(I)FY,-(E)FY	to make
Lat.	-ILE/YLE	pertaining to
Lat.	-INE	pertaining to
Lat.	-ION	act of
Gr.	-ISM,-YSM	belief in
Gr.	-IST/YST	One who believes in
Lat.	-ITUDE	quality of, state, condition
Lat.	-IVE	tending to
Lat.	-LINGUAL	language, tongue
Lat./Gr.	-LOGUE	speech, conversation
Gr.	-LOGUE	word, speech
Lat/Gr.	-LOGY	science of, speech
Gr.	-MANIAC	one who has madness, passion
Lat.	-MESTER	month
Gr.	-METER	measure
Lat/Gr.	-METRE	measure
Gr.	-METRY	art, science of measuring
Lat.	-MONY,-(I) MONY	condition
Lat/Gr.	-NAUT	ship, navigation
Gr.	-NOMY	science of, speech
Gr.	-ODE	electrical conductor
Lat/Gr.	-ODE	song, lyric
Gr.	-OID,-OIDS	like, similar
Gr.	-OMA	tumor
Gr.	-ONYM	name, word
Lat.	-OR	one who does
Lat.	--(U)LENCE,-(O)LENCE	state or quality of
Lat.	-(U)LENT,-(O)LENT	full of
Lat.	-OR	state of
Lat.	-ORY	place
Lat.	-ORY	place
Lat.	-ORY	tending to
Lat.	-OSE,-(LOSE)	full of
Gr.	-OSIS	diseased condition
Lat.	-OUS,-IOUS, ETC.	full of
Lat.	-PAROUS	to produce (children)
Gr.	-PATHY	disease of
Lat.	-PED	foot
Gr.	-PHILIA	love

Gr.	-PHOBIA	fear, hatred
Gr.	-PHONE	sound
Lat.	-PLE	fold,-(pl(us)
Gr.	-POLIS	city, state
Lat/Gr.	-RRHEA	fluid discharge
Lat/Gr.	-SAURUS	lizard
Gr.	-SCOPY	instrument to view
Gr.	-SIS	result of, action
Gr.	-SOPHY	wise, clever
Gr.	-SPHERE	globe, ball
Gr.	-STOLE	contraction, dilation
Gr.	-STROPHE	turning, twisting
Gr.	-THERAPY	treatment
Lat	-TIC	pertaining to
Lat.	-TION	expressing action, process
Lat.	-TION	action, process, result
Lat.	-TRESS	feminine of "tor"
Lat.	-TRIX,-RIX	she who does
Lat.	-TUDE	state, condition
Lat.	-TUDE (etude)	state or condition, quality of
Lat.	-TY	quality, state, condition
Lat.	-TY (-ETY,-ITY)	quality of
Gr.	-TYPE	image, model, impression
Lat.	-ULE	little
Lat.	-ULT	commotion, disturbing
Lat.	-UM	nominative neuter nouns
Lat.	-UND	producing, capable to produce
Lat.	-UOUS	tending to
Lat.	-URE	act of
Lat.	-US	masculine nouns and adjectives of
Lat.	-US	second declension
Lat.	-VOROUS	to swallow, to eat
Lat.	-Y	quality of

Notes

ENGLISH-ITALIAN LEXICAL CONVERTER IN DESINENCE ORDER

-ABLE	-ABILE
able	abile
abominable	abominabile
acceptable*	accettabile
accusable	accusabile
adaptable*	adattabile
admirable*	ammirabile
adorable	adorabile
adoptable*	adottabile
affable	affabile
alienable	alienabile
amiable*	amabile
annullable	annullabile
applicable	applicabile
appreciable*	apprezzabile
arable	arabile
bankable*	bancabile
comfortable*	c confortabile
commensurable	commensurabile
communicable*	comunicabile
comparable	comparabile
computable	computabile
considerable	considerabile
curable	curabile
desirable*	desiderabile
determinable	determinabile
disputable	disputabile
expiable*	espiabile
formidable	formidabile
friable	friabile
habitable*	abitabile
honorable*	onorabile
identifiable*	identificabile
imaginable*	immaginabile
imitable	imitabile
immutable	immutabile
impalpable	impalpabile
impeccable	impeccabile
impenetrable	impenetrabile
impermeable	impermeabile
imperturbable	imperturbabile
implacable	implacabile

imponderable	imponderabile
impracticable*	impraticabile
impressionable	impressionabile
improbable	improbabile
imputable	imputabile
inadaptable	inadattabile
inalienable	inalienabile
inalterable	inalterabile
inapplicable	inapplicabile
incalculable*	incalcolabile
incommensurable	incommensurabile
incommunicable*	incomunicabile
incomparable	incomparabile
inconsiderable	inconsiderabile
inconsolable	inconsolabile
incontestable	incontestabile
incontrollable	incontrollabile
inculpable*	incolpabile
incurable	incurabile
indecipherable*	indecifrabile
indeterminable	indeterminabile
indispensable	indispensabile
indisputable	indisputabile
indomitable*	indomabile
ineffable	ineffabile
ineluctable*	ineluttabile
inestimable	inestimabile
inevitable	inevitabile
inexorable*	inesorabile
inexpiable*	inespiabile
inexplicable*	inesplicabile
inexpugnable*	inespugnabile
inextricable*	inestricabile
inflammable*	infiammabile
inimitable	inimitabile
innumerable	innumerabile
insatiable*	insaziabile
inscrutable	inscrutabile
inseparable	inseparabile
insuperable	insuperabile
insurmountable*	insormontabile
interminable	interminabile

intolerable*	intollerabile	separable	separabile
intractable*	intrattabile	specifiable*	specificabile
invariable	invariabile	stable	stabile
inviolable	inviolabile	superable	superabile
irrealizable*	irrealizzabile	supportable*	sopportabile
irreconcilable	irreconciliabile	taxable*	tassabile
irrecoverable*	irrecuperabile	terminable	terminabile
irrecusable	irrecusabile	tolerable*	tollerabile
irrefragable	irrefragabile	tractable*	trattabile
irrefutable	irrefutabile	transportable*	trasportabile
irremediable*	irrimediabile	unable*	inabile
irreparable	irreparabile	unappealable*	inappellabile
irrevocable	irrevocabile	undecipherable*	indecifrabile
irrigable	irrigabile	undeclinable*	indeclinabile
irritable	irritabile	unpardonable*	imperdonabile
justifiable*	giustificabile	unreconciliable*	irreconciliabile
lamentable	lamentabile	unstable*	instabile
malleable	malleabile	untouchable*	intoccabile
measurable*	misurabile	usable	usabile
memorable	memorabile	utilizable*	utilizzabile
miserable	miserabile	variable	variabile
mutable	mutabile	venerable	venerabile
navigable	navigabile	verifiable*	verificabile
negotiable*	negoziabile	violable	violabile
notable	notabile	volatizable	volatilizzabile
numerable	numerabile	vulnerable	vulnerabile
observable*	osservabile	*but:*	
palpable	palpabile	durable	duraturo
penetrable	penetrabile	*Exceptions:*	
pensionable	pensionabile	capable	capace
permeable	permeabile	conformable	conforme
personable	personabile	hospitable	ospitale
placable	placabile	incapable	incapace
ponderable	ponderabile	inequitable	ineguale
portable	portabile	inhospitable	inospitale
potable	potabile	vegetable	vegetale
practicable*	praticabile	**-ABLE**	**-IBILE**
presentable	presentabile	Note: "-able" changes to "-ibile"	
probable	probabile	(Verbs of II or III conjugation)	
qualifiable*	qualificabile	attributable*	attribuibile
recyclable*	reciclabile	extractable*	estraibile
remediable*	rimediabile	inconceivable*	inconcepibile
respectable*	rispettabile	indefinable	indefinibile
revocable	revocabile	indescribable*	indescrivibile
salvable	salvabile	indistinguishable*	indistinguibile
savable*	salvabile	irrecognizable*	irriconoscibile

irredeemable*	irredimibile
irremovable	irremovibile
movable	movibile
obtainable*	ottenibile
perceivable*	percettibile
preferable	preferibile
recognizable*	riconoscibile
transferable*	trasferibile
translatable*	traducibile
uncontainable*	incontenibile
unrepeatable*	irripetibile
untranslatable*	intraducibile

-ABLE / **-EVOLE**

amicable *	amichevole
charitable *	caritatevole
culpable*	colpevole
durable	durevole
favorable*	favorevole
laudable *	lodevole
sociable	socievole

-AC / **-ACO**

aphrodisiac*	afrodisiaco
cardiac	cardiaco
demoniac	demoniaco
Dionysiac*	dionisiaco
elegiac	elegiaco
hypochondriac*	ipocondriaco
iliac	iliaco
maniac	maniaco
paradisiac	paradisiaco
sacroiliac	sacroiliaco
Syriac	siriaco
zodiac	zodiaco

Exceptions:

insomniac	insonne
kleptomaniac	cleptomane
paranoi(a)c	paranoico
pyromaniac	piromane

-ACT / **-ATTO**

abstract*	astratto
act*	atto
compact	compatto
contact	contatto
contract	contratto
exact*	esatto
extract*	estratto
fact	fatto
impact	impatto
inexact*	inesatto
intact	intatto
pact	patto
tact	tatto

Exception:

cateract	cateratta

-ACY / **-ACIA**

efficacy	efficacia
fallacy	fallacia
inefficacy	inefficacia
pharmacy*	farmacia

Exception:

piracy	pirateria

-ACY / **-ATEZZA**

accuracy	accuratezza
adequacy*	adeguatezza
delicacy	delicatezza
effeminacy	effeminatezza
inadequacy*	inadeguatezza
indelicacy	indelicatezza

-ACY / **-ATO**

celibacy	celibato
episcopacy	episcopato
papacy	papato
primacy	primato

-ACY / **-ATURA**

advocacy*	avvocatura
candidacy	candidatura
magistracy	magistratura

-ACY / **-AZIA**

diplomacy	diplomazia
supremacy	supremazia

-ACY / **-AZIONE**

confederacy	confederazione
conspiracy*	cospirazione
degeneracy	degenerazione
obstinacy*	ostinazione

-ACY / **-ITÀ**

illegitimacy*	illegittimità
intimacy	intimità
legitimacy*	legittimità

-AD / **-ADE**

Iliad	Iliade
monad	monade

myriad*	miriade
pentad	pentade
triad	triade
-ADE	**-ADA**
alidade	alidada
charade*	sciarada
jade*	giada
Exceptions:	
blockade	blocco
cannonade	cannoneggiamento
decade	decade
-ADE	**-ATA**
arcade	arcata
balustrade*	balaustrata
barricade	barricata
blockade*	bloccata
brigade	brigata
cannonade	cannonata
cascade	cascata
cavalcade	cavalcata
colonnade	colonnata
crusade*	crociata
fanfaronade	fanfaronata
grenade*	granata
lemonade*	limonata
motorcade*	autoparata
parade	parata
pomade	pomata
serenade	serenata
-AGE	**-AGGIO**
advantage*	vantaggio
amperage	amperaggio
anchorage*	ancoraggio
apanage*	appannaggio
arbitrage	arbitraggio
careenage*	carenaggio
counterespionage*	controspionaggio
courage*	coraggio
dosage	dosaggio
drainage*	drenaggio
equipage	equipaggio
espionage*	spionaggio
forage	foraggio
hostage*	ostaggio
massage	massaggio
message	messaggio

mirage	miraggio
montage	montaggio
outrage*	oltraggio
passage	passaggio
patronage	patronaggio
personage	personaggio
photomontage*	fotomontaggio
pilgrimage*	pellegrinaggio
plumage*	piumaggio
porterage*	facchinaggio
sabotage	sabotaggio
savage*	selvaggio
tonnage*	tonnellaggio
vantage	vantaggio
vassalage*	vassallaggio
village	villaggio
voltage	voltaggio
voyage*	viaggio
Some exceptions:	
adage	adagio
assemblage	assemblea
baggage	bagaglio
brokerage	mediazione
camouflage	camuffamento
carnage	carneficina
Carthage	Cartagine
cartilage	cartilagine
concubinage	concubinato
damage	danno
foliage	fogliame
fuselage	fusoliera
hemorrhage	emorragia
heritage	eredità
image	immagine
language	lingua
luggage	bagaglio
marriage	matrimonio
mortgage	ipoteca
mucilage	mucilaggine
orphanage	orfanotrofio
page	pagina
percentage	percentuale
postage	tariffa postale
presage	presagio
tutelage	tutela
usage	uso

verbiage	verbosità
vicarage	vicariato
vintage	vendemmia
-AGOGUE	**-AGOGO**
demagogue	demagogo
pedagogue	pedagogo
-AIN	**-ANO**
captain*	capitano
villain	villano
but:	
chieftain	capo
-AIRE	**-ARIO**
concessionaire	concessionario
doctrinaire*	dottrinario
millionaire*	milionario
-AL	**-ALE**
-ial	
-ennial	
-social	
abdominal*	addominale
abnormal*	anormale
abyssal*	abissale
accidental	accidentale
additional*	addizionale
adjectival*	aggettivale
alluvial	alluviale
amoral	amorale
anal	anale
ancestral	ancestrale
animal	animale
annual	annuale
anticonstitutional*	anticostituzionale
antisocial	antisociale
arbitral	arbitrale
arsenal	arsenale
artificial	artificiale
ascensional*	ascensionale
asexual*	asessuale
astral	astrale
attitudinal	attitudinale
austral	australe
autumnal*	autunnale
axial*	assiale
bacchanal*	baccanale
banal	banale
baptismal*	battesimale

basal	basale
bestial	bestiale
bicentennial	bicentennale
biennial	biennale
bilateral	bilaterale
bronchial	bronchiale
brutal	brutale
cadastral*	catastale
canal	canale
cannibal	cannibale
capital	capitale
cardinal	cardinale
carnal	carnale
carnival*	carnevale
carpal	carpale
casual	casuale
cathedral*	cattedrale
causal	causale
celestial	celestiale
centennial	centennale
centesimal	centesimale
central	centrale
cereal	cereale
cerebral	cerebrale
cerebrospinal	cerebrospinale
ceremonial*	cerimoniale
choral*	corale
circumstantial*	circostanziale
cloistral*	claustrale
coaxial*	coassiale
collateral	collaterale
collegial	collegiale
colloquial	colloquiale
colonial	coloniale
colossal	colossale
commercial	commerciale
conceptual*	concettuale
conditional*	condizionale
confessional	confessionale
confidential*	confidenziale
congenial	congeniale
congressional*	congressuale
conjugal*	coniugale
consensual	consensuale
constitutional*	costituzionale
contextual*	contestuale

continental	continentale	feudal	feudale
contractual*	contrattuale	filial	filiale
conventional*	convenzionale	final	finale
convivial	conviviale	fiscal	fiscale
cordial	cordiale	floral	floreale
coronal	coronale	fluvial	fluviale
criminal	criminale	focal	focale
crucial	cruciale	formal	formale
cultural	culturale	frontal	frontale
decennial*	decennale	frugal	frugale
decimal	decimale	functional*	funzionale
decretal	decretale	fundamental*	fondamentale
deferential*	deferenziale	funeral	funerale
dental	dentale	general	generale
departmental*	dipartimentale	genital	genitale
detrimental	detrimentale	germinal	germinale
diagonal	diagonale	gingival*	gengivale
dialectal*	dialettale	glacial	glaciale
dictatorial*	dittatoriale	gradual	graduale
differential*	differenziale	grammatical	grammaticale
dimensional	dimensionale	gravitational*	gravitazionale
divisional	divisionale	gubernatorial*	governatoriale
doctrinal*	dottrinale	guttural	gutturale
dorsal	dorsale	habitual*	abituale
dual	duale	hexagonal*	esagonale
ducal	ducale	homosexual*	omosessuale
duodecimal	duodecimale	horizontal*	orizzontale
duodenal	duodenale	ideal	ideale
editorial	editoriale	illegal	illegale
electoral*	elettorale	immaterial	immateriale
episcopal	episcopale	immoral	immorale
equinoctial*	equinoziale	immortal	immortale
equrial	equriale	impartial*	imparziale
essential*	essenziale	imperial	imperiale
eventual	eventuale	impersonal	impersonale
exceptional*	eccezionale	inaugural	inaugurale
existential*	esistenziale	incidental	incidentale
exterritorial*	estraterritoriale	individual	individuale
extraterritorial	extraterritoriale	industrial	industriale
facial*	facciale	infernal	infernale
fatal	fatale	initial*	iniziale
fecal	fecale	institutional*	istituzionale
federal	federale	insurrectional*	insurrezionale
feral	ferale	integral	integrale
ferial	feriale	intellectual*	intellettuale
fetal	fetale	intentional*	intenzionale

intercontinental	intercontinentale	naval	navale
intercostal	intercostale	neural	neurale
interdigital	interdigitale	neutral	neutrale
international*	internazionale	nodal	nodale
intestinal	intestinale	nominal	nominale
irrational*	irrazionale	normal	normale
journal*	giornale	numeral	numerale
jovial*	gioviale	nuptial*	nuziale
judicial*	giudiziale	occasional	occasionale
jurisdictional*	giurisdizionale	occidental	occidentale
labial	labiale	occipital	occipitale
legal	legale	octagonal*	ottagonale
lethal*	letale	official*	ufficiale
lexical*	lessicale	ogival	ogivale
liberal	liberale	opal	opale
literal*	letterale	optional*	opzionale
local	locale	oral	orale
manual	manuale	orchestral	orchestrale
marginal	marginale	ordinal	ordinale
marital	maritale	oriental	orientale
marsupial	marsupiale	original	originale
martial*	marziale	ornamental	ornamentale
material	materiale	oval	ovale
maternal	maternale	palatal	palatale
matrimonial	matrimoniale	papal	papale
medicinal	medicinale	parochial*	parrocchiale
medieval	medievale	partial*	parziale
memorial	memoriale	pastoral	pastorale
menstrual*	mestruale	patriarchal*	patriarcale
mental	mentale	pectoral*	pettorale
mercurial	mercuriale	pedal	pedale
meridional	meridionale	penal	penale
mineral	minerale	penitential*	penitenziale
ministerial	ministeriale	pentagonal	pentagonale
missal*	messale	pestilential*	pestilenziale
modal	modale	phenomenal*	fenomenale
monaural*	monoaurale	pineal	pineale
monumental	monumentale	plural	plurale
moral	morale	postal	postale
mortal	mortale	potential*	potenziale
municipal	municipale	preferential*	preferenziale
mural	murale	prenatal	prenatale
nasal	nasale	presidential*	presidenziale
natal	natale	primordial	primordiale
national*	nazionale	principal	principale
natural	naturale	procedural	procedurale

professional	professionale	superficial	superficiale
professiorial*	professorale	supernational*	supernazionale
pronominal	pronominale	supernatural*	soprannaturale
proportional*	proporzionale	supra-national*	supernazionale
proverbial	proverbiale	temporal	temporale
providential*	provvidenziale	terminal	terminale
provincial	provinciale	territorial	territoriale
puerperal	puerperale	textual*	testuale
punctual*	puntuale	thermal*	termale
pyramidal*	piramidale	tonal	tonale
quadrennial*	quadriennale	torrential*	torrenziale
Quirinal	Quirinale	total	totale
racial*	razziale	traditional*	tradizionale
radial	radiale	transversal*	traversale
rational*	razionale	tribal	tribale
real	reale	tribunal	tribunale
rectal*	rettale	triennial*	triennale
regal	regale	triumphal*	trionfale
regicidal	regicidale	unequal*	ineguale
regimental*	reggimentale	unicameral	unicamerale
regional	regionale	unilateral	unilaterale
renal	renale	universal	universale
ritual	rituale	unnatural*	innaturale
rival	rivale	unreal*	irreale
rural	rurale	usual	usuale
sacerdotal	sacerdotale	vaginal	vaginale
sacramental	sacramentale	vasal	vasale
scriptural*	scritturale	vegetal	vegetale
secretarial*	segretariale	venal	venale
semifinal	semifinale	venial	veniale
seminal	seminale	ventral	ventrale
semiofficial*	semiufficiale	vertebral	vertebrale
sensational*	sensazionale	vestal	vestale
sensorial	sensoriale	vicarial	vicariale
sentimental	sentimentale	viceregal*	vicerale
septennial*	settennale	vicinal	vicinale
sepulchral*	sepolcrale	Viminal	Viminale
sexual*	sessuale	viral	virale
signal*	segnale	virginal*	verginale
social	sociale	virtual	virtuale
spatial*	spaziale	visceral	viscerale
special	speciale	visual	visuale
spectral*	spettrale	vital	vitale
spinal	spinale	vocal	vocale
spiral	spirale	zenithal*	zenitale
structural*	strutturale	zonal	zonale

but:	
aerial	aereo
demoniacal	demoniaco
financial	finanziario
skeletal	scheletrico
suicidal	suicida
-AL	**-ALLO**
coral	corallo
crystal*	cristallo
interval	intervallo
jackal	sciacallo
metal	metallo
pedestal*	piedistallo
vassal	vassallo
but:	
appeal*	appello
-AL	**-ALO**
Nouns:	
cymbal*	cembalo
petal	petalo
sandal	sandalo
scandal	scandalo
serval (zool.)	servalo
vandal	vandalo
-AL	**-ARIO**
centennial	centenario
financial*	finanziario
fractional*	frazionario
-AL	**-ICO**
-physical	fisico
anecdotal*	aneddotico
architectural*	architettonico
bacterial*	batterico
beneficial	benefico
critical	critico
ectodermal	ectodermico
epidermal	epidermico
geophysical*	geofisico
isothermal*	isotermico
malarial	malarico
medical	medico
metaphysical*	metafisico
ovarial	ovarico
paroxysmal*	parossistico
physical*	fisico
political	politico
polyhedral*	poliedrico
thermal	termico
typical*	tipico
-AL	**-IMO**
infinitesimal	infinitesimo
millesimal	millesimo
minimal	minimo
-AL	**-IVO**
arrival	arrivo
governmental*	governativo
intuitional*	intuitivo
recreational*	ricreativo
volitional*	volitivo
-AL	**-O**
diurnal	diurno
eternal	eterno
external*	esterno
fraternal	fraterno
internal	interno
maternal	materno
nocturnal*	notturno
paternal	paterno
-AL	**-ORIO**
ambassadorial*	ambasciatorio
censorial	censorio
conspiratorial*	cospiratorio
inquisitorial	inquisitorio
piscatorial	piscatorio
provisional	provvisorio
vibrational*	vibratorio
-AL	**-OSO**
arterial	arterioso
substantial*	sostanzioso
venal	venoso
-AL	**-VARIOUS**
(NOUNS AND ADJECTIVES:)	
aboriginal	aborigeno
admiral*	ammiraglio
agricultural*	agricolo
apocryphal	apocrifo
approval	approvazione
archiepiscopal*	arcivescovile
arrival	arrivo
aural*	auricolare
binomial	binomio
centripetal	centripeto

coastal*	costiero	charlatan*	ciarlatano
congenital	congenito	Cordovan	cordovano
continual	continuo	cosmopolitan	cosmopolitano
controversial	controverso	Cuban	cubano
ephemeral*	effimero	diocesan	diocesano
equilateral	equilatero	divan	divano
equivocal	equivoco	Dominican*	domenicano
influential	influente	Franciscan*	francescano
mammal	mammifero	German	germano
medal	medaglia	human*	umano
mutual	mutuo	inhuman*	inumano
perennial	perenne	interurban	interurbano
perpetual	perpetuo	Koran*	Corano
polynomial*	polinomio	Lutheran*	luterano
prefectorial*	prefettizio	Magellan	Magellano
prejudicial*	pregiudizievole	Mantuan*	mantovano
prodigal	prodigo	metropolitan	metropolitano
professional	professionista	Mexican*	messicano
proposal	proposta	Milan	Milano
quadrilateral	quadrilatero	Mohican*	moicano
reciprocal	reciproco	Mussulman*	musulmano
remittal*	remissione	Neapolitan*	napoletano
seneschal*	siniscalco	organ	organo
supplemental	supplementare	orphan*	orfano
survival*	sopravvivenza	Ottoman	ottomano
tactual*	tattile	Paduan*	padovano
terrestrial	terrestre	pagan	pagano
transposal	trasposizione	Parmesan*	parmigiano
trigeminal	trigemino	partisan*	partigiano
trilateral	trilatero	pelican*	pellicano
trinomial	trinomio	platan	platano
unconditional*	incondizionato	Puritan	puritano
univocal	univoco	republican*	repubblicano
urinal*	orinatorio	sacristan*	sagrestano
zeal*	zelo	silvan	silvano
-AN	**-ANO**	Spartan	spartano
See also-IAN-IANO		suburban	suburbano
African	africano	sultan	sultano
American	americano	sylvan*	silvano
Anglican	Anglicano	talisman	talismano
Aristotelian	Aristoteliano	Texan	texano
artisan*	artigiano	Theban*	tebano
caiman	caimano	Titan	Titano
cardan	cardano	Tristan	Tristano
castellan	castellano	uhlan*	ulano
catamaran	catamarano	urban	urbano

112

Vatican	Vaticano
veteran	veterano
-ANCE	**-AMENTO**
advance	avanzamento
maintainance	mantenimento
sustenance	sostentamento
-ANCE /-ANCY	**-ANZA**
abundance*	abbondanza
alliance*	alleanza
ambulance	ambulanza
arrogance	arroganza
assonance	assonanza
circumstance*	circostanza
concordance	concordanza
consonance	consonanza
constancy*	costanza
dance	danza
discrepancy	discrepanza
dissonance	dissonanza
distance	distanza
elegance	eleganza
equidistance	equidistanza
exorbitance*	esorbitanza
extravagance*	stravaganza
exuberance*	esuberanza
finance	finanza
flagrancy	flagranza
fragrance	fragranza
ignorance	ignoranza
importance	importanza
inconstancy	inconstanza
inelegance	ineleganza
inobservance*	inosservanza
intemperance	intemperanza
intolerance*	intolleranza
observance*	osservanza
perseverance	perseveranza
predominance	predominanza
preponderance	preponderanza
protuberance	protuberanza
redundance*	ridondanza
redundancy*	ridondanza
reluctance*	riluttanza
remonstrance*	rimostranza
repugnance*	ripugnanza
resemblance*	rassomiglianza

resonance*	risonanza
semblance*	sembianza
substance*	sostanza
surveillance*	sorveglianza
temperance	temperanza
tolerance*	tolleranza
usance	usanza
vacancy	vacanza
vigilance	vigilanza
-ANCE	**-AZIONE**
assurance*	assicurazione
hesitance*	esitazione
irradiance	irradiazione
variance	variazione
-ANCE	**-ENZA**
appearance*	apparenza
appurtenance*	appartenenza
assistance	assistenza
connivance	connivenza
obedience*	ubbidienza
penance* (eccl.)	penitenza
provenance*	provenienza
Exceptions:	
cognizance	conoscenza
continuance	continuità
discordance	discordia
disturbance	disturbo
lance	lancia
parlance	linguaggio
radiance	radiosità
romance	romanzo
significance	significato
-ANCY	**-ANZIA**
cartomancy	cartomanzia
chiromancy	chiromanzia
infancy	infanzia
necromancy	necromanzia
rhabdomancy	rabdomanzia
but:	
malignancy	malignità
occupancy	occupazione
-ANGLE	**-ANGOLO**
angle*	angolo
equiangle	equiangolo
quadrangle	quadrangolo
rectangle*	rettangolo

triangle	triangolo	immigrant	immigrante
-ANT	**-ANTE**	important	importante
aberrant	aberrante	incessant	incessante
abundant*	abbondante	inconsonant	inconsonante
accusant	accusante	inconstant*	incostante
arrogant	arrogante	inelegant	inelegante
aspirant	aspirante	infant	infante
assonant	assonante	inhabitant*	abitante
attestant	attestante	inhalant*	inalante
brilliant*	brillante	inobservant*	inosservante
carburant	carburante	insignificant	insignificante
celebrant	celebrante	instant*	istante
coagulant	coagulante	intolerant*	intollerante
commandant*	comandante	intrigant	intrigante
concomitant	concomitante	irradiant	irradiante
concordant	concordante	irritant	irritante
consonant	consonante	jubilant*	giubilante
constant*	costante	Levant	Levante
cosecant	cosecante	lubricant	lubricante
deodorant	deodorante	mandant	mandante
determinant	determinante	mendicant	mendicante
discordant	discordante	migrant	migrante
disinfectant*	disinfettante	militant	militante
disputant	disputante	observant*	osservante
dissonant	dissonante	occupant	occupante
distant	distante	officiant	officiante
dominant	dominante	participant*	partecipante
elegant	elegante	pedant	pedante
elephant*	elefante	perseverant	perseverante
emigrant	emigrante	postulant	postulante
equidistant	equidistante	predominant	predominante
errant	errante	preponderant	preponderante
excitant*	eccitante	Protestant	protestante
exorbitant*	esorbitante	protuberant	protuberante
expectorant*	espettorante	quadrant	quadrante
exuberant*	esuberante	radiant*	raggiante
figurant	figurante	recalcitrant*	ricalcitrante
flagrant	flagrante	redundant*	ridondante
fragrant	fragrante	refrigerant	refrigerante
fulgurant*	folgorante	reluctant*	riluttante
fulminant	fulminante	repugnant*	ripugnante
giant*	gigante	resonant*	risonante
habitant*	abitante	restaurant*	ristorante
hesitant*	esitante	resultant*	risultante
hydrant*	idrante	retardant*	ritardante
ignorant	ignorante	ruminant	ruminante

secant	secante	auricular	auriculare
secant (geom.)	secante	basilar	basilare
sextant*	sestante	cellular	cellulare
sibilant	sibilante	circular*	circolare
significant	significante	collar	collare
stagnant	stagnante	consular*	consolare
stimulant*	stimolante	corpuscular*	corpuscolare
supplicant	supplicante	crepuscular*	crepuscolare
sycophant*	sicofante	equiangular*	equiangolare
tolerant*	tollerante	exemplar*	esemplare
triumphant*	trionfante	familiar	familiare
vacant	vacante	follicular*	follicolare
verdant*	verdeggiante	funicular*	funicolare
vibrant	vibrante	glandular*	ghiandolare
vigilant	vigilante	granular	granulare
-ANT	**-ENTE**	insular	insulare
appurtenant*	appartenente	interlinear	interlineare
ascendant	ascendente	interpolar	interpolare
clairvoyant*	chiaroveggente	irregular*	irregolare
combatant*	combattente	jugular*	giugulare
confidant	confidente	linear	lineare
dependant*	dipendente	lumbar*	lombare
descendant*	discendente	lunar	lunare
pendant	pendente	modular	modulare
sergeant*	sergente	molar	molare
Some exceptions:		molecular*	molecolare
benignant	benigno	muscular*	muscolare
malignant	maligno	nuclear	nucleare
indignant	indignato	ocular	oculare
tyrant	tiranno	oracular*	oracolare
valiant	valoroso	ovular	ovulare
significant	significativo	particular*	particolare
informant	informatore	peculiar	peculiare
assailant	assalitore	peninsular	peninsulare
-ANTHROPE	**-ANTROPO**	perpendicular*	perpendicolare
misanthrope	misantropo	polar	polare
philanthrope *	filantropo	popular*	popolare
-ANTHROPY	**-ANTROPIA**	premolar	premolare
misanthropy	misantropia	rectangular*	rettangolare
philanthropy*	filantropia	regular*	regolare
-AR	**-ARE**	reticular*	reticolare
-ular		scapular*	scapolare
alar	alare	secular*	secolare
angular*	angolare	semicircular*	semicircolare
annular*	anulare	singular*	singolare
articular*	articolare	solar	solare

spectacular*	spettacolare	leopard	leopardo
tentacular*	tentacolare	Lollard	lollardo
thermonuclear*	termonucleare	Lombard	lombardo
triangular*	triangolare	petard	petardo
tubercular*	tubercolare	retard*	ritardo
tubular*	tubolare	Richard*	Riccardo
tutelar	tutelare	Savoyard*	savoiardo
unicellular	unicellulare	standard*, n.	stendardo
unpopular*	impopolare	*Exceptions*:	
valvular*	valvolare	courtyard	cortile
vascular*	vascolare	guard	guardia
vehicular*	veicolare	mustard	mostarda
velar	velare	standard, adj.	standard
ventricular*	ventricolare	vanguard	avanguardia
vermicular*	vermicolare	**-ARIAN**	**-ARIANO**
vesicular*	vescicolare	arian/arian	ariano
vestibular*	vestibolare	rotarian	rotariano
vulgar*	volgare	unitarian	unitariano
vulvar	vulvare	vegetarian	vegetariano
but:		**-ARIAN**	**-ARIO**
mortar	mortaio	agrarian	agrario
vicar	vicario	antiquarian	antiquario
-ARCH	**-ARCA**	authoritarian*	autoritario
matriarch	matriarca	centenarian	centenario
monarch	monarca	equalitarian*	egualitario
patriarch	patriarca	humanitarian*	umanitario
Petrarch	Petrarca	librarian*	bibliotecario
Note:		nonagenarian	nonagenario
Plutarch	Plutarco	octogenarian*	ottogenario
-ARCHY	**-ARCHIA**	octonarian*	ottonario
anarchy	anarchia	proletarian	proletario
diarchy	diarchia	sectarian*	settario
hierarchy*	gerarchia	sexagenarian*	sessagenario
monarchy	monarchia	totalitarian	totalitario
oligarchy	oligarchia	trinitarian	trinitario
Some exceptions:		utilitarian	utilitario
matriarchy	matriarcato	valetudinarian	valetudinario
patriarchy	patriarcato	*Some exceptions:*	
plutarchy	plutocrazia	barbarian	barbarico
-ARD	**-ARDO**	parliamentarian	parlamentare
bastard	bastardo	**-ARY**	**-ARE**
Bernard	Bernardo	basilary	basilare
Edward*	Edoardo	capillary	capillare
goliard	goliardo	disciplinary	disciplinare
lard	lardo	elementary	elementare
Leonard	Leonardo	epistolary	epistolare

exemplary*	esemplare
medullary*	midollare
military	militare
nobiliary	nobiliare
parliamentary*	parlamentare
preliminary	preliminare
pulmonary*	polmonare
salivary	salivare
salutary	salutare
supplementary	supplementare

Note:

library	biblioteca
bookcase	libreria
bookstore	libreria

Exceptions:

contemporary	contemporaneo
february	febbraio
inflationary	inflazionistico
momentary	momentaneo
notary	notaio
ovary	ovaia
temporary	temporaneo
termitary	termitaio

-ARY   **-ARIO**

Nouns and adjectives

adversary*	avversario
alimentary	alimentario
anniversary	anniversario
arbitrary	arbitrario
auxiliary*	ausiliario
beneficiary	beneficiario
binary	binario
breviary	breviario
centenary	centenario
commentary	commentario
commissary	commissario
complementary	complementario
contrary	contrario
corollary	corollario
culinary	culinario
depositary	depositario
diary	diario
dictionary*	dizionario
dignitary	dignitario
dispensary	dispensario

documentary	documentario
dromedary	dromedario
emissary	emissario
estuary	estuario
fiduciary	fiduciario
functionary*	funzionario
funerary	funerario
glossary	glossario
granary	granario
hereditary*	ereditario
imaginary*	immaginario
incendiary	incendiario
intermediary	intermediario
interplanetary	interplanetario
involuntary*	involontario
itinerary	itinerario
lapidary	lapidario
legendary*	leggendario
legionary	legionario
mammary	mammario
mandatary	mandatario
mercenary	mercenario
millenary	millenario
missionary	missionario
monetary	monetario
mortuary	mortuario
necessary	necessario
ordinary	ordinario
ossuary*	ossario
ovary (bot.)	ovario
pecuniary	pecuniario
pituitary	pituitario
planetary	planetario
plenary	plenario
plenipotentiary*	plenipotenziario
presidiary	presidiario
primary	primario
reactionary*	reazionario
reliquary	reliquario
revolutionary*	rivoluzionario
rosary	rosario
salary	salario
sanctuary*	santuario
sanguinary	sanguinario
sanitary	sanitario
secondary	secondario

secretary*	segretario	concordat	concordato
sectary*	settario	ducat	ducato
sedentary	sedentario	format	formato
sedimentary	sedimentario	muscat*	moscato
seminary	seminario	proletariat	proletariato
septenary*	settenario	rheostat*	reostato
solitary	solitario	secretariat*	segretariato
stationary*	stazionario	Serbo-Croat	serbo-croato
statuary	statuario	thermostat*	termostato
subsidiary*	sussidiario	*but:*	
summary*	sommario	diplomat	diplomatico
sumptuary*	suntuario	hemostat	ermostatico
syllabary*	sillabario	**-ATE**	**-ATA**
tercentenary*	tricentenario	apostate	apostata
tertiary*	terziario	date	data
tributary	tributario	frigate*	fregata
tricentenary*	trecentenario	grate	grata
unitary	unitario	pirate	pirata
urinary	urinario	prostate	prostata
veterinary	veterinario	Vulgate	Volgata
visionary	visionario	*Exceptions:*	
vocabulary*	vocabolario	celibate	celibe
voluntary*	volontario	climate	clima
Exceptions:		illegitimate	illegittimo
library	biblioteca	intimate	intimo
bookstore	libreria	debate	dibattito
-ASM	**-ASMA**	**-ATE**	**-ATO**
-plasm		accurate	accurato
cataplasm (med.)	cataplasma	Adequate*	adeguato
cytoplasm*	citoplasma	adulterate	adulterato
ectoplasm	ectoplasma	affectionate*	affezionato
phantasm*	fantasma	aggregate	aggregato
plasm	plasma	agnate	agnato
protoplasm	protoplasma	alternate	alternato
-ASM	**-ASMO**	animate	animato
enthusiasm*	entusiasmo	apostolate	apostolato
orgasm	orgasmo	appropriate	appropriato
pleonasm	pleonasmo	approximate*	approssimato
sarcasm	sarcasmo	arcuate	arcuato
spasm	spasmo	articulate*	articolato
-AT	**-ATO**	associate	associato
-stat		bicarbonate	bicarbonato
aerostat	aerostato	candidate	candidato
attentat	attentato	carbonate	carbonato
carat	carato	certificate	certificato
commissariat	commissariato	chocolate*	cioccolato

chordate* (zool.)	cordato	inspectorate*	ispettorato
citrate	citrato	insubordinate	insubordinato
commensurate	commensurato	intestate	intestato
concentrate	concentrato	intricate	intricato
confederate	confederato	invertebrate	invertebrato
consecrate*	consacrato	inveterate	inveterato
consulate*	consolato	inviolate	inviolato
coordinate	coordinato	irate	irato
curate	curato	Italianate*	italianizzato
degenerate	degenerato	lacerate	lacerato
delegate	delegato	laminate	laminato
delicate	delicato	lanceolate	lanceolato
designate	designato	literate*	letterato
desolate	desolato	lobate	lobato
desperate*	disperato	magistrate	magistrato
diaconate	diaconato	mandate	mandato
discriminate	discriminato	marquisate*	marchesato
disparate	disparato	matriculate*	immatricolato
doctorate*	dottorato	mediate	mediato
duplicate	duplicato	moderate	moderato
effeminate	effeminato	nitrate	nitrato
elaborate	elaborato	noviciate*	noviziato
episcopate	episcopato	oblate	oblato
exaggerate*	esagerato	obstinate*	ostinato
expatriate*	espatriato	ornate	ornato
exudate*	essudato	palate	palato
fate	fato	palmate	palmato
fortunate	fortunato	phosphate*	fosfato
fulminate	fulminato	Pilate	Pilato
geminate	geminato	Pontificate	Pontificato
hydrate*	idrato	Pontius Pilate*	Ponzio Pilato
illiterate*	illetterato	postulate	postulato
immaculate*	immacolato	predicate	predicato
immediate	immediato	prelate	prelato
impregnate	impregnato	primate	primato
inadequate*	inadeguato	priorate	priorato
inanimate	inanimato	private	privato
inarticulate*	inarticolato	proportionate*	proporzionato
incarnate	incarnato	prostrate	prostrato
inconsiderate	inconsiderato	protectorate*	protettorato
indelicate	indelicato	quadrate	quadrato
indeterminate	indeterminato	quadruplicate	quadruplicato
indiscriminate	indiscriminato	renegate*	rinnegato
ingrate	ingrato	reticulate*	reticolato
initiate*	iniziato	sedate	sedato
innate	innato	semiprivate	semiprivato

119

senate	senato	**-CENTER**	**-CENTRO**
separate	separato	center	centro
situate	situato	epicenter (amer.)	epicentro
state	stato	orthocenter*	ortocentro
striate	striato	**-CENTRE**	**-CENTRO**
subordinate	subordinato	barycentre*	baricentro
sulphate*	solfato	centre	centro
sultanate	sultanato	epicentre	epicentro
syncopate*	sincopato	**-CEPHALIC**	**-CEFALO**
syndicate*	sindacato	acephalic	acefalo
temperate	temperato	brachycephalic*	brachicefalo
tractate*	trattato	hydrocephalic*	idrocefalo
triplicate	triplicato	macrocephalic	macrocefalo
triumvirate	triumvirato	microcephalic	microcefalo
uncinate	uncinato	*Exception*:	
vertebrate	vertebrato	cephalic	cefalico
-AX	**-ACE**	**-CEPHALY**	**-CEFALIA**
anthrax*	antrace	acephaly	acefalia
borax	borace	brachycephaly*	brachicefalia
pneumothorax*	pneumotorace	hydrocephaly*	idrocefalia
thorax*	torace	macrocephaly *	macrocefalia
Exceptions:		microcephaly	microcefalia
climax	clima	**-CIDAL**	**-CIDA**
syntax	sintassi	(adjective)	
tax	tassa	fratricidal	fratricida
-BER	**-BRE**	genocidal	genocida
december*	dicembre	homicidal*	omicida
november	novembre	matricidal	matricida
october*	ottobre	parricidal	parricida
september*	settembre	patricidal	patricida
-BLE	**-BILE**	sororicidal	sororicida
(preceded by e/o/u)	(preceduta da e/o/u)	suicidal	suicida
ignoble	ignobile	uxoricidal	uxoricida
noble	nobile	uxoricidal	ussoricida
dissoluble	dissolubile	**-CIDE**	**-CIDA/-CIDIO**
insoluble	insolubile	*NOTE:*	
resoluble*	risolubile	*-cide = "killer" and "the act of killing"*	
soluble	solubile	*-cidio = the act of killing*	
Nouns:		*-cida = the killer*	
rouble	rublo	Example: *Gianni è un fratricida*	
double	doppio	*perchè ha commesso un fratricidio.*	
Note:		bactericide*	battericida
Marital status:		deicide	deicida
single woman	nubile	deicide	deicidio
single man	celibe	filicide	filicida
		filicide	filicidio

120

fratricide	fratricida	kilocicle	kilociclo
fratricide	fratricidio	miracle	miracolo
fungicide	fungicida	monocle	monocolo
genocide	genocidio	muscle	muscolo
germicide	germicida	obstacle*	ostacolo
homicide*	omicida	oracle	oracolo
homicide*	omicidio	peduncle	peduncolo
infanticide	infanticida	pinnacle	pinnacolo
infanticide	infanticidio	receptacle*	ricettacolo
insecticide*	insetticida	spectacle*	spettacolo
matricide	matricida	tabernacle	tabernacolo
matricide	matricidio	tentacle	tentacolo
pesticide	pesticida	testicle	testicolo
parricide	parricida	tubercle	tubercolo
parricide	parricidio	vehicle*	veicolo
patricide	patricida	ventricle	ventricolo
patricide	patricidio	*Some exceptions*:	
regicide	regicida	circle	cerchio
regicide	regicidio	cronicle	cronaca
sororicide	sororicida	particle	particella
sororicide	sororicidio	radicle (bot.)	radichetta
suicide	suicida	semicircle	semicerchio
suicide	suicidio	**-CORN**	**-CORNO**
tyrannicide*	tirannicida	Capricorn	Capricorno
tyrannicide*	tirannicidio	unicorn	unicorno
uxoricide*	uxoricida	*but:*	
uxoricide*	ussoricida	corn	granturco
uxoricide*	uxoricidio	**-COSM**	**-COSMO**
uxoricide*	ussoricidio	cosm	cosmo
Note:		macrocosm	macrocosmo
massacre	eccidio	mcrocosm	microcosmo
-CLE	**-COLA**	**-CRACY**	**-CRAZIA**
clavicle	clavicola	aristocracy	aristocrazia
conventicle	conventicola	autocracy	autocrazia
cuticle	cuticola	bureaucracy*	burocrazia
pellicle	pellicola	democracy	democrazia
-CLE	**-COLO**	plutocracy	plutocrazia
-acle,-icle		theocracy*	teocrazia
article	articolo	**-CRAT**	**CRATE/-**
circle	circolo		**CRATICO**
corpuscle	corpuscolo	autocrat	autocrate
fascicle	fascicolo	bureaucrat*	burocrate
follicle	follicolo	plutocrat	plutocrate
funicle	funicolo	theocrat*	teocrate
furuncle*	foruncolo	aristocrat	aristocratico
kilocicle	chilociclo	democrat	democratico

121

-CRE/-CHRE	-CRO
fulcre	fulcro
massacre	massacro
sepulchre*	sepolcro
-CYCLE	**-CICLO**
cycle*	ciclo
epicycle*	epiciclo
hemicycle*	emiciclo
kilocycle*	chilociclo
motorcycle*	motociclo
tricycle*	triciclo
Exceptions:	
bicycle	bicicletta
motorcycle	motocicletta
-DERM	**-DERMA**
ectoderm	ectoderma
pachyderm*	pachiderma
-DOX	**-DOSSO**
heterodox*	eterodossoosso
orthodox*	ortodossoosso
paradox	paradossoosso
-DOXY	**-DOSSIA**
heterodoxy*	eterodossia
orthodoxy*	ortodossia
-DROME	**-DROMO**
aerodrome*	aerodromo
airdrome*	aerodromo
autodrome	autodromo
hippodrome*	ippodromo
palindrome	palindromo
velodrome	velodromo
-DUCT	**-DOTTO**
aqueduct*	acquedotto
product	prodotto
viaduct	viadotto
-EAL	**-EO**
arboreal	arboreo
ethereal*	etereo
funereal	funereo
incorporeal	incorporeo
lacteal*	latteo
laryngeal*	laringeo
marmoreal	marmoreo
rectilineal	rettilineo
venereal	venereo
-EAN	**-EO**

Aegean*	egeo
cerulean	ceruleo
cetacean	cetaceo
crustacean*	crostaceo
epicurean	epicureo
Euclidean	euclideo
European	europeo
herculean*	erculeo
Mediterranean	Mediterraneo
pigmean	pigmeo
subterranean*	sotterraneo
Some exceptions:	
Korean	coreano
Achean	Acheo
Dantean	dantesco
Mephistophelean	mefistofelico
Tyrolean	tirolese
Andean	andino
Cyclopean	ciclopico
Ethiopean	etiopico
Pythagorean	pitagorico
Note:	
ocean	oceano
-ECT	**-ETTO**
-spect	
abject*	abietto
architect	architetto
aspect	aspetto
circumspect*	circospetto
correct	corretto
defect*	difetto
dialect	dialetto
direct	diretto
effect	effetto
elect	eletto
imperfect	imperfetto
incorrect	incorretto
indirect	indiretto
insect	insetto
intellect	intelletto
object*	oggetto
perfect	perfetto
prefect	prefetto
project*	progetto
prospect	prospetto
respect*	rispetto

English	Italian
select	seletto
subject*	soggetto
suspect*	sospetto
Exception:	
sect	setta
-ECTOMY ECTOMIA	**-ETOMIA/ ECTOMIA**
appendectomy*	appendicetomia
mastectomy	mastectomia
ovariectomy	ovariectomia
thyroidectomy*	tiroidectomia
tonsillectomy	tonsillectomia
vasectomy	vasectomia
-EE	**-ATARIO**
assignee*	assegnatario
consignee*	consegnatario
-EM	**-EMA**
apothem*	apotema
diadem	diadema
emblem	emblema
poem	poema
problem	problema
system*	sistema
theorem*	teorema
but:	
gem	gemma
phlem (med.)	flemma
stratagem	stratagemma
-ENCE	**-ENZA**
-escence	
-valence	
absence*	assenza
abstinence*	astinenza
acquiescence	acquiescenza
adherence*	aderenza
adjacence*	adiacenza
adolescence	adolescenza
affluence	affluenza
ambivalence	ambivalenza
antecedence	antecedenza
appetence	appetenza
audience*	udienza
beneficence	beneficenza
benevolence	benevolenza
cadence	cadenza
circumference*	circonferenza
clairvoyance*	chiaroveggenza
coalescence	coalescenza
coexistence*	coesistenza
coherence*	coerenza
coincidence	coincidenza
competence	competenza
concupiscence	concupiscenza
conference	conferenza
confidence	confidenza
confluence	confluenza
congruence	congruenza
conscience*	coscienza
consequence*	conseguenza
consistence	consistenza
continence	continenza
convalescence	convalescenza
convenience	convenienza
convergence	convergenza
corpulence	corpulenza
correspondence*	corrispondenza
decadence	decadenza
deference	deferenza
dependence*	dipendenza
desinence	desinenza
difference	differenza
diffidence	diffidenza
diligence	diligenza
disobedience*	disubbidienza
dissidence	dissidenza
divergence	divergenza
ebullience*	ebollienza
effervescence	effervescenza
eloquence	eloquenza
emergence	emergenza
eminence	eminenza
equivalence	equivalenza
essence	essenza
evanescence	evanescenza
evidence	evidenza
excellence*	eccellenza
excrescence*	escrescenza
exigence*	esigenza
existence*	esistenza
experience*	esperienza
flatulence	flatulenza
fluorescence	fluorescenza

fraudulence*	fraudolęnza	omniscience*	onniscięnza
immanence	immanęnza	opalescence	opalescęnza
imminence	imminęnza	opulence	opulęnza
impatience*	impazięnza	patience*	pazięnza
impenitence	impenitęnza	penitence	penitęnza
impertinence	impertinęnza	permanence	permanęnza
impotence	impotęnza	persistence	persistęnza
imprudence	imprudęnza	pertinence	pertinęnza
impudence	impudęnza	pestilence	pestilęnza
incandenscence	incandenscęnza	phosphorescence*	fosforescęnza
incidence	incidęnza	potence	potęnza
incoherence*	incoeręnza	precedence	precedęnza
incompetence	incompetęnza	preeminence*	preminęnza
inconseguence*	inconseguęnza	preference	preferęnza
inconsistence	inconsistęnza	prepotence	prepotęnza
incontinence	incontinęnza	prescience	prescięnza
inconvenience	inconvenięnza	presence	presęnza
independence*	indipendęnza	prevalence	prevalęnza
indifference	indifferęnza	prominence	prominęnza
indigence	indigęnza	provenience	provenięnza
indolence	indolęnza	prudence	prudęnza
indulgence	indulgęnza	pubescence	pubescęnza
inexperience*	inesperięnza	quintessence	quintessęnza
influence	influęnza	recrudescence	recrudescęnza
inherence*	ineręnza	recurrence*	ricorręnza
innocence	innocęnza	reference	referęnza
insipience	insipięnza	resistence	resistęnza
insistence	insistęnza	respondence*	rispondęnza
insolence	insolęnza	reticence	reticęnza
intelligence	intelligęnza	reverence*	riveręnza
interference	interferęnza	sapience	sapięnza
intermittence	intermittęnza	science	scięnza
intransigence	intransigęnza	senescence	senescęnza
iridescence	iridescęnza	sentence	sentęnza
irreverence*	irriveręnza	sequence	sequęnza
jurisprudence*	giurisprudęnza	somnolence*	sonnolęnza
licence	licęnza	subsistence*	sussistęnza
luminiscence	luminiscęnza	succulence	succulęnza
magnificence	magnificęnza	superintendence*	sovrintendęnza
magniloquence	magniloquęnza	transparence*	trasparęnza
malevolence	malevolęnza	turbulence*	turbolęnza
munificence	munificęnza	valence*	valęnza
negligence	negligęnza	vehemence*	veemęnza
obedience*	ubbidięnza	violence	violęnza
omnipotence*	onnipotęnza	virescence	virescęnza
omnipresence*	onnipresęnza	virulence	virulęnza

Some exceptions:

abhorrence	aborrimento
ambience	ambiente
belligerence	belligeranza
condolence*	condoglianza
credence	credito
defense	difesa
Florence	Firenze
Lawrence	Lorenzo
offence	offesa
pretence	pretesa
recompence	ricompensa
reference	riferimento
resurgence	risurrezione
silence	silenzio
transference	trasferimento
transience	transitorietà
translucence	traslucidità
univalence	monovalenza
-ENCY	**-ENZA**
adjacency*	adiacenza
astringency	astringenza
clemency	clemenza
coefficiency	coefficienza
contingency	contingenza
decency	decenza
deficiency	deficienza
delinquency	delinquenza
dependency*	dipendenza
efficiency	efficienza
emergency	emergenza
Excellency*	Eccellenza
flatulency	flatulenza
frequency	frequenza
inclemency	inclemenza
indecency	indecenza
inefficiency	inefficienza
infrequency	infrequenza
insolvency	insolvenza
insufficiency	insufficienza
persistency	persistenza
presidency	presidenza
regency*	reggenza
sufficiency	sufficienza
superintendency*	sovrintendenza
tangency	tangenza

transparency*	trasparenza
urgency	urgenza
valency	valenza

Some exceptions:

agency	agenzia
ascendency	ascendente
belligerency	belligeranza
fluency	fluidità
solvency	solvibilità
-END	**-ENDO**
addend	addendo
dividend	dividendo
reverend	reverendo
-ENSE	**-ENSO**
dense	denso
immense	immenso
intense	intenso
Nouns:	
incense	incenso
sense	senso

Exception:

recompense	ricompensa
-ENSE	**-ESA**
defense	difesa
offense	offesa
-ENT	**-ENTE**

Nouns and adjectives

absent*	assente
absorbent*	assorbente
abstinent*	astinente
accident	accidente
adherent*	aderente
adjacent*	adiacente
adolescent	adolescente
agent	agente
ambivalent	ambivalente
antecedent	antecedente
apparent	apparente
ardent	ardente
ascendent	ascendente
assentient*	assenziente
astringent	astringente
benevolent	benevolente
bivalent	bivalente
Clement	Clemente
clement	clemente

125

client	cliente	evanescent	evanescente
coefficient	coefficiente	evident	evidente
coexistent*	coesistente	excellent*	eccellente
coherent*	coerente	exigent*	esigente
coincident	coincidente	existent*	esistente
competent	competente	expedient*	espediente
component	componente	exponent*	esponente
concupiscent	concupiscente	fervent	fervente
concurrent*	concorrente	flatulent	flatulente
confluent	confluente	fluent	fluente
congruent	congruente	fluorescent	fluorescente
consentient*	consenziente	frequent	frequente
consequent*	conseguente	immanent	immanente
constituent*	costituente	imminent	imminente
contangent	contangente	impatient*	impaziente
continent	continente	impellent	impellente
contingent	contingente	impenitent	impenitente
convalescent	convalescente	impertinent	impertinente
convenient	conveniente	impotent	impotente
convergent	convergente	imprudent	imprudente
correspondent*	corrispondente	impudent	impudente
crescent	crescente	incandescent	incandenscente
current*	corrente	incident	incidente
decadent	decadente	incipient	incipiente
decent	decente	inclement	inclemente
deferent	deferente	incoherent*	incoerente
deficient	deficiente	incompetent	incompetente
defluent	defluente	inconsequent*	inconseguente
delinquent	delinquente	inconsistent	inconsistente
dependent*	dipendente	incontinent	incontinente
deponent	deponente	inconvenient	inconveniente
detergent	detergente	incumbent*	incombente
different	differente	indecent	indecente
diffident	diffidente	independent*	indipendente
diligent	diligente	indifferent	indifferente
disobedient*	disubbidiente	indigent	indigente
dissident	dissidente	indolent	indolente
dissolvent	dissolvente	indulgent	indulgente
divergent	divergente	inefficient	inefficiente
effervescent	effervescente	infrequent	infrequente
efficient	efficiente	ingredient	ingrediente
eloquent	eloquente	inherent*	inerente
eminent	eminente	innocent	innocente
emollient	emolliente	insistent	insistente
equipollent	equipollente	insolent	insolente
equivalent	equivalente	insolvent	insolvente

insufficient	insufficiente	regent*	reggente
intelligent	intelligente	resistent	resistente
intermittent	intermittente	respondent*	rispondente
interpendent	interpendente	resurgent*	risorgente
intervenient	interveniente	reticent	reticente
intransigent	intransigente	reverent*	riverente
iridescent	iridescente	salient	saliente
irreverent*	irriverente	sapient	sapiente
latent	latente	senescent	senescente
lucent	lucente	sentient*	senziente
luminiscent	luminiscente	sequent*	seguente
magniloquent	magniloquente	serpent	serpente
nascent	nascente	solvent	solvente
negligent	negligente	strident	stridente
nutrient	nutriente	student	studente
obedient*	ubbidiente	subsistent*	sussistente
Occident	Occidente	sufficient	sufficiente
omnipotent*	onnipotente	tangent	tangente
omnipresent*	onnipresente	torrent	torrente
omniscient*	onnisciente	transcendent*	trascendente
opalescent	opalescente	transparent*	trasparente
orient	oriente	trident	tridente
parturient*	partoriente	urgent	urgente
patient*	paziente	vehement*	veemente
penitent	penitente	virescent	virescente
permanent	permanente	*Some exceptions*:	
persistent	persistente	abolishment	abolizione
pertinent	pertinente	announcement	annuncio
pestilent	pestilente	arrangement	sistemazione
phosphorescent*	fosforescente	ascent	ascesa
potent	potente	assent	assenso
precedent	precedente	belligerent	belligerante
preeminent*	preminente	beneficent	benefico
prepotent	prepotente	benevolent	benevolo
present	presente	cent	centesimo
president	presidente	consent	consenso
prevalent	prevalente	content	contenuto
prominent	prominente	descent	discesa
prudent	prudente	dissent	dissenso
pubescent	pubescente	esculent	commestibile
pungent	pungente	government	governo
putrescent	putrescente	jurisprudent	giurisperito
quiescent	quiescente	magnificent	magnifico
quotient*	quoziente	malevolent	malevolo
recent	recente	punishment	punizione
recurrent*	ricorrente	refreshment	rinfresco

retirement	ritiro
rodent	roditore
silent	silenzioso
tournament	torneo
transient	transitorio
translucent	traslucido
Vincent	Vincenzo
but:	
parent	padre o madre
parents	genitori
-ENT	**-ENTO**
-lent	
-ment	
-ulent	
accent*	accento
accompaniment*	accompagnamento
adjournment*	aggiornamento
advancement*	avanzamento
advent*	avvento
aliment	alimento
amendment*	amendamento
annullment*	annullamento
apartment*	appartamento
appointment*	appuntamento
argument*	argomento
attachment*	attaccamento
cement	cemento
commandment*	comandamento
comment	commento
compartment*	compartimento
compliment	complimento
condiment	condimento
convent	convento
corpulent	corpulento
deferment*	differimento
department*	dipartimento
derailment*	deragliamento
detriment	detrimento
disarmament	disarmamento
discernment*	discernimento
document	documento
emolument	emolumento
encouragement*	incoraggiamento
equipment*	equipaggiamento
event	evento
excitement*	eccitamento
excrement*	escremento

experiment*	esperimento
ferment	fermento
filament	filamento
firmament	firmamento
fragment*	frammento
fraudulent *	fraudolento
fundament*	fondamento
impediment	impedimento
impugment*	impugnamento
incitement*	incitamento
increment	incremento
intent	intento
internment*	internamento
investment*	investimento
lament	lamento
lineament	lineamento
liniment	linimento
malcontent	malcontento
maltreatment*	maltrattamento
medicament	medicamento
moment	momento
monument	monumento
movement*	movimento
nutriment	nutrimento
opulent	opulento
ornament	ornamento
parliament*	parlamento
pavement*	pavimento
portent	portento
presentiment	presentimento
purulent	purulento
rearmament*	riarmamento
regiment*	reggimento
rudiment	rudimento
sacrament	sacramento
sediment	sedimento
segment	segmento
sentiment	sentimento
somnolent*	sonnolento
succulent	succulento
supplement	supplemento
talent	talento
temperament	temperamento
testament	testamento
torment	tormento
treatment*	trattamento

Trent	Trento
turbulent*	turbolento
violent	violento
virulent	virulento
-EPT	**-ETTO**
concept	concetto
except*	eccetto
inept	inetto
transept	transetto
-ER	**-ORE**
accuser	accusatore
amplifier	amplificatore
announcer*	annunciatore
cauliflower*	cavolfiore
comforter*	confortatore
composer	compositore
condenser	condensatore
converter	convertitore
examiner*	esaminatore
finisher	finitore
founder*	fondatore
informer	informatore
miner	minatore
multiplier*	moltiplicatore
offender	offensore
planter*	piantatore
producer	produttore
promoter	promotore
rectifier*	rettificatore
repeater*	ripetitore
silencer	silenziatore
tempter*	tentatore
-ERN	**-ERNA**
cavern	caverna
cistern	cisterna
lantern	lanterna
tavern	taverna
-ERSE	**-ERSO**
adverse*	avverso
averse*	avverso
diverse	diverso
inverse	inverso
perverse	perverso
terse	terso
transverse*	traverso
traverse	traverso

universe	universo
verse	verso
-ERY	**-ERIA**
artillery*	artiglieria
buffoonery*	buffoneria
chancellery*	cancelleria
cutlery*	coltelleria
devilry*	diavoleria
distillery	distilleria
misery	miseria
perfumery*	profumeria
periphery*	periferia
Exceptions:	
machinery*	macchinario
scenery	scenario
slavery	schiavitù
-ERY	**-ERIO**
adultery	adulterio
cautery	cauterio
presbytery*	presbiterio
psaltery*	salterio
-ERY	**-ERO**
baptistery*	battistero
cemetery*	cimitero
mistery	mistero
monastery	monastero
-ESE	**-ESE**
Chinese*	cinese
Genoese*	genovese
Japanese*	giapponese
Lebanese	lebanese
Siamese	siamese
Tyrolese*	tirolese
-ESQUE	**-ESCO**
arabesque	arabesco
burlesque	burlesco
Dantesque	dantesco
grotesque*	grottesco
Moresque	moresco
picaresque	picaresco
picturesque*	pittoresco
Some exceptions:	
Romanesque	romanico
statuesque	statuario
-ESS	**-ERA**
adulteress	adultera

adventuress* — avventuriera

Exceptions:

governess — governante

-ESS — **-ESSA**

archiduchess* — arciduchessa
baroness — baronessa
countess* — contessa
deaconess* — diaconessa
duchess — duchessa
giantess* — gigantessa
lioness* — leonessa
poetess — poetessa
princess* — principessa
prophetess* — profetessa

but:

authoress — autrice

-ESS — **-ESSO**

-gress
abscess* — ascesso
access — accesso
congress — congresso
egress — egresso
excess* — eccesso
express* — espresso
ingress — ingresso
progress — progresso
regress — regresso
success — successo

-ESS — **-EZZA**

absolutness* — assolutezza
caress — carezza
fineness* — finezza
firmness* — fermezza
fortress* — fortezza
promptness* — prontezza
pureness* — purezza
resoluteness* — risolutezza
robustness* — robustezza

-ESS — **-ITÀ**

generousness* — generosità
genuiness* — genuinità
ingeniousness* — ingegnosità
ingenuousness* — ingenuità
licentiousness* — licenziosità
obsequiousness* — ossequiosità
obtuseness* — ottusità

odiousness* — odiosità
ponderousness* — ponderosità
positiveness* — positività
precariousness* — precarietà
preciousness* — preziosità
rareness* — rarità
sensuousness* — sensuosità
soberness* — sobrietà
temporariness* — temporaneità
uniqueness* — unicità
variableness* — variabilità
vastness* — vastità

-ET — **-ETA/-ETTA**

comet — cometa
diet — dieta
planet* — pianeta
poet — poeta
prophet* — profeta
barret* — berretta
bayonet* — baionetta
cornet — cornetta
cutlet* — cotoletta
egret — egretta
genet — genetta
hatchet* — accetta
Juliet* — Giulietta
spinet — spinetta
toilet* — toletta

Exceptions:

electromagnet* — elettromagnete
magnet — magnete

-ET — **-ETO**

alphabet * — alfabeto
amulet — amuleto
epithet* — epiteto
indiscreet* — indiscreto
minaret — minareto
quiet — quieto
secret* — segreto
unquiet* — inquieto

-ET — **-ETTO**

aglet* — aghetto
ballet* — balletto
banquet* — banchetto
baronet* — baronetto
bracelet* — braccialetto

brevet	brevetto
cabinet*	gabinetto
cadet*	cadetto
clarinet*	clarinetto
corselet*	corsaletto
duet*	duetto
helmet*	elmetto
minuet*	minuetto
net*	netto
octet*	ottetto
parapet*	parapetto
quartet*	quartetto
quintet*	quintetto
sachet*	sacchetto
sextet*	sestetto
sonnet*	sonetto
valet*	valetto
verset*	versetto
violet	violetto
zibet*	zibetto
but:	
dulcet	dolce
-ETTE	**-ETTA**
brunette	brunetta
cigarette*	sigaretta
corvette	corvetta
croquette*	crocchetta
etiquette*	etichetta
gazette*	gazzetta
lunette	lunetta
marionette	marionetta
pirouette*	piroetta
rosette	rosetta
statuette	statuetta
vignette	vignetta
-ETUDE	**SEE-TUDE**
-EX	**-ESSO**
annex	annesso
complex	complesso
convex	convesso
perplex	perplesso
sex* [1]	sesso
simplex	simplesso

[1]

Latin	English	Italian
sex	*>six*	*>sei*

sexus	*>sex-*	*>sesso*
-EX		**-ICE**
-plex		
apex		apice
duplex		duplice
index		indice
latex		latice
multiplex*		molteplice
murex		murice
pollex		pollice
quadruplex		quadruplice
triplex		triplice
vertex		vertice
vortex		vortice
-FICE		**-FICIO**
artifice		artificio
benefice		beneficio
sacrifice		sacrificio
-FICENT		**-FICO**
beneficent		benefico
magnificent		magnifico
maleficent		malefico
munificent		munifico
-FIX		**-FISSO**
affix		affisso
crucifix		crocifisso
prefix		prefisso
profix		profisso
suffix		suffisso
-FLECTION		**-FLESSIONE**
flection		flessione
genuflection		genuflessione
inflection		inflessione
reflection*		riflessione
-FLEX/FLUX		**-FLESSO/ FLUSSO**
circumflex*		circonflesso
reflex*		riflesso
afflux		afflusso
efflux		efflusso
flux		flusso
influx		influsso
reflux*		riflusso
-FOIL		**-FOGLIO**
quatrefoil*		quadrifoglio
trefoil*		trifoglio

-FORM	-FORME
-iform	
aeriform	aeriforme
cubiform	cubiforme
cuneiform	cuneiforme
fibriform	fibriforme
linguiform	linguiforme
multiform	multiforme
oviform	oviforme
pisciform	pisciforme
uniform	uniforme

Exceptions:

platform	piattaforma
reform	riforma

-FUGAL	-FUGO
febrifugal*	febbrifugo
centrifugal	centrifugo
vermifugal	vermifugo

-FUGE	-FUGIO
refuge*	rifugio
subterfuge*	sotterfugio

-GAMY	-GAMIA
bigamy	bigamia
endogamy	endogamia
monogamy	monogamia
polygamy*	poligamia

-GEN	-GENO
carcinogen*	cancerogeno
halogen*	alogeno
hydrogen*	idrogeno
oxygen*	ossigeno

-GON	-GONO
decagon	decagono
hexagon*	esagono
octagon*	ottagono
pentagon	pentagono
polygon	poligono

-GRADE	-GRADO
Belgrade	Belgrado
centigrade	centigrado
grade	grado
plantigrade	plantigrado
retrograde	retrogrado

-GRAM	-GRAMMA

Note: Denoting "written" or "drawn"

anagram*	anagramma
cablegram*	cablogramma
cardiogram	cardiogramma
diagram	diagramma
echocardiogram*	ecocardiogramma
electrocardiogram*	elettrocardiogramma
epigram	epigramma
hologram*	ologramma
ideogram	ideogramma
monogram	monogramma
parallelogram	parallelogramma
pentagram	pentagramma
phonogram*	fonogramma
program	programma
radiogram	radiogramma
telegram	telegramma

-GRAM	-GRAMMO

Note: denoting metric system

centigram	centigrammo
decagram	decagrammo
decigram	decigrammo
gram	grammo
hectogram*	ettogrammo
kilogram*	chilogrammo
microgram	microgrammo
milligram	milligrammo

-GRAPH	-GRAFIA
lithograph*	litografia
monograph	monografia
oleograph	oleografia
photograph*	fotografia
radiograph	radiografia
xylograph*	silografia
zincograph	zincografia

-GRAPH	-GRAFO
autograph	autografo
calligrapher	calligrafo
chirograph	chirografo
chronograph*	cronografo
cinematograph	cinematografo
heliograph*	eliografo
holograph*	olografo
pantograph	pantografo
paragraph	paragrafo
phonograph*	fonografo
polygraph*	poligrafo
seismograph*	sismografo
spectrograph*	spettrografo

telegraph — telegrafo

Exceptions:

cryptograph — crittogamma
graph — grafico
epigraph — epigrafe

-GRAPHER — **-GRAFISTA**

epigrapher — epigrafista
heliographer* — eliografista
pantographer — pantografista
telegrapher — telegrafista

but:

radiographer — radiologo

-GRAPHER — **-GRAFO**

autobiographer — autobiografo
bibliographer — bibliografo
biographer — biografo
calligrapher — calligrafo
cartographer — cartografo
chalcographer* — calcografo
choreographer* — coreografo
chromatographer* — cromatografo
cryptographer* — crittografo
demographer — demografo
ethnographer* — etnografo
geographer — geografo
hagiographer* — agiografo
historiographer* — storiografo
hydrographer* — idrografo
iconographer — iconografo
lexicographer* — lessicografo
lithographer* — litografo
oceanographer — oceanografo
photographer* — fotografo
pornographer — pornografo
scenographer — scenografo
stenographer — stenografo
stratigrapher — stratigrafo
topographer — topografo
typographer* — tipografo
xylographer* — silografo
zincographer — zincografo

-GRAPHICAL — **-GRAFICO**

autobiographical — autobiografico
bibliographical — bibliografico
biographical — biografico
calligraphical — calligrafico

cartographical — cartografico
chalcographical* — calcografico
cryptographical* — crittografico
ethnographical* — etnografico
geographical — geografico
hagiographical* — agiografico
heliographical* — eliografico
historiographical* — storiografico
iconographical — iconografico
lexicographical* — lessicografico
lithographical* — litografico
monographical — monografico
oceanographical — oceanografico
orographical — orografico
orthographical* — ortografico
phonographical* — fonografico
photographical* — fotografico
radiographical* — radiografico
scenographical — scenografico
seismographical* — sismografico
stenographical — stenografico
stratigraphical — stratigrafico
telegraphical — telegrafico
topographical — topografico
typographical* — tipografico
xylographical* — silografico
zincographical — zincografico

-GRAPHY — **-GRAFIA**

autobiography — autobiografia
bibliography — bibliografia
biography — biografia
calligraphy — calligrafia
cacography — cacografia
cartography — cartografia
chalcography* — calcografia
choreography* — coreografia
chromatography* — cromatografia
cinematography — cinematografia
cryptography* — crittografia
demography — demografia
echocardiography* — echocardiografia
epigraphy — epigrafia
ethnography* — etnografia
geography — geografia
hagiography* — agiografia
heliography* — eliografia

133

historiography*	storiografia	Albania	Albania
holography*	olografia	albuminuria	albuminuria
hydrography*	idrografia	Alexandria*	Alessandria
iconography	iconografia	alexia*	alessia
lexicography*	lessicografia	Algeria	Algeria
lithography*	litografia	alleluia	alleluia
mammography	mammografia	amblyopia*	ambliopia
oceanography	oceanografia	ambrosia	ambrosia
oleography	oleografia	ametropia	ametropia
orography	orografia	amnesia	amnesia
orthography*	ortografia	anaemia*	anemia
pantography	pantografia	anaesthesia*	anestesia
phonography*	fonografia	analgesia	analgesia
photography*	fotografia	anemia	anemia
pornography	pornografia	anorexia	anoressia
radiography	radiografia	anosmia	anosmia
scenography	scenografia	antonomasia	antonomasia
seismography*	sismografia	aphasia*	afasia
siderography	siderografia	aphonia*	afonia
spectrography*	spettrografia	aplasia	aplasia
stenography	stenografia	apologia	apologia
stratigraphy	stratigrafia	araucaria	araucaria
telegraphy	telegrafia	aria	aria
topography	topografia	Armenia	Armenia
typography*	tipografia	arrhythmia*	aritmia
xylography*	silografia	artemisia	artemisia
zincography	zincografia	Asia	Asia
-IA	**-IA**	asphyxia*	asfissia
-aesthesia		asthenia*	astenia
-algia		Australia	Australia
-anemia		Austria	Austria
-asia		azotemia	azotemia
-emia		begonia	begonia
-leukemia		bibliomania	bibliomania
-lexia		Bolivia	Bolivia
-mania		bulimia	bulimia
-mnesia		California	California
-noia		camellia*	camelia
-opia		cassia	cassia
-orexia		Columbia*	Colombia
-phoria		cornucopia	cornucopia
-(r)rhytmia		curia	curia
-somnia		dahlia*	dalia
-thanasia		Dalmatia*	Dalmazia
abulia	abulia	diplopia	diplopia
acacia	acacia	dyslexia*	dislessia

134

dyspepsia*	dispepsia	Mauretania	Mauretania
dysphoria*	disforia	megalomania	megalomania
encyclopedia*	enciclopedia	militia*	milizia
erotomania	erotomania	Mongolia	Mongolia
Ethiopia*	Etiopia	monomania	monomania
euphoria*	euforia	multimedia	multimedia
Eurasia	Eurasia	myopia*	miopia
euthanasia*	eutanasia	neuralgia*	nevralgia
fantasia	fantasia	New Caledonia*	Nuova Caledonia
fascia	fascia	Nigeria	Nigeria
freesia*	fresia	nostalgia	nostalgia
fuchsia*	fucsia	Nova Scotia*	Nuova Scozia
gardenia	gardenia	nymphomania*	ninfomania
Georgia*	Giorgia	Oceania	Oceania
Gloria	Gloria	odontalgia	odontalgia
gloxinia	gloxinia	Olympia*	Olimpia
glycoemia*	glicemia	paramnesia	paramnesia
hemiplegia*	emiplegia	paranoia	paranoia
hernia*	ernia	Persia	Persia
Hymalaia*	Imalaia	petunia	petunia
hyperemia	iperemia	phantasmagoria*	fantasmagoria
hypermetropia*	ipermetropia	pizzeria	pizzeria
hypochondria*	ipocondria	Polynesia*	Polinesia
hypothermia*	ipotermia	presbyopia*	presbiopia
hysteria*	isteria	pyromania*	piromania
India	India	Rhodesia*	Rodesia
Indonesia	Indonesia	Romania	Romania
inertia*	inerzia	Russia	Russia
insomnia*	insonnia	salvia	salvia
ischemia	ischemia	sarracenia	sarracenia
jealousy*	gelosia	Scandinavia	Scandinavia
Kenia	Kenia	scoria	scoria
kleptomania*	cleptomania	sepia* (zool.)	seppia
Laetitia*	Letizia	septicaemia*	setticemia
lamia	lamia	Serbia	Serbia
leuk(a)emia*	leucemia	Siberia	Siberia
leukemia*	leucemia	tibia	tibia
Liberia	Liberia	uremia	uremia
Lithuania*	Lituania	utopia	utopia
loggia	loggia	Venezia	Venezia
Macedonia	Macedonia	via	via
magnesia	magnesia	Virginia	Virginia
magnolia	magnolia	zinnia	zinnia
malaria	malaria	*Exceptions:*	
Manchuria*	Manciuria	ammonia	ammoniaca
mania	mania	insignia	insegna

diphtheria*	difterite	Persian (1)*	persiano
pneumonia	polmonite	Peruvian	peruviano
-IAD	**-IADE**	Politian*	Poliziano
Iliad	Iliade	Polynesian*	polinesiano
myriad*	miriade	Pompeian	pompeiano
Olympiad*	olimpiade	postmeridian*	pomeridiano
-IAN	**-ESE**	praetorian*	pretoriano
Albanian	albanese	Presbyterian*	presbiteriano
Athenian	ateniese	quotidian	quotidiano
Calabrian	calabrese	Rhodesian*	rodesiano
Canadian	canadese	Siberian	siberiano
Hungarian*	ungherese	Sicilian	siciliano
Norwegian*	norvegese	Syrian*	siriano
Palestinian	palestinese	Tasmanian	tasmaniano
-IAN	**-IANO**	Titian*	Tiziano
Ambrosian	ambrosiano	Trajan*	Traiano
antediluvian*	antidiluviano	Trojan*	troiano
antemeridian*	antimeridiano	Venetian*	veneziano
Arian	Ariano	venusian	venusiano
Aristotelian	Aristoteliano	Vesuvian	vesuviano
artesian	artesiano	(1) Persian*	
Aryan*	ariano	*Used with geographic expressions.*	
Augustinian*	agostiniano	*Ex: Persian gulf = Golfo persico.*	
Australian	australiano		
Cartesian	cartesiano	*Exceptions*:	
Darwinian*	darviniano	librarian	bibliotecario
Diocletian*	Diocleziano	plebeian	plebeo
Egyptian*	egiziano	**-IAN**	**-ICO**
episcopalian	episcopaliano	arcadian	arcadico
Eurasian	eurasiano	Aristotelian	aristotelico
Gregorian	gregoriano	Asian*	asiatico
guardian	guardiano	Balkan*	balcanico
Indian	indiano	barbarian	barbarico
Indonesian	indonesiano	historian*	storico
Italian	italiano	Iberian	iberico
Justinian*	Giustiniano	isthmian*	istmico
Kantian	kantiano	lesbian	lesbico
Laotian	laotiano	Lybian*	libico
Lilliputian*	lillipuziano	Machiavellian	machiavellico
Lithuanian*	lituano	ovarian	ovarico
Martian*	marziano	Persian (1)*	persico
median	mediano	politician*	politico
meridian	meridiano	uranian	uranico
Nigerian	nigeriano	**-IATRY**	**-IATRA**
Palladian	palladiano	-latry	
Paraguayan*	paraguaiano	bibliolatry	bibliolatria

idolatry	idolatria	ineligible*	ineleggibile
podiatry	podiatria	inexhaustible*	inesauribile
psychiatry*	psichiatria	inexpressible*	inesprimibile
-IBLE	**-IBILE**	infallible	infallibile
accessible	accessibile	inflexible*	inflessibile
admissible*	ammissibile	infrangible	infrangibile
audible*	udibile	infusible	infusibile
combustible	combustibile	insensible	insensibile
compatible	compatibile	intangible	intangibile
comprehensible*	comprensibile	intelligible	intelligibile
convertible	convertibile	invincible	invincibile
corrodible	corrodibile	invisible	invisibile
corruptible*	corruttibile	irascible	irascibile
credible	credibile	irreducible*	irriducibile
digestible*	digeribile	irremissible	irremissibile
dirigible	dirigibile	irreprehensible*	irreprensibile
divisible	divisibile	irrepressible	irrepressibile
eligible*	eleggibile	irresistible	irresistibile
exigible*	esigibile	irreversible	irreversibile
flexible*	flessibile	legible*	leggibile
fusible	fusibile	ostensible	ostensibile
horrible*	orribile	permissible	permissibile
illegible*	illeggibile	plausible	plausibile
impassible	impassibile	possible	possibile
imperceptible*	impercettibile	reducible*	riducibile
impossible	impossibile	refrangible*	rifrangibile
imprescriptible*	imprescrittibile	remissible	remissibile
inaccessible	inaccessibile	reversible	reversibile
inadmissible*	inammissibile	susceptible*	suscettibile
inaudible	inaudibile	tangible	tangibile
incoercible	incoercibile	terrible	terribile
incombustible	incombustibile	visible	visibile

Note:"-ible changes to "-abile":

impressible*	impressionabile
irresponsible	irresponsabile
responsible	responsabile
suggestible*	suggestionabile
unresponsible*	irresponsabile

Exceptions:

indelible	indelebile
sensible	pratico, saggio
-IC	**-ICA**
arithmetic*	aritmetica
chiropractic*	chiropratica
clinic	clinica

colic	colica	-utic	
ethic*	etica	academic*	accademico
logic	logica	acephalic	acefalo
music	musica	achromatic*	acromatico
philippic*	filippica	acoustic*	acustico
republic*	repubblica	acrobatic	acrobatico
rhetoric*	retorica	acrostic	acrostico
rubric	rubrica	acyclic*	aciclico
subtonic*	sottotonica	Adriatic	Adriatico
tunic	tunica	aerodynamic*	aerodinamico
-IC-	**ICO**	aerostatic	aerostatico
-anthropic		aesthetic*	estetico
-astic		agnostic	agnostico
-atic		agonistic	agonistico
-centric		alcoholic*	alcolico
-cosmic		algebraic*	algebrico
-cratic		allegoric	allegorico
-demic		allergic	allergico
-etic		alphabetic*	alfabetico
-fic		altruistic	altruistico
-genic		anachronistic*	anacronistico
-glyphic		anaemic*	anemico
-graphic		anaesthetic*	anestetico
-iatric		analcoholic*	analcolico
-istic		analgesic	analgesico
-itic		analytic*	analitico
-logic		anarchic	anarchico
-metric		anatomic	anatomico
-morphic		angelic	angelico
-otic		anorexic	anoressico
-pathic		antagonistic	antagonistico
-pedic		Antarctic*	antartico
-periodic		antithetic*	antitetico
-phonic		anthropic*	antropico
-plegic		anthropocentric*	antropocentrico
-psychic		antiballistic*	antiballistico
-scopic		antibiotic	antibiotico
-seismic		antidemocratic	antidemocratico
-sonic		antineuralgic*	antinevralgico
-sophic		antiphlogistic*	antiflogistico
-spheric		antiseptic*	antisettico
-static		antitoxic*	antitossico
-technic		apathetic*	apatico
-thoracic		apocalyptic*	apocalittico
-tic		apod(e)ictic*	apodittico
-tomic		apologetic	apologetico

apostolic	apostolico	biographic	biografico
aprioristic	aprioristico	biologic	biologico
aquatic*	acquatico	biometric	biometrico
Arabic	arabico	biotic	biotico
archaeozoic*	archeozoico	bolshevic*	bolscevico
archaic*	arcaico	boric	borico
architectonic*	architettonico	botanic	botanico
arctic*	artico	brachycephalic*	brachicefalo
arhythmic*	aritmico	bubonic*	bubbonico
aristocratic	aristocratico	bucolic	bucolico
aromatic	aromatico	bureaucratic*	burocratico
arrhythmic*	aritmico	cacophonic	cacofonico
arsenic	arsenico	cadaveric	cadaverico
arthritic*	artritico	calligraphic	calligrafico
artistic	artistico	caloric	calorico
ascetic	ascetico	calorific	calorifico
ascorbic	ascorbico	Calvanistic	calvanistico
aseptic*	asettico	capitalistic	capitalistico
Asiatic	asiatico	carbonic	carbonico
asthmatic*	asmatico	cardiopathic*	cardiopatico
astigmatic	astigmatico	cartographic	cartografico
astronomic	astronomico	catastrophic*	catastrofico
atavic	atavico	categoric	categorico
atheistic*	ateistico	catholic*	cattolico
athletic*	atletico	caustic	caustico
Atlantic	Atlantico	Celtic	celtico
atmosphereric*	atmosferico	chalcographic*	calcografico
atomic	atomico	chaotic*	caotico
atonic	atonico	characteristic*	caratteristico
attic	attico	chloric*	clorico
aulic	aulico	choreographic*	coreografico
authentic*	autentico	chromatic*	cromatico
autobiographic	autobiografico	chronic*	cronico
autocratic	autocratico	chronographic*	cronografico
autodidactic*	autodidattico	cinematographic	cinematografico
automatic	automatico	civic	civico
axiomatic*	assiomatico	classic	classico
Bacchic	Bacchico	climatic	climatico
bacteriologic*	batteriologico	clinic	clinico
ballistic*	balistico	comic	comico
balsamic	balsamico	communistic*	comunistico
Baltic	Baltico	concentric	concentrico
barbaric	barbarico	conic	conico
barometric	barometrico	cosmetic	cosmetico
basic	basico	cosmic	cosmico
bibliographic	bibliografico	critic	critico

139

cryptographic*	crittografico	emblematic	emblematico
cubic	cubico	embryogenetic*	embriogenetico
cyanotic*	cianotico	embryonic*	embrionico
cyclic*	ciclico	emetic	emetico
cyclonic*	ciclonico	emphatic*	enfatico
cynic*	cinico	empiric	empirico
Cyrillic*	cirillico	encyclopedic*	enciclopedico
decasyllabic*	decasillabico	endemic	endemico
deistic	deistico	energetic	energetico
demagogic	demagogico	energetic*	energico
democratic	democratico	enthusiastic*	entusiastico
demographic	demografico	entomologic	entomologico
despotic*	dispotico	epic	epico
diabetic	diabetico	epidemic	epidemico
diabolic	diabolico	epidermic	epidermico
diagnostic	diagnostico	epiglottic	epiglottico
diagrammatic	diagrammatico	epigrammatic	epigrammatico
dialogic	dialogico	epigraphic	epigrafico
dialogistic	dialogistico	epileptic*	epilettico
diatonic	diatonico	episodic	episodico
didactic*	didattico	erotic	erotico
dielectric*	dielettrico	erratic	erratico
dietetic	dietetico	esoteric	esoterico
dioptric*	diottrico	ethnic*	etnico
diplomatic	diplomatico	ethnographic*	etnografico
diuretic	diuretico	ethnologic*	etnologico
dogmatic	dogmatico	etymologic*	etimologico
domestic	domestico	eugenic*	eugenetico
dramatic*	drammatico	euphemistic*	eufemistico
drastic	drastico	euphonic	eufonico
dynamic*	dinamico	euphuistic*	eufuistico
dynastic*	dinastico	evangelic	evangelico
eccentric	eccentrico	exotic*	esotico
ecclesiastic	ecclesiastico	fanatic	fanatico
eclectic*	eclettico	fascistic	fascistico
ecliptic*	eclittico	forensic	forensico
ecologic	ecologico	Frederic	Federico
economic	economico	frenetic	frenetico
ecstatic*	estatico	Gaelic	Gaelico
egocentric	egocentrico	galvanic	galvanico
egoistic	egoistico	gastric	gastrico
elastic	elastico	gastronomic	gastronomico
electric*	elettrico	generic	generico
electronic*	elettronico	genetic	genetico
electrostatic*	elettrostatico	geocentric	geocentrico
elliptic*	ellittico	geographic	geografico

geologic	geologico	hydroelectric*	idroelettrico
geometric	geometrico	hydrographic*	idrografico
geopolitic	geopolitico	hydrologic*	idrologico
geriatric	geriatrico	hydropic*	idropico
Germanic	germanico	hydrostatic*	idrostatico
glutamic*	glutammico	hygienic*	igienico
gnomic	gnomico	hygroscopic*	igroscopico
Gothic*	gotico	hyperbolic*	iperbolico
grammatic	grammatico	hypercritic*	ipercritico
graphic	grafico	hypnotic*	ipnotico
graphologic*	grafologico	hypodermic*	ipodermico
gynaecologic*	ginecologico	hypostatic*	ipostatico
haematic*	ematico	hypotetic*	ipotetico
haemostatic*	emostatico	hysteric*	isterico
hagiographic*	agiografico	iconographic	iconografico
harmonic*	armonico	idealistic	idealistico
Hebraic	ebraico	ideologic	ideologico
hedonic*	edonico	idiomatic	idiomatico
hedonistic*	edonistico	idyllic*	idillico
heliocentric*	eliocentrico	imperialistic	imperialistico
heliographic*	eliografico	impressionistic	impressionistico
Hellenic*	ellenico	individualistic	individualistico
Hellenistic*	ellenistico	infrasonic	infrasonico
Helvetic*	elvetico	inorganic	inorganico
hemorrhagic*	emorragico	interoceanic	interoceanico
hepatic*	epatico	ionic	ionico
heretic*	eretico	ironic	ironico
hermetic*	ermetico	Islamic	Islamico
heroic*	eroico	italic	italico
hierarchic*	gerarchico	journalistic*	giornalistico
hieratic*	ieratico	kaleidoscopic*	caleidoscopico
hieroglyphic*	geroglifico	kinetic*	cinetico
Hippocratic*	ippocratico	laconic	laconico
Hispanic*	ispanico	laic	laico
histologic*	istologico	lethargic*	letargico
historic*	storico	lexicographic*	lessicografico
historiographic*	storiografico	lexicologic*	lessicologico
histrionic*	istrionico	linguistic	linguistico
holographic*	olografico	lithographic*	litografico
homeopatic*	omeopatico	lithologic*	litologico
Homeric*	omerico	liturgic	liturgico
honorific*	onirifico	logarithmic*	logaritmico
humanistic*	umanistico	logistic	logistico
humoristic*	umoristico	luetic	luetico
hydraulic*	idraulico	lunatic	lunatico
hydrocephalic*	idrocefalo	lymphatic*	linfatico

lyric*	lirico	Mosaic	mosaico
macaronic*	maccheronico	mystic*	mistico
macrocephalic	macrocefalo	mythic*	mitico
macroscopic	macroscopico	mythologic*	mitologico
magic	magico	Napoleonic	napoleonico
magnetic	magnetico	narcotic	narcotico
malefic	malefico	necrologic	necrologico
manneristic*	manieristico	neoclassic	neoclassico
mathematic*	matematico	neolithic*	neolitico
mechanic*	meccanico	nephritic*	nefritico
megalithic*	megalitico	neuralgic*	nevralgico
melancholic*	malinconico	neuroleptic*	neurolettico
melodic	melodico	neurologic	neurologico
melodramatic*	melodrammatico	neuropsychic*	neuropsichico
mesmeric	mesmerico	neurotic*	nevrotico
Messianic	messianico	Nipponic	Nipponico
metallic	metallico	nitric	nitrico
metallurgic	metallurgico	Nordic	Nordico
metamorphic*	metamorfico	nostalgic	nostalgico
metaphoric*	metaforico	numismatic	numismatico
meteoric	meteorico	obstetric*	ostetrico
meteorologic	meteorologico	oceanographic	oceanografico
metric	metrico	oenologic*	enologico
michrophonic*	microfonico	oleographic	oleografico
microbiologic	microbiologico	oligarchic	oligarchico
microcephalic	microcefalo	Olympic*	olimpico
microcosmic	microcosmico	onomatopoeic*	onomatopeico
microscopic	microscopico	ophthalmic*	oftalmico
microseismic*	microsismico	ophthalmologic*	oftalmologico
mimetic	mimetico	optic*	ottico
mineralogic	mineralogico	organic	organico
misanthropic*	misantropico	orgiastic	orgiastico
mnemonic	mnemonico	ornithologic*	ornitologico
monarchic	monarchico	orographic	orografico
monastic	monastico	orthodontic*	ortodontico
monatomic	monatomico	orthogenetic*	ortogenetico
monochromatic*	monocromatico	orthographic*	ortografico
monogrammatic	monogrammatico	orthopaedic*	ortopedico
monographic	monografico	orthopedic*	ortopedico
monolithic*	monolitico	osteologic	osteologico
monopolistic	monopolistico	osteopathic*	osteopatico
monosyllabic*	monosillabico	oxalic*	ossalico
monotheistic*	monoteistico	pacific	pacifico
moralistic	moralistico	pacific	pacifico
morganatic	morganatico	paediatric*	pediatrico
morphologic*	morfologico	pancreatic	pancreatico

142

pandemic	pandemico	poetic	poetico
panoramic	panoramico	polemic	polemico
pantographic	pantografico	politechnic*	politecnico
parabolic	parabolico	politic	politico
paralytic*	paralitico	polychromatic*	policromatico
paraphrastic*	parafrastico	polyclinic*	policlinico
paraplegic	paraplegico	polyphonic*	polifonico
parasitic*	parassitico	polytheistic*	politeistico
pathetic*	patetico	pornographic	pornografico
pathologic*	patologico	pragmatic	pragmatico
patriotic*	patriottico	prehistoric*	preistorico
patronymic*	patronimico	prismatic	prismatico
pedagogic	pedagogico	problematic	problematico
pediatric	pediatrico	prognostic*	pronostico
pelvic	pelvico	prolific	prolifico
peptic*	pettico	prophetic*	profetico
periodic	periodico	prosaic	prosaico
peripatetic	peripatetico	prosthetic*	prostetico
peripheric*	periferico	protoplasmic*	protoplasmatico
periphrastic*	perifrastico	prussic	prussico
phallic*	fallico	psychiatric*	psichiatrico
pharmacologic*	farmacologico	psychic*	psichico
philanthropic*	filantropico	psychoanalytic*	psicanalitico
philarmonic*	filarmonico	psychoanalytic*	psicoanalitico
philatelic*	filatelico	psychologic*	psicologico
philologic*	filologico	psychopathic*	psicopatico
philosophic*	filosofico	psychopathologic*	psicopatologico
phlegmatic*	flemmatico	psychosomatic*	psicosomatico
phobic*	fobico	psychotic*	psicopatico
phonetic*	fonetico	psycopatic*	psicopatico
phonic	fonico	Ptolemaic*	tolemaico
phonographic*	fonografico	pubic	pubico
phonologic*	fonologico	public*	pubblico
photoelectric*	fotoelettrico	Punic	punico
photogenic*	fotogenico	pyrotechnic*	pirotecnico
photographic*	fotografico	quadriplegic	quadriplegico
phraseologic*	fraseologico	rabbinic	rabbinico
phrenic*	frenico	rachitic	rachitico
physiognomic*	fisionomico	radiographic*	radiografico
Pindaric	pindarico	radiologic	radiologico
plastic	plastico	radiometric	radiometrico
Platonic	platonico	realistic	realistico
pleonastic	pleonastico	rhapsodic*	rapsodico
pleuritic	pleuritico	rheumatic*	reumatico
plutocratic	plutocratico	rhombic*	rombico
pneumatic	pneumatico	rhythmic*	ritmico

romantic	romantico	stereoscopic	stereoscopico
runic	runico	stethoscopic*	stetoscopico
rustic	rustico	stigmatic	stigmatico
Salic	salico	stoic	stoico
Sapphic*	saffico	strategic	strategico
sarcastic	sarcastico	stratigraphic	stratigrafico
sardonic	sardonico	stratospheric*	stratosferico
satanic	satanico	strophic*	strofico
satiric	satirico	stylistic*	stilistico
scenographic	scenografico	subarctic*	subartico
sceptic*	scettico	subsonic	subsonico
schematic	schematico	sulphuric*	solforico
schizophrenic*	schizofrenico	supersonic	supersonico
scholastic*	scolastico	sybaritic*	sibaritico
sciatic	sciatico	syllabic*	sillabico
scientific	scientifico	syllogistic*	sillogistico
scorbutic	scorbutico	symbolic*	simbolico
seismic*	sismico	symmetric*	simmetrico
seismographic*	sismografico	symphonic*	sinfonico
seismologic*	sismologico	symptomatic*	sintomatico
semantic	semantico	synchronic*	sincronico
Semitic	semitico	synoptic*	sinottico
septic*	settico	syntactic*	sintattico
simplistic*	semplicistico	synthetic*	sintetico
skeptic*	scettico	syphilitic*	sifilitico
sociologic	sociologico	systaltic*	sistaltico
Socratic	socratico	systematic*	sistematico
somatic	somatico	systolic*	sistolico
sonic	sonico	tannic	tannico
sophistic*	sofistico	tautologic	tautologico
spasmodic	spasmodico	technic*	tecnico
spastic	spastico	technologic*	tecnologico
spathic*	spatico	tectonic*	tettonico
specific	specifico	telegraphic	telegrafico
spectrographic*	spettrografico	teleologic	teleologico
spectroscopic*	spettroscopico	telepathic*	telepatico
spermatic	spermatico	telephonic	telefonico
spheric*	sferico	telescopic	telescopico
sporadic	sporadico	telluric	tellurico
stalactic*	stalattico	tetanic	tetanico
stannic	stannico	Teutonic	teutonico
static	statico	theistic*	teistico
statistic	statistico	thematic*	tematico
stearic	stearico	theologic*	teologico
stenographic	stenografico	theosophic*	teosofico
stereophonic	stereofonico	therapeutic*	terapeutico

thermoelectric*	termoelettrico	embryonic	embrionale
thermostatic*	termostatico	epic, n.	poema epico
thoracic	toracico	extrinsic	estrinseco
titanic	titanico	geomorphic	geomorfologico
tonic	tonico	gigantic	gigantesco
topographic	topografico	grammatic/al	grammaticale
toxic*	tossico	Guelfic	guelfo
traffic	traffico	Guelphic	guelfo
tragic	tragico	hallucinogenic	allucinogeno
transatlantic	transatlantico	holographic*	olografo
traumatic	traumatico	hydrocloric	cloridrico
tropic	tropico	hydrophobic	idrofobo
typographic*	tipografico	hypermetric	ipermetro
typologic*	tipologico	hypocritic	ipocrita
ultrasonic	ultrasonico	idiotic	idiota
urbanistic	urbanistico	intrinsic	intrinseco
uric	urico	majestic	maestoso
urologic	urologico	myopic	miope
vicarapostolic*	vicario apostolico	Ostrogothic	ostrogoto
		parisyllabic	parisillabo
vitriolic*	vetriolico	pedantic	pedantesco
vocalic	vocalico	Plutonic	plutoniano
volcanic*	vulcanico	polysyllabic	polisillabo
voltaic	voltaico	pulmonic	polmonare
volumetric	volumetrico	Quixotic	donchisciottesco
xylographic*	silografico	sadistic	sadico
zincographic	zincografico	Slavic	slavo
zygomatic*	zigomatico	Slavonic	slavo
Exceptions:		socialistic	socialista
acidic	acido	soporific	soporifero
alembic	alambicco	subaquatic	subacqueo
anthropomorphic*	antropomorfo	subtonic	sottotonica
anticonformistic	anticonformista	sudorific	sudorifero
aphonic	afono	sympathetic	comprensivo
archibishopric	arcivescovado	**-ICAL**	**-ALE**
arithmetic	arithmetica	diametrical	diametrale
auric	aureo	paradoxical*	paradossale
camphoric	canforato	theatrical*	teatrale
carcinogenic	cancerogeno	**-ICAL**	**-ICALE**
cephalic	cefalico	anticlerical	anticlericale
chiropractic	chiropratica	basilical	basilicale
climacteric	climaterico	clerical	clericale
clinic, n.	clinica	cortical	corticale
congeneric	congenere	dominical*	domenicale
Coptic	copto	grammatical	grammaticale
diametric	diametrale	musical	musicale

pontifical — pontificale
radical — radicale
subtropical — subtropicale
tropical — tropicale
umbilical* — ombelicale
vertical — verticale
vortical — vorticale

-ICAL — **-ICO**

academical* — accademico
alphabetical* — alfabetico
anagogical — anagogico
analytical* — analitico
anarchical — anarchico
anatomical — anatomico
antarctical* — antartico
apolitical — apolitico
apologetical — apologetico
arithmetical* — aritmetico
aromatical — aromatico
astronautical — astronautico
astronomical — astronomico
asymmetrical* — asimmetrico
atheistical* — ateistico
barometrical — barometrico
biblical — biblico
bibliographical* — bibliografico
biographical* — biografico
biological — biologico
botanical — botanico
canonical — canonico
categorical — categorico
chemical* — chimico
chimerical — chimerico
classical — classico
clinical — clinico
comical — comico
conical — conico
critical — critico
cyclical* — ciclico
cylindrical* — cilindrico
cynical* — cinico
demagogical — demagogico
diabolical — diabolico
dialectical* — dialettico
dramatical* — drammatico
dynamical* — dinamico

eccentrical — eccentrico
economical — economico
ecumenical — ecumenico
electrical* — elettrico
empirical — empirico
encyclical* — enciclico
epical — epico
epistemological — epistemologico
erotical — erotico
ethical* — etico
ethnical* — etnico
evangelical — evangelico
exegetical* — esegetico
fanatical — fanatico
genealogical — genealogico
heretical* — eretico
hydrographical* — idrografico
hypercritical* — ipercritico
iconographical* — iconografico
identical — identico
ironical — ironico
juridical* — giuridico
laical — laico
lexicographical* — lessicografico
logistical — logistico
lyrical* — lirico
magical — magico
majestical* — magestico
mechanical* — meccanico
medical — medico
metaphysical* — metafisico
methodical* — metodico
mystical* — mistico
mythical* — mitico
nautical — nautico
numerical — numerico
optical* — ottico
paleontological — paleontologico
parabolical — parabolico
parasitical* — parassitico
periodical — periodico
pharmaceutical* — farmaceutico
philosophical* — filosofico
physical* — fisico
polemical — polemico
political — politico

146

practical*	pratico	police	polizia
pragmatical*	prammatico	**-ICE**	**-IZIO**
problematical	problematico	armistice	armistizio
prophetical*	profetico	hospice*	ospizio
psychical*	psichico	interstice	interstizio
rhapsodical*	rapsodico	Maurice	Maurizio
rhetorical*	retorico	novice	novizio
rhythmical*	ritmico	orifice	orifizio
sabbatical*	sabatico	precipice	precipizio
satirical	satirico	prejudice*	pregiudizio
sceptical*	scettico	service	servizio
skeptical*	scettico	solstice	solstizio
sophistical*	sofistico	**-ICIAN**	**-ICO**
sporadical	sporadico	academician*	accademico
statistical	statistico	arithmetician*	aritmetico
stoical	stoico	dialectician*	dialettico
symbolical*	simbolico	logician	logico
symmetrical*	simmetrico	mathematician*	matematico
symptomatical*	sintomatico	metaphysician*	metafisico
synoptical*	sinottico	obstetrician*	ostetrico
tactical*	tattico	optician*	ottico
technical*	tecnico	tactician*	tattico
theosophical*	teosofico	technician*	tecnico
topical	topico	theoretician*	teorico
toxicological*	tossicologico	*but:*	
tragical	tragico	beautician	estetista
trigonometrical	trigonometrico	patrician	patrizio
typical*	tipico	politician	uomo politico
tyrannical*	tirannico	**-ICIAN**	**-ISTA**
-ICE	**-ICIO**	cosmetician	cosmetista
-fice		electrician*	elettricista
artifice	artificio	musician*	musicista
auspice	auspicio	*but:*	
benefice	beneficio	dietician	dietologo
dentifrice	dentifricio	geometrician	geometra
edifice	edificio	paediatrician	pediatra
office*	ufficio	pediatrician	pediatra
sacrifice	sacrificio	**-ICS**	**-IA**
but:		-iatrics	
practice	pratica	agronomics	agronomia
-ICE	**-IZIA**	economics	economia
avarice	avarizia	eurhythmics	euritmia
injustice*	ingiustizia	geriatrics	geriatria
justice*	giustizia	obstetrics	ostetricia
liquorice*	liquirizia	orthopedics	ortopedia
malice	malizia	pedagogics	pedagogia

pediatrics	pediatrịa	orthoptics*	ortọttica
-ICS	**-ICA**	phonetics*	fonẹtica
-physics		physics*	fịsica
-statics		poetics	poẹtica
-therapeutics		polemics	polẹmica
acoustics*	acụstica	politics	polịtica
acrobatics*	acrobạtica	propaedeutics*	propedẹutica
aerodynamics*	aerodinạmica	psychotechnics*	psicotẹcnica
aerostatics	aerostạtica	pyrotechnics*	pirotẹcnica
aesthetics*	estẹtica	semantics	semạntica
astronautics	astronạutica	statics	stạtica
astrophysics*	astrofịsica	statistics	statịstica
athletics*	atlẹtica	tactics*	tạttica
ballistics*	balịstica	tectonics*	tettọnica
biophysics*	biofịsica	therapeutics*	terapẹutica
ceramics	cerạmica	thermionics*	termiọnica
cybernetics*	cibernẹtica	thermodynamics*	termodinạmica
dialectics*	dialẹttica	zootechnics*	zootẹcnica
didactics*	didạttica	*Exception*:	
dietetics	dietẹtica	orthodontics	ortodonzịa
dioptrics*	diọttrica	**-ID**	**-IDE**
dramatics*	drammạtica	Aeneid*	Enẹide
dynamics*	dinạmica	carotid	carọtide
electronics*	elettrọnica	chrysalid*	crisạlide
electrostatics*	elettrostạtica	Euclid	Euclịde
ethics*	ẹtica	Nereid	Nerẹide
eugenics*	eugenẹtica	pyramid*	pirạmide
genetics	genẹtica	*Exceptions*:	
geophysics*	geofịsica	orchid	orchidẹa
geopolitics	geopolịtica	typhoid*	tifọide
glyphtics*	glịttica	chambermaid*	camerịera
graphics*	grạfica	Ovid	Ovịdio
gymnastics*	ginnạstica	Brigid	Brịgida
hermeneutics*	ermenẹutica	**-ID**	**IDO**
hydraulics*	idrạulica	-acid	
hydrostatics*	idrostạtica	*NOTE:From Latin: fervid-us, liquid-us,*	
hydrotherapeutics*	idroterapẹutica	*etc. These words drop the "us" in English*	
kinematics*	cinemạtica	acid	ạcido
kinetics*	cinẹtica	antacid*	antiạcido
linguistics	linguịstica	arid	ạrido
logistics	logịstica	avid	ạvido
mathematics*	matemạtica	candid	cạndido
mechanics*	meccạnica	Cupid	Cupịdo
metaphysics*	metafịsica	cupid	cụpido
metrics	mẹtrica	fervid	fẹrvido
numismatics	numismạtica	fetid	fẹtido

flaccid	flaccido	cavalier	cavaliere
florid	florido	chandelier*	candeliere
fluid	fluido	courier*	corriere
frigid	frigido	financier*	finanziere
gelid	gelido	fusilier*	fuciliere
gravid	gravido	gondolier	gondoliere
hispid*	ispido	grenadier*	granatiere
horrid*	orrido	halberdier*	alabardiere
humid*	umido	*Exception*:	
hybrid*	ibrido	amplifier	amplificatore
insipid	insipido	**-ILE/YLE**	**-ILE**
intrepid	intrepido	-atile	
invalid	invalido	-febrile	
languid	languido	-fertile	
limpid	limpido	-mobile	
liquid	liquido	fragile	fragile
livid	livido	protractile*	protrattile
lucid	lucido	retractile*	retrattile
lurid	lurido	versatile	versatile
pallid	pallido	volatile	volatile
placid	placido	aedile*	edile
putrid	putrido	erectile*	erettile
rancid	rancido	fertile	fertile
rapid	rapido	prehensile*	prensile
solid	solido	projectile*	proiettile
sordid	sordido	reptile*	rettile
splendid	splendido	cyclostyle*	ciclostile
squalid*	squallido	facsimile	facsimile
stupid	stupido	febrile*	febbrile
tepid*	tiepido	juvenile*	giovanile
timid	timido	infantile	infantile
torpid	torpido	nitrile (chem.)	nitrile
torrid	torrido	hostile*	ostile
tumid	tumido	senile	senile
turbid*	torbido	style*	stile
turgid	turgido	virile	virile
valid	valido	automobile	automobile
viscid	viscido	docile	docile
vivid	vivido	immobile	immobile
Exceptions:		mobile	mobile
morbid	morboso	ductile*	duttile
pinguid	pingue	futile	futile
rabid	rabbioso	*Exceptions*:	
-IER	**-IERE**	camomile	camomilla
brazier*	braciere	chamomile	camomilla
cashier*	cassiere	crocodile	coccodrillo

domicile	domicilio	Augustin*	Agostino
exile	esilio	baldaquin*	baldacchino
gentile	gentile	basin*	bacino
imbecile	imbecille	Berlin	Berlino
infertile	infecondo	bulletin*	bollettino
mile	miglio	Capuchin*	cappuccino
Nile	Nilo	cousin*	cugino
profile	profilo	cretin	cretino
textile	tessile	dolphin*	delfino
-ILLA	**-IGLIA**	Dublin	Dublino
cedilla	cediglia	kaolin*	caolino
flotilla*	flottiglia	Latin	latino
guerilla*	guerriglia	lupin	lupino
mantilla	mantiglia	mandarin	mandarino
vanilla	vaniglia	mandolin	mandolino
-IN	**-INA**	mannequin*	manechino
adrenalin	adrenalina	Martin	Martino
albumin	albumina	Merlin	Merlino
aspirin	aspirina	mocassin	mocassino
bobbin*	bobina	Odin	Odino
cabin	cabina	paladin	paladino
casein	caseina	penguin*	pinguino
cousin*	cugina	tannin	tannino
Evelin	Evelina	Turin*	Torino
haemoglobin*	emoglobina	violin	violino
hemoglobin*	emoglobina	**-INA**	**-INA**
heroin*	eroina	angina	angina
insulin	insulina	concertina	concertina
lanolin	lanolina	ocarina	ocarina
nitroglycerin*	nitroglicerina	vagina	vagina
paraffin	paraffina	*but:*	
penicillin	penicillina	semolina	semolino
pepsin	pepsina	**-INE**	**-INA**
ptyalin*	ptialina	adrenaline	adrenalina
resin	resina	aniline	anilina
ruin*	rovina	benzoline*	benzina
saccharin*	saccarina	brilliantine*	brillantina
streptomycin*	streptomicina	caffeine	caffeina
terramycin*	terramicina	carbine*	carabina
-IN	**-INE**	Caroline	Carolina
margin	margine	Catharine*	Caterina
origin	origine	Catherine*	Caterina
virgin*	vergine	cocaine	cocaina
-IN	**-INO**	concubine	concubina
Angevin*	Angioino	crinoline	crinolina
assassin	assassino	discipline	disciplina

doctrine*	dottrina	Philippine	filippino
galantine	galantina	quarantine	quarantena
gelatine	gelatina	sanguine	sanguigno
glycerine*	glicerina	Seine	Senna
guillotine*	ghigliottina	**-INE**	**-INO**
heroine*	eroina	adamantine	adamantino
histamine*	istamina	alexandrine*	alessandrino
indiscipline	indisciplina	alkaline*	alcalino
Katharine*	Caterina	alpine*	alpino
latrine	latrina	aquamarine*	acquamarino
machine*	macchina	aquiline	aquilino
margarine	margarina	argentine	argentino
medicine	medicina	asinine	asinino
mine	mina	azurine*	azzurrino
morphine*	morfina	bovine	bovino
nicotine	nicotina	brigantine	brigantino
olivine	olivina	bulletin*	bollettino
opaline	opalina	Byzantine*	bizantino
Palestine	Palestina	canine	canino
pantomime	pantomina	cisalpine	cisalpino
Proserpine	Proserpina	clandestine	clandestino
quinine* (chem.)	chinina	crystalline*	cristallino
rapine	rapina	decliine*	declino
saccharine*	saccarina	divine	divino
sardine	sardina	endocrine	endocrino
sordine	sordina	equine	equino
spine	spina	feline	felino
strychnine*	stricnina	feminine*	femminino
turbine	turbina	Florentine*	fiorentino
Ukraine*	Ucraina	genuine	genuino
urine*	urina	Ghibelline	ghibellino
vaseline*	vasellina	intestine	intestino
Some exceptions:		leonine	leonino
airline	aerolinea	leporine	leporino
antihistamine	antistaminico	Levantine	levantino
bromine	bromo	libertine	libertino
carmine	carminio	marine	marino
chlorine	cloro	mezzanine	mezzanino
cosine	coseno	nervine	nervino
elephantine	elefantesco	ovine	ovino
feminine	femminile	pine	pino
gabardine	gabardine	Pontine	pontino
iodine	iodo	porcupine*	porcospino
line	linea	pristine	pristino
masculine	maschile	Sabine	sabino
mine	miniera	saline	salino

151

serpentine	serpentino	communion*	comunione
subalpine	subalpino	comprehension*	comprensione
supine	supino	compression	compressione
sybilline*	sibillino	compulsion	compulsione
trampoline	trampolino	concession	concessione
transalpine	transalpino	concision	concisione
travertine	travertino	conclusion	conclusione
trentine	trentino	confession	confessione
Tridentine	tridentino	confusion	confusione
triestine	triestino	connexion*	connessione
trine	trino	contusion	contusione
ultramarine*	oltremarino	conversion	conversione
uterine	uterino	corrosion	corrosione
vaccine	vaccino	crucifixion*	crocifissione
Valentine	Valentino	decision	decisione
vespertine	vespertino	declension*	declinazione
vulpine*	volpino	decompression	decompressione
zibeline*	zibellino	delusion	delusione
-ION	**-IONE**	depression	depressione
-flexion		derision	derisione
-pulsion		detersion	detersione
-sion		diffusion	diffusione
-vision		dimension	dimensione
abrasion	abrasione	discussion	discussione
accession	accessione	disillusion	disillusione
adhesion*	adesione	dispersion	dispersione
admission*	ammissione	dissension	dissensione
affixion*	affissione	disunion	disunione
aggression	aggressione	diversion	diversione
Albion	Albione	division	divisione
allusion	allusione	effusion	effusione
alluvion	alluvione	elision	elisione
ascension	ascensione	elusion	elusione
aspersion	aspersione	emersion	emersione
aversion*	avversione	emission	emissione
avulsion	avulsione	emulsion	emulsione
battalion*	battaglione	erosion	erosione
centurion	centurione	Eurovision	eurovisione
cession	cessione	evasion	evasione
champion*	campione	exclusion*	esclusione
circumcision*	circoncisione	excursion*	escursione
coercion*	coercizione	expansion*	espansione
cohesion*	coesione	explosion*	esplosione
collision	collisione	expression*	espressione
collusion	collusione	expulsion*	espulsione
commission	commissione	extension*	estensione

extroversion*	estroversione	possession	possessione
fission	fissione	postil(l)ion	postil(l)ione
flexion*	flessione	precision	precisione
fluxion*	flussione	pression	pressione
fusion	fusione	prevision	previsione
genuflexion*	genuflessione	procession	processione
histrion*	istrione	profession	professione
hypertension*	ipertensione	profusion	profusione
hypotension*	ipotensione	progression	progressione
illusion	illusione	prolusion	prolusione
immersion	immersione	propulsion	propulsione
imprecision	imprecisione	Pygmalion*	Pigmalione
impression	impressione	quadrillion	quadrillione
incision	incisione	rebellion*	ribellione
inclusion	inclusione	recession	recessione
incomprehension*	incomprensione	reflexion*	riflessione
incursion	incursione	region	regione
indecision	indecisione	regression	regressione
inflexion*	inflessione	religion	religione
infusion	infusione	remission	remissione
intercession	intercessione	repercussion*	ripercussione
intermission	intermissione	repression	repressione
intromission	intromissione	repulsion	repulsione
introversion	introversione	rescission	rescissione
intrusion	intrusione	retrocession	retrocessione
invasion	invasione	retrogression	retrogressione
inversion	inversione	retroversion	retroversione
ion	ione	reunion*	riunione
legion	legione	revision	revisione
lesion	lesione	scansion	scansione
manumission*	manomissione	scission	scissione
medallion*	medaglione	scorpion	scorpione
million*	milione	secession	secessione
mission	missione	session	sessione
obsession*	ossessione	subdivision*	suddivisione
occasion	occasione	submission*	sottomissione
occlusion	occlusione	subversion*	sovversione
omission	omissione	succession	successione
opinion	opinione	suppression*	soppressione
oppression	oppressione	suspension*	sospensione
passion	passione	television	televisione
pavilion*	padiglione	tension	tensione
pension	pensione	torsion	torsione
percussion	percussione	transfusion*	trasfusione
persuasion	persuasione	transgression*	trasgressione
perversion	perversione	transmission*	trasmissione

trillion*	trilione
union	unione
version	versione
vision	visione
Some exceptions:	
aphelion	afelio
companion	compagno
compulsion	costrizione
criterion	criterio
cushion*	cuscino
dominion	dominio
exhaustion	esaurimento
impulsion	impulso
intension	intensificazione
lion	leone
oblivion	oblio
permission	permesso
possession	possesso
stallion	stallone
television(set)	televisore
Zion	Sion
-IQUE	**-ICA**
critique	critica
technique*	tecnica
but:	
oblique	obliquo
physique*	fisico
-ISK	**-ISCO**
asterisk	asterisco
basilisk	basilisco
disk	disco
obelisk	obelisco
tamarisk	tamarisco
-ISM	**-ESIMO**
Catholicism	cattolicesimo
feudalism	feudalesimo
Germanism	germanesimo
humanism	umanesimo
-ISM/YSM	**-ISMA**
aneurism	aneurisma
aphorism	aforisma
cataclysm	cataclisma
microseism*	microsisma
prism	prisma
schism	scisma
chrism	crisma

-ISM/YSM	**-ISMO**
-theism	
abolitionism*	abolizionismo
absenteeism*	assenteismo
absolutism*	assolutismo
abstractionism*	astrazionismo
activism*	attivismo
aestheticism*	esteticismo
agnosticism	agnosticismo
alarmism*	allarmismo
alcoholism*	alcolismo
altruism	altruismo
Americanism	americanismo
anachronism*	anacronismo
anarchism	anarchismo
Anglicanism	anglicanismo
Anglicism	anglicismo
animatism*	animismo
antagonism	antagonismo
anthropocentrism*	antropocentrismo
anthropomorphism*	antropomorfismo
anticommunism*	anticomunismo
anticonformism	anticonformismo
antifascism	antifascismo
antimilitarism*	anti-militarismo
anti-Semitism*	antisemitismo
apriorism	apriorismo
archaism*	arcaismo
Aristotelianism	aristotelianismo
astigmatism	astigmatismo
atavism	atavismo
atheism*	ateismo
authoritarianism*	autoritarianismo
autism	autismo
automatism	automatismo
barbarism	barbarismo
bolshevism*	bolscevismo
bradyseism*	bradisismo
Buddhism*	buddismo
Calvanism	calvanismo
cannibalism	cannibalismo
capitalism	capitalismo
catechism	catechismo
Chartism*	cartismo
chauvinism*	sciovinismo
classicism	classicismo

154

clericalism	clericalismo	gallicism	gallicismo
collectivism*	collettivismo	geotropism	geotropismo
colloquialism	colloquialismo	giantism*	gigantismo
colonialism	colonialismo	hedonism*	edonismo
communism*	comunismo	helioncentricism*	eliocentrismo
conservatism	conservatismo	Hellenism*	ellenismo
constitutionalism*	costituzionalismo	hermaphroditism*	ermafroditismo
criticism	criticismo	heroism*	eroismo
cubism	cubismo	hypnotism*	ipnotismo
cynism*	cinismo	historicism*	storicismo
dadaism	dadaismo	humanitarianism*	umanitarismo
Darwinism*	darvinismo	hybridism*	ibridismo
defeatism*	disfattismo	hypnotism*	ipnotismo
deism	deismo	idealism	idealismo
despotism*	dispotismo	imperialism	imperialismo
determinism	determinismo	impressionism	impressionismo
deviationism*	deviazionismo	individualism	individualismo
dogmatism	dogmatismo	infantilism	infantilismo
dualism	dualismo	intellectualism*	intellettualismo
dynamism*	dinamismo	internationalism*	internazionalismo
eclecticism*	eclettismo	irredentism	irredentismo
egalitarianism*	egualitarianismo	isolationism*	isolazionismo
egocentrism	egogentrismo	Islamism	islamismo
egoism	egoismo	journalism*	giornalismo
egotism	egotismo	Judaism*	giudaismo
empiricism*	empirismo	labourism*	laburismo
Epicureanism*	epicureismo	Latinism	latinismo
eroticism*	erotismo	legalism	legalismo
euphemism*	eufemismo	liberalism	liberalismo
euphuism*	eufuismo	libertinism	libertinismo
Europeanism*	europeismo	Lutheranism*	luteranismo
Evangelicalism*	evangelismo	lyricism*	lirismo
existentialism*	esistenzialismo	Machiavellism	machiavellismo
exorcism*	esorcismo	magnetism	magnetismo
exoticism*	esotismo	mannerism*	manierismo
expansionism*	espansionismo	Marxism	marxismo
expressionism*	espressionismo	masochism	masochismo
extremism*	estremismo	materialism	materialismo
fanaticism*	fanatismo	mechanism*	meccanismo
Fascism	fascismo	mesmerism	mesmerismo
fatalism	fatalismo	metabolism	metabolismo
favoritism*	favoritismo	meteorism	meteorismo
federalism	federalismo	Methodism*	metodismo
feminism*	femminismo	micro-organism*	microorganismo
fetishism*	feticismo	militarism	militarismo
futurism	futurismo	mithridatism*	mitridatismo

modernism	modernismo	protectionism*	protezionismo
Mongolism	mongolismo	Protestantism	protestantismo
monism	monismo	provincialism	provincialismo
monotheism*	monoteismo	pugilism	pugilismo
mutism	mutismo	purism	purismo
mysticism*	misticismo	Puritanism	puritanismo
narcissism*	narcisismo	quietism	quietismo
nationalism*	nazionalismo	racialism*	razzismo
naturalism	naturalismo	racism*	razzismo
naturism	naturismo	radicalism	radicalismo
Nazism	nazismo	rationalism*	razionalismo
neoclassicism	neoclassicismo	realism	realismo
neologism	neologismo	relativism	relativismo
nepotism	nepotismo	rheumatism*	reumatismo
nervosism	nervosismo	rhotacism*	rotacismo
neutralism	neutralismo	rigorism	rigorismo
nihilism*	nichilismo	ritualism	ritualismo
nomadism	nomadismo	romanticism	romanticismo
nudism	nudismo	sadism	sadismo
obscurantism*	oscurantismo	scepticism*	scetticismo
obstructionism*	ostruzionismo	sensationalism*	sensazionalismo
Occidentalism	occidentalismo	sentimentalism	sentimentalismo
occultism	occultismo	separatism	separatismo
opportunism	opportunismo	skepticism*	scetticismo
optimism*	ottimismo	socialism	socialismo
organism	organismo	somnambulism*	sonnambulismo
Orientalism	orientalismo	sophism*	sofismo
ostracism	ostracismo	statism*	statalismo
pacifism	pacifismo	stoicism	stoicismo
papalism*	papalismo	surrealism	surrealismo
paroxism*	parossismo	syllogism*	sillogismo
patriotism*	patriottismo	symbolism*	simbolismo
perfectionism*	perfezionismo	synchronism*	sincronismo
pessimism	pessimismo	syncretism*	sincretismo
Philistinism*	filiteismo	synchronism*	sincronismo
pietism	pietismo	syndicalism*	sindacalismo
Platonism	platonismo	terrorism	terrorismo
pluralism	pluralismo	theism*	teismo
polymorphism*	polimorfismo	Thomism*	tomismo
polytheism*	politeismo	tourism*	turismo
positivism	positivismo	traditionalism	traditionalismo
Postimpressionism	postimpressionismo	transcendentalism*	trascendentalismo
pragmatism	pragmatismo	transvestism*	travestismo
Presbyterianism*	presbiterianismo	transvestitism*	travestitismo
professionalism	professionalismo	truism	truismo
prohibitionism*	proibizionismo	Unitarianism*	unitarismo

utilitarianism*	utilitarismo	alchemist	alchemista
vampirism	vampirismo	alienist	alienista
vandalism	vandalismo	alpinist	alpinista
vocalism	vocalismo	altruist	altruista
voodooism*	vuduismo	amethist*	ametista
vorticism	vorticismo	analogist	analogista
vulgarism*	volgarismo	anaesthetist*	anestesista
Zionism*	sionismo	anesthetist*	anestesista
Some exceptions:		analyst	analista
baptism	battesimo	anarchist	anarchista
Briticism	anglismo	anatomist	anatomista
Catholicism	cattolicesimo	anglicist	anglicista
charisma	carisma	annalist	annalista
charlatanism	ciarlataneria	antagonist	antagonista
criticism	critica	anthologist*	antologista
libertinism	libertinaggio	anticommunist*	anticomunista
opiumism	oppiomania	antifascist	antifascista
plagiarism	plagio	antimilitarist	antimilitarista
propagandism	propaganda	apologist	apologista
recidivism	recidività	archivist	archivista
scholasticism	scolastica	artist	artista
ventriloquism	ventriloquio	atheist*	ateista
-IST	**-ICO**	Baptist*	battista
antimonarchist	antimonarchico	botanist	botanista
autist	autistico	Buddhist*	buddista
botanist	botanico	Calvanist	calvanista
chemist*	chimico	canonist	canonista
philatelist *	filatelico	capitalist	capitalista
physicist*	fisico	caricaturist	caricaturista
metallurgist	metallurgico	catechist	catechista
numismatist	numismatico	classicist	classicista
orthopaedist*	ortopedico	colonist	colonista
orthopedist*	ortopedico	colorist*	colorista
sadist	sadico	colourist*	colorista
satirist	satirico	communist*	comunista
theorist*	teorico	conformist	conformista
-IST/YST	**-ISTA**	contortionist*	contorsionista
-gamist		copyist*	copista
-graphist		defeatist*	disfattista
-linguist		dentist	dentista
-theist		dogmatist	dogmatista
abolitionist*	abolizionista	dualist	dualista
absolutist*	assolutista	duellist	duellista
academist*	accademista	economist	economista
activist*	attivista	egoist	egoista
alarmist*	allarmista	egotist	egotista

emblematist	emblematista	linotypist*	linotipista
epigraphist	epigrafista	list	lista
equilibrist	equilibrista	lyrist*	lirista
evangelist	evangelista	machinist*	macchinista
exhibitionist*	esibizionista	mannerist*	manierista
exorcist*	esorcista	Marxist	marxista
expansionist*	espansionista	masochist	masochista
expressionist*	espressionista	materialist	materialista
extremist*	estremista	medallist*	medaglista
fabulist*	favolista	metallurgist	metallurgista
Fascist	fascista	Methodist*	metodista
fatalist	fatalista	militarist	militarista
federalist	federalista	mineralist	mineralista
feminist*	femminista	miniaturist	miniaturista
finalist	finalista	monarchist	monarchista
flautist	flautista	monotheist*	monoteista
florist*	fiorista	monotypist*	monotipista
flutist*	flautista	moralist	moralista
formalist	formalista	mosaicist	mosaicista
futurist	futurista	nationalist*	nazionalista
geneticist*	genetista	naturalist	naturalista
Germanist	germanista	naturist	naturista
guitarist*	chitarrista	nihilist*	nichilista
harpist*	arpista	nudist	nudista
hedonist*	edonista	obscurantist*	oscurantista
hellenist*	ellenista	obstructionist*	ostruzionista
herbalist*	erborista	occultist	occultista
herborist*	erborista	oculist	oculista
humanist*	umanista	opportunist	opportunista
humorist*	umorista	optimist*	ottimista
hygienist*	igienista	organist	organista
hypnotist*	ipnotista	Orientalist	orientalista
idealist	idealista	pacifist	pacifista
imperialist	imperialista	parachutist*	paracadutista
impressionist	impressionista	parodist	parodista
individualist	individualista	perfectionist*	perfezionista
integrationist*	integrazionista	pessimist	pessimista
intellectualist*	intellettualista	pharmacist*	farmacista
internationalist*	internazionalista	philatelist*	filatelista
ironist	ironista	physicist*	fisicista
irredentist	irredentista	physiognomist*	fisionomista
journalist*	giornalista	pianist	pianista
jurist*	giurista	pietist	pietista
Latinist	latinista	pluralist	pluralista
librettist	librettista	polemist	polemista
linguist	linguista	polytheist*	politeista

positivist	positivista	xylophonist*	silofonista
pragmatist	pragmatista	Zionist*	sionista
progressist	progressista	*Some exceptions*:	
propagandist	propagandista	accompanist	accompagnatore
protagonist	protagonista	agronomist	agronomo
protectionist*	protezionista	antichrist	anticristo
psalmist*	salmista	atheist	ateo
psalmodist*	salmista	bigamist	bigamo
psychoanalyst*	psicanalista	calligraphist	calligrafo
publicist*	pubblicista	catalyst	catalizzatore
pugilist	pugilista	dramatist	drammaturgo
purist	purista	duellist	duellante
racialist*	razzista	eulogist	elogiatore
racist*	razzista	floricolturalist	floricultore
rationalist*	razionalista	funambulist	funambolo
realist	realista	gastronomist	gastronomo
rhapsodist*	rapsodista	hagiographist*	agiografo
ritualist	ritualista	hypnotist	ipnotizzatore
satirist	satirista	industrialist	industriale
segregationist*	segregazionista	manicurist	manicure
seminarist	seminarista	philanthropist	filantropo
sensationalist*	sensazionalista	plagiarist	plagiario
sensualist	sensualista	podiatrist	podologo
sentimentalist	sentimentalista	polygamist	poligamo
separatist	separatista	psychiatrist	psichiatra
socialist	socialista	recidivist	recidivo
soloist*	solista	sacrist	sagrestano
sophist*	sofista	schist	scisto
specialist	specialista	scientist	scienziato
stenotypist*	stenotipista	somnambulist	sonnambulo
stylist*	stilista	strategist	stratega
surrealist	surrealista	theosophist	teosofo
symbolist*	simbolista	therapist	terapeuta
syndicalist*	sindacalista	tobacconist	tabaccaio
taxidermist*	tassidermista	ventriloquist	ventriloquo
telegraphist*	telegrafista	**-IT**	**-ITO**
telephonist*	telefonista	ambit	ambito
terrorist	terrorista	bandit	bandito
theist*	teista	bipartite	bipartito
tourist*	turista	circuit	circuito
traditionalist	traditionalista	credit	credito
transcendentalist*	trascendentalista	cubit	cubito
urbanist	urbanista	debit	debito
violinist	violinista	decrepit	decrepito
violoncellist	violoncellista	demerit	demerito
vocalist	vocalista	deposit	deposito

discredit	discredito	stalactite*	stalattite
explicit*	esplicito	*Exceptions*:	
habit*	abito	despite	dispetto
illicit*	illecito	opposite	opposto
implicit	implicito	**-ITE/YTE**	**-ITO**
introit	introito	aconite	aconito
licit*	lecito	appetite	appetito
merit	merito	contrite	contrito
pulpit	pulpito	electrolyte*	elettrolito
Sanskrit*	sanscrito	erudite	erudito
tacit	tacito	exquisite*	squisito
transit	transito	favo(u)rite*	favorito
tripartite	tripartito	granite	granito
vomit	vomito	hermaphrodite*	ermafrodito
Exceptions:		heteroclite*	eteroclito
culprit	colpevole	indefinite	indefinito
hermit*	eremita	infinite	infinito
Jesuit	gesuita	nitrite	nitrito
orbit	orbita	phosphite*	fosfito
limit	limite	plebiscite	plebiscito
-ITE	**-ITA**	preterite	preterito
-site		proselyte	proselito
anti-Semite*	antisemita	quadripartite	quadripartito
cenobite	cenobita	recondite	recondito
cosmopolite	cosmopolita	requisite	requisito
eremite	eremita	rite	rito
hypocrite*	ipocrita	sulphite*	solfito
Islamite	islamita	transvestite*	travestito
Israelite	israelita	trite	trito
Jabobite*	giacobita	unite	unito
marguerite*	margherita	*Exception*:	
Muscovite*	moscovita	polite	educato
parasite*	parassita	polite	cortese
Pre-Raphaelite*	preraffaellita	**-ITIS**	**-ITE**
sodomite	sodomita	appendicitis	appendicite
sybarite*	sibarita	arthritis*	artrite
-ITE	**-ITE**	bronchitis	bronchite
anthracite*	antracite	bursitis*	borsite
Aphrodite*	Afrodite	cellulitis	cellulite
bakelite*	bachelite	cholecystitis	colecistite
ballistite*	balistite	colitis	colite
dynamite*	dinamite	conjunctivitis	congiuntivite
ebonite*	ebanite	cystitis*	cistite
graphite*	grafite	diverticulitis*	diverticolite
haematite*	ematite	encephalitis*	encefalite
hematite*	ematite	enteritis	enterite

gastritis	gastrite	affective*	affettivo
gingivitis*	gengivite	affirmative*	affermativo
glossitis	glossite	aggressive	aggressivo
hepatitis*	epatite	allusive	allusivo
laryngitis*	laringite	apprehensive*	apprensivo
mastitis	mastite	assertive	assertivo
meningitis	meningite	associative	associativo
myelitis*	mielite	attractive*	attrattivo
nephritis*	nefrite	attributive	attributivo
otitis	otite	auditive	auditivo
peritonitis	peritonite	coagulative	coagulativo
phlebitis*	flebite	coercive*	coercitivo
poliomyelitis*	poliomielite	cogitative	cogitativo
sinusitis	sinusite	cognitive	cognitivo
synovitis*	sinovite	collective*	collettivo
tonsillitis	tonsillite	commemorative	commemorativo
vaginitis	vaginite	communicative*	comunicativo
-IVE	**-IVA**	comparative	comparativo
alternative	alternativa	competitive	competitivo
initiative	iniziativa	comprehensive	comprensivo
invective	invettiva	compulsive	compulsivo
locomotive	locomotiva	concessive	concessivo
prerogative	prerogativa	conclusive	conclusivo
Exceptions:		conjunctive*	congiuntivo
electromotive	elettromotore	consecutive	consecutivo
motive	motivo	conservative	conservativo
-IVE	**-IVO**	constructive*	costruttivo
-ative		contemplative	contemplativo
-itive		contributive	contributivo
-tive		cooperative	cooperativo
-utive		copulative	copulativo
abductive*	adduttivo	corrective*	correttivo
ablative	ablativo	correlative	correlativo
abortive	abortivo	corroborative	corroborativo
abrasive	abrasivo	corrosive	corrosivo
abusive	abusivo	curative	curativo
accumulative	accumulativo	cursive*	corsivo
accusative	accusativo	dative	dativo
active*	attivo	decisive	decisivo
additive	additivo	decorative	decorativo
adhesive*	adesivo	deductive*	deduttivo
adjective*	aggettivo	defective*	difettivo
adjunctive*	aggiuntivo	defensive*	difensivo
administrative*	amministrativo	definitive	definitivo
adoptive*	adottivo	degenerative	degenerativo
adversative*	avversativo	deliberative	deliberativo

demonstrative*	dimostrativo	incisive	incisivo
derivative	derivativo	inclusive	inclusivo
derogative	derogativo	indicative	indicativo
descriptive*	descrittivo	inexpressive*	inespressivo
destructive*	distruttivo	infective*	infettivo
determinative	determinativo	informative	informativo
diffusive	diffusivo	inoffensive	inoffensivo
digestive	digestivo	inquisitive	inquisitivo
diminutive	diminutivo	insinuative	insinuativo
directive*	direttivo	instinctive*	istintivo
disgressive	disgressivo	instructive*	istruttivo
disjunctive*	disgiuntivo	intensive	intensivo
dispersive	dispersivo	interpretative	interpretativo
distributive	distributivo	interrogative	interrogativo
educative	educativo	intransitive	intransitivo
elective*	elettivo	introductive*	introduttivo
emotive	emotivo	introspective*	introspettivo
eradicative	eradicativo	intuitive	intuitivo
eruptive*	eruttivo	inventive	inventivo
evasive	evasivo	inversive	inversivo
evocative	evocativo	investigative	investigativo
excessive*	eccessivo	irreflective*	irriflessivo
exclusive*	esclusivo	iterative	iterativo
executive*	esecutivo	justificative*	giustificativo
explicative*	esplicativo	laxative*	lassativo
explosive*	esplosivo	lucrative	lucrativo
expressive*	espressivo	meditative	meditativo
extensive*	estensivo	motive	motivo
facultative*	facoltativo	narrative	narrativo
festive	festivo	native	nativo
figurative	figurativo	negative	negativo
formative	formativo	nominative	nominativo
fugitive*	fuggitivo	normative	normativo
furtive	furtivo	objective*	oggettivo
generative	generativo	obsessive*	ossessivo
genitive	genitivo	offensive	offensivo
gustative	gustativo	operative	operativo
hypertensive*	ipertensivo	oppressive	oppressivo
illuminative	illuminativo	optative*	ottativo
illustrative	illustrativo	palliative	palliativo
imaginative*	immaginativo	partitive	partitivo
imitative	imitativo	passive	passivo
imperative	imperativo	pejorative*	peggiorativo
impulsive	impulsivo	perceptive*	percettivo
inactive*	inattivo	persuasive	persuasivo
incentive	incentivo	positive	positivo

English	Italian	English	Italian
possessive	possessivo		congiuntivo
preclusive	preclusivo	substantive*	sostantivo
predicative	predicativo	subversive*	sovversivo
prejudicative*	pregiudicativo	successive	successivo
preservative	preservativo	superlative	superlativo
preventive	preventivo	transitive	transitivo
primitive	primitivo	unproductive*	improduttivo
productive*	produttivo	vegetative	vegetativo
progressive	progressivo	vindictive*	vendicativo
prohibitive*	proibitivo	vocative	vocativo
propulsive	propulsivo	votive	votivo
prospective*	prospettivo	*Some exceptions*:	
protective*	protettivo	attentive	attento
protractive*	protrattivo	authoritative	autoritario
provocative	provocativo	authoritative	autorevole
punitive	punitivo	calmative	calmante
purgative	purgativo	deceptive	illusorio
putative	putativo	derisive	derisorio
qualitative	qualitativo	exhaustive	esauriente
quantitative	quantitativo	hypersensitive	ipersensibile
radioactive*	radioattivo	illusive	illusorio
reactive*	reattivo	indecisive	indeciso
receptive*	ricettivo	indigestive	indigesto
recessive	recessivo	insensitive	insensibile
recitative	recitativo	pensive	pensoso
reflective*	riflessivo	preparative	preparatorio
reflexive*	riflessivo	promotive	promotore
regenerative*	rigenerativo	provocative	provocante
relative	relativo, parente	reflective	riflessivo
remunerative*	rimunerativo	restive	restio
representative*	rappresentativo	rotative	rotatorio
reproductive*	riproduttivo	ruminative	ruminante
repulsive*	ripulsivo	sensitive	sensibile
respective*	rispettivo	solutive	lassativo
restorative	restorativo	**-IX /-YX**	**-ICE**
restrictive*	restrittivo	appendix	appendice
retributive	retributivo	calyx	calice
retroactive*	retroattivo	cervix	cervice
retrogressive	retrogressivo	onyx	onice
retrospective*	retrospettivo	phoenix*	fenice
sedative	sedativo	radix	radice
seductive*	seduttivo	spadix	spadice
selective*	selettivo	varix	varice
significative	significativo	*but:*	
speculative	speculativo	coccyx	coccige
subjunctive*	soggiuntivo,	helix	elica

prolix	prolisso	gynecological*	ginecologico
pyx	pisside	histological*	istologico
Styx	Stige	hydrological*	idrologico
-IZER	**-IZZATORE**	ideological	ideologico
atomizer	atomizzatore	lexicological*	lessicologico
monopolizer	monopolizzatore	lithological*	litologico
organizer	organizzatore	logical	logico
stabilizer	stabilizzatore	meteorological	meteorologico
sterilizer	sterilizzatore	metrological	metrologico
totalizer	totalizzatore	microbiological	microbiologico
vaporizer	vaporizzatore	morphological*	morfologico
Exceptions:		mythological*	mitologico
fertilizer	fertilizzante	necrological	necrologico
tranquillizer	tranquillante	neurological	neurologico
-LEGE	**-LEGIO**	oenological*	enologico
college	collegio	oncological	oncologico
florilege	florilegio	ophthalmological*	oftalmologico
privilege	privilegio	ornithological*	ornitologico
sacrilege	sacrilegio	pathological*	patologico
-LINGUAL	**-LINGUE**	pharmacological*	farmacologico
bilingual	bilingue	philological*	filologico
multilingual	multilingue	phonological*	fonologico
trilingual	trilingue	phraseological*	fraseologico
-LITRE	**-LITRO**	physiological*	fisiologico
decalitre	decalitro	psychological*	psicologico
centilitre	centilitro	psychopathological*	psicopatologico
hectolitre	ettolitro	radiological	radiologico
-LOGICAL	**-LOGICO**	seismological*	sismologico
analogical	analogico	sociological	sociologico
archaeological*	archeologico	tautological	tautologico
astrological	astrologico	technological*	tecnologico
bacteriological*	batteriologico	teleological	teleologico
chronological*	cronologico	terminological	terminologico
cosmological	cosmologico	theological*	teologico
ecological	ecologico	typological*	tipologico
embryological*	embriologico	virological	virologico
entomological	entomologico	zoological	zoologico
epidemiological	epidemiologico	**-LOGIST**	**-LOGISTA**
ethnological*	etnologico	chronologist*	cronologista
etymological*	etimologico	dialogist	dialogista
genealogical	genealogico	genealogist	genealogista
geological	geologico	mineralogist	mineralogista
gnoseological	gnoseologico	mythologist*	mitodologista
gnosiological	gnosiologico	necrologist	necrologista
graphological*	grafologico	**-LOGIST**	**-LOGO**
gynaecological*	ginecologico	anthropologist*	antropologo
		archaeologist*	archeologo

bacteriologist*	batteriologo	urologist	urologo
biologist	biologo	virologist	virologo
cardiologist	cardiologo	zoologist	zoologo
chronologist*	cronologo	*Exception*:	
cosmologist	cosmologo	eulogist	elogiatore
criminologist	criminologo	**-LOGUE**	**-LOGO**
dermatologist	dermatologo	apologue	apologo
ecologist	ecologo	catalogue	catalogo
Egyptologist*	egittologo	Decalogue	decalogo
embryologist*	embriologo	dialogue	dialogo
entomologist	entomologo	duologue*	dialogo
ethnologist*	etnologo	epilogue	epilogo
etymologist*	etimologo	monologue	monologo
geologist	geologo	prologue	prologo
gerontologist	gerontologo	**-LOGY**	**-LOGIA**
graphologist*	grafologo	analogy	analogia
gynaecologist*	ginecologo	anthology*	antologia
gynecologist*	ginecologo	anthropology*	antropologia
histologist*	istologo	apology	apologia
hydrologist*	idrologo	archaeology*	archeologia
ideologist	ideologo	astrology	astrologia
lexicologist*	lessicologo	bacteriology*	batteriologia
lithologist*	litologo	biology	biologia
meteorologist	meteorologo	brachylogy*	brachilogia
microbiologist	microbiologo	cardiology	cardiologia
musicologist	musicologo	chronology*	cronologia
neurologist	neurologo	cosmology	cosmologia
oenologist*	enologo	criminology	criminologia
oncologist	oncologo	chronology*	cronologia
ophthalmologist*	oftalmologo	dermatology	dermatologia
ornithologist*	ornitologo	ecology	ecologia
paleontologist	paleontologo	Egyptology*	egittologia
pathologist*	patologo	embryology*	embriologia
pharmacologist*	farmacologo	entomology	entomologia
philologist*	filologo	epidemiology	epidemiologia
phonologist*	fonologo	epistemology	epistemologia
phrenologist*	frenologo	ethnology*	etnologia
psychologist*	psicologo	etymology*	etimologia
psychopathologist*	psicopatologo	genealogy	genealogia
radiologist	radiologo	geology	geologia
seismologist*	sismologo	gerontology	gerontologia
sinologist	sinologo	glottology	glottologia
sociologist	sociologo	gnoseology	gnoseologia
speleologist	speleologo	gnosiology	gnosiologia
technologist*	tecnologo	graphology*	grafologia
toxicologist*	tossicologo	gynaecology*	ginecologia

gynecology*	ginecologia	zoology	zoologia
histology*	istologia	*Exception*:	
hydrobiology*	idrobiologia	eulogy	
hydrology*	idrologia	martyrology	
ideology	ideologia	**-MA**	**-MA**
insectology*	insettologia	-coma	
lexicology*	lessicologia	-drama	
lithology*	litologia	-emma	
meteorology	meteorologia	-oma	
methodology*	metodologia	-orama	
metrology	metrologia	-rama	
micro-biology*	microbiologia	asthma*	asma
mineralogy	mineralogia	anathema*	anatema
morphology*	morfologia	angioma	angioma
musicology	musicologia	aroma	aroma
mythology*	mitologia	charisma*	carisma
necrology	necrologia	coma (med.)	coma
oenology*	enologia	dilemma	dilemma
oncology	oncologia	diorama	diorama
oneirology*	onirologia	diploma	diploma
ophthalmology*	oftalmologia	dogma	dogma
ornithology*	ornitologia	drama*	dramma
osteology	osteologia	enigma	enigma
paleontology	paleontologia	fibroma	fibroma
pathology*	patologia	glaucoma	glaucoma
pharmacology*	farmacologia	hematoma*	ematoma
philology*	filologia	lymphoma*	linfoma
phonology*	fonologia	melanoma	melanoma
phraseology*	fraseologia	melodrama*	melodramma
physiology*	fisiologia	mimodrama*	mimodramma
posology	posologia	myoma*	mioma
psychology*	psicologia	neuroma	neuroma
psychopathology*	psicopatologia	osteoma	osteoma
radiology	radiologia	panorama	panorama
seismology*	sismologia	plasma	plasma
sinology	sinologia	sarcoma	sarcoma
sociology	sociologia	stigma	stigma
speleology	speleologia	trauma	trauma
technology*	tecnologia	*but:*	
teleology	teleologia	enema	clistere
terminology	terminologia	**-MANIAC**	**-MANE**
theology*	teologia	kleptomaniac*	cleptomane
toxicology*	tossicologia	megalomaniac	megalomane
trilogy	trilogia	monomaniac	monomane
typology*	tipologia	nymphomaniac*	ninfomane
virology	virologia	pyromaniac*	piromane

166

Exceptions:

maniac	maniaco

-ME / **-ME**

legume	legume
volume	volume

but:

clime	clima
programme	programma

-ME / **-MO**

extreme*	estremo
prime	primo
supreme	supremo

-MESTER / **-MESTRE**

bimester	bimestre
trimester	trimestre
semester	semestre

-METER / **-METRO**

altimeter	altimetro
anemometer	anemometro
barometer	barometro
decameter	decametro
diameter	diametro
dynamometer*	dinamometro
chronometer*	cronometro
electrometer*	elettrometro
goniometer	goniometro
hectometer*	ettometro
hexameter*	esametro
hydrometer*	idrometro
hygrometer*	igrometro
inclinometer	inclinometro
kilometer*	chilometro
meter	metro
micrometer	micrometro
odometer	odometro
parameter	parametro
pentameter	pentametro
perimeter	perimetro
pluviometer	pluviometro
radiogoniometer	radiogoniometro
spectrometer*	spettrometro
tachometer	tachometro
taximeter*	tassametro
thermometer*	termometro
voltameter	voltametro

-METRE / **-METRO**

centimetre	centimetro
millimetre	millimetro

-METRY / **-METRIA**

asymmetry*	asimmetria
geometry	geometria
symmetry*	simmetria
trigonometry	trigonometria

-MONY/-IMONY / **-MONIA/-IMONIA**

acrimony	acrimonia
alimony	alimonia
ceremony*	cerimonia
harmony*	armonia

Exception:

patrimony*	patrimonio

-NAUT / **-NAUTA**

argonaut	argonauta
astronaut	astronauta
cosmonaut	cosmonauta

-NOMY / **-NOMIA**

-gnomy	
agronomy	agronomia
antinomy	antinomia
astronomy	astronomia
autonomy	autonomia
economy	economia
gastronomy	gastronomia
physiognomy*	fisionomia

-ODE / **-ODE**

cathode*	catode
ode	ode

Exceptions:

code	codice
episode	episodio

-ODE / **-ODO**

anode	anodo
diode	diodo
electrode*	elettrodo
Kathode*	catodo
mode	modo
node	nodo

-OID/-OIDS / **-OIDE/-OIDI**

alkaloid*	alcaloide
anthropoid*	antropoide
asteroid	asteroide
cancroid	cancroide

celluloid	celluloide	festoon*	festone
colloid	colloide	gabion*	gabbione
conoid	conoide	gallon	gallone
geoid	geoide	glutton*	ghiottone
hyoid*	ioide	gnomon	gnomone
mastoid	mastoide	gonfalon	gonfalone
metalloid	metalloide	griffon*	grifone
Mongoloid	mongoloide	harpoon*	arpione
negroid	negroide	Jason*	Giasone
ovoid	ovoide	lemon*	limone
paratyphoid*	paratifoide	lesson*	lezione
rhomboid*	romboide	medallion*	medaglione
saccharoid*	saccaroide	melon	melone
schizoid	schizoide	million*	milione
spermatozoid	spermatozoide	monsoon*	monsone
spheroid*	sferoide	Mormon*	mormone
steroid	steroide	Napoleon	Napoleone
trochoid*	trocoide	neutron	neutrone
Note: generally plural		nucleon	nucleone
adenoids	adenoidi	pennon	pennone
haemorrhoids	emorroidi	photon*	fotone
hemorrhoids	emorroidi	piston	pistone
-ON	**-ONE**	platoon*	plotone
Agamemnon*	Agamennone	pontoon*	pontone
amphitryon*	anfitrione	proton	protone
Anglo-Saxon*	anglosassone	pylon*	pilone
baron	barone	python*	pitone
baton*	bastone	salmon	salmone
buffoon*	buffone	Sampson*	Sansone
button*	bottone	Saxon*	sassone
cannon	cannone	sermon	sermone
canon (1)	canone	siphon*	sifone
canton	cantone	squadron	squadrone
capon*	cappone	synchrotron*	sincrotrone
carbon	carbone	tampon	tampone
cartoon*	cartone	tenon	tenone
cordon	cordone	Triton	tritone
cotton*	cotone	typhoon*	tifone
coupon*	cupone	zircon	zircone
cyclotron	ciclotrone	Note: embryo	embrione
demon	demone	*Exceptions*:	
dragon	dragone	archdeacon*	arcidiacono
dungeon*	dongione	argon	argo
electron*	elettrone	autochthon*	autoctono
falcon	falcone	automaton	automa
fanon	fanone	canon (1)	canonico

cinnamon — cinnamono
deacon* — diacono
horizon* — orizzonte
mastodon — mastodonte
matron — matrona
patron — patrono
phenomenon — fenomeno
silicon — silicio
unison — unisono
Xenophon* — Senofonte

-ON — **-ONTE**
Acheron — Acheronte
Anacreon — Anacreonte
bison — bisonte
chameleon* — camaleonte
Charon* — Caronte
horizon* — orizzonte

-ONE — **-ONE**
acetone (chem.) — acetone
cyclone* — ciclone
hormone* — ormone
ketone* — chetone
quinone* (chem.) — chinone
trombone — trombone

-ONE — **-ONO**
-tone
baritone — baritono
cone — cono
epigone — epigono
ozone (chem.) — ozono
semitone — semitono
throne* — trono
tone — tono
Exception:
zone — zona

-ONYM — **-ONIMO**
acronym — acronimo
anonym — anonimo
antonym — ontonimo
homonym* — omonimo
pseudonym — pseudonimo
synonym* — sinonimo

-OR — **-ORE**
-ator
-color
-ior

-motor
-tor
accelerator — acceleratore
accumulator — accumulatore
actor* — attore
administrator* — amministratore
adulator — adulatore
aggressor — aggressore
agitator — agitatore
alternator — alternatore
ambassador* — ambasciatore
annunciator — annunciatore
anterior — anteriore
ardor — ardore
auditor* — uditore
author* — autore
aviator — aviatore
benefactor* — benefattore
bicolor — bicolore
bimotor — bimotore
candor — candore
cantor — cantore
carburator — carburatore
censor — censore
clamor — clamore
collaborator — collaboratore
collector* — collettore
color — colore
commentator — commentatore
commutator — commutatore
competitor — competitore
compositor — compositore
compressor — compressore
conductor* — conduttore
confessor — confessore
connector* — connettore
conqueror* — conquistatore
conservator — conservatore
contractor* — contrattore
contributor — contributore
convector* — convettore
creator — creatore
creditor — creditore
debtor* — debitore
decorator — decoratore
delator — delatore

demonstrator*	dimostratore	instigator*	istigatore
denominator	denominatore	instructor*	istruttore
depressor	depressore	insulator*	isolatore
desertor*	disertore	interceptor*	intercettatore
detonator	detonatore	interior*	interiore
dictator*	dittatore	interlocutor	interlocutore
director*	direttore	inventor	inventore
divisor	divisore	investigator	investigatore
doctor*	dottore	investor*	investitore
donator	donatore	irrigator	irrigatore
donor*	donatore	isolator	isolatore
duplicator	duplicatore	languor	languore
editor	editore	legislator	legislatore
educator	educatore	liberator	liberatore
elector*	elettore	lictor*	littore
equator	equatore	liquidator	liquidatore
error	errore	liquor	liquore
evaporator	evaporatore	locomotor	locomotore
exactor*	esattore	lubricator	lubricatore
executor*	esecutore	major*	maggiore
exterior*	esteriore	malefactor*	malfattore
extractor*	estrattore	mediator	mediatore
factor*	fattore	mentor	mentore
favor	favore	minor	minore
fervor	fervore	moderator	moderatore
fetor	fetore	modulator	modulatore
furor	furore	motor	motore
generator	generatore	multicolor	multicolore
gladiator	gladiatore	narrator	narratore
governor*	governatore	navigator	navigatore
Hector*	Ettore	negotiator*	negoziatore
honor*	onore	numerator	numeratore
horror*	orrore	objector*	obiettore
humor*	umore	odor	odore
illustrator	illustratore	operator	operatore
imitator	imitatore	oppressor	oppressore
impostor	impostore	orator	oratore
improvisator*	improvvisatore	oscillator	oscillatore
incubator	incubatore	pallor	pallore
indicator	indicatore	pastor	pastore
inferior	inferiore	perpetrator	perpetratore
injector*	iniettore	persecutor	persecutore
innovator	innovatore	possessor	possessore
inoculator	inoculatore	posterior	posteriore
inspector*	ispettore	praetor*	pretore
inspirator	inspiratore	preceptor*	precettore

precursor	precursore	vasodilator*	vasodilatore
predecessor	predecessore	vasonstrictor*	vasocostrittore
primogenitor*	progenitore	vector*	vettore
proctor*	procuratore	vendor*	venditore
procurator	procuratore	ventilator	ventilatore
professor	professore	versificator	versificatore
progenitor	progenitore	vibrator	vibratore
projector*	proiettore	vigor	vigore
prosecutor	prosecutore	vindicator*	rivendicatore
protector*	protettore	violator	violatore
protractor*	protrattore	visitor*	visitatore
radiator	radiatore	*Exceptions*:	
reactor*	reattore	calculator	calcolatrice
rector*	rettore	camphor	canfora
reflector*	riflettore	chancellor	cancelliere
refractor*	rifrattore	corridor	corridoio
regulator*	regolatore	guarantor	garante
renovator*	rinnovatore	juror	giurato
resistor	resistore	metaphor	metafora
resonator*	risonatore	meteor	meteora
respirator	respiratore	proprietor	proprietario
sculptor*	scultore	refrigerator	frigorifero
sector*	settore	technicolor	tecnicolor
senator	senatore	**-ORY**	**-IVO**
sergeant-major*	sergente maggiore	exclamatory*	esclamativo
spectator*	spettatore	imprecatory	imprecativo
speculator	speculatore	indicatory	indicativo
squalor*	squallore	investigatory	investigativo
stupor	stupore	introductory*	introduttivo
successor	successore	modificatory	modificativo
superior	superiore	olfactory*	olfattivo
tenor	tenore	*Exceptions*:	
terror	terrore	benedictory	benedicente
torpor	torpore	depository*	deposito
tractor*	trattore	inauguratory	inaugurale
traitor*	traditore	incriminatory	incriminante
translator*	traduttore	refractory *	refrattario
tremor	tremore	satisfactory*	soddisfacente
tricolor	tricolore	sensory	sensoriale
trimotor	trimotore	statutory*	statutario
tumor	tumore	suppository*	supposta
tutor	tutore	**-ORY**	**-ORIA**
ulterior	ulteriore	allegory	allegoria
vaccinator	vaccinatore	category	categoria
valor	valore	chicory*	cicoria
vapor	vapore	euphory*	euforia

glory	gloria	promontory	promontorio
hystory*	storia	purgatory	purgatorio
memory	memoria	refectory*	refettorio
prehistory*	preistoria	reformatory*	riformatorio
story	storia	repertory	repertorio
theory*	teoria	respiratory	respiratorio
trajectory*	traiettoria	responsory*	responsorio
vainglory*	vanagloria	rotatory	rotatorio
-ORY	**-ORIO**	suspensory*	sospensorio
accessory	accessorio	territory	territorio
admonitory*	ammonitorio	transitory	transitorio
aleatory	aleatorio	usurpatory	usurpatorio
amatory	amatorio	*exception*:	
ambulatory	ambulatorio	inventory	inventario
auditory*	uditorio	**-OSE**	**-OSO**
conciliatory	conciliatorio	-icose	
conservatory	conservatorio	-ulose	
consistory*	concistorio	adipose	adiposo
contradictory*	contraddittorio	bellicose	bellicoso
crematory	crematorio	comatose	comatoso
depilatory	depilatorio	fructose*	fruttosio
deprecatory	deprecatorio	gibbose	gibboso
derogatory	derogatorio	globose	globoso
dilatory	dilatorio	grandiose	grandioso
directory*	direttorio	jocose*	giocoso
discriminatory	discriminatorio	lachrymose*	lacrimoso
dormitory	dormitorio	nodose	nodoso
extrasensory*	estrasensorio	repose*	riposo
illusory	illusorio	succose	succoso
inflammatory*	infiammatorio	varicose	varicoso
inhibitory*	inibitorio	verbose	verboso
interlocutory	interlocutorio	*Exceptions*:	
intimidatory	intimidatorio	cellulose	cellulosa
laboratory	laboratorio	glucose	glucosio
locutory	locutorio	nose	naso
masticatory	masticatorio	pose	posa
migratory	migratorio	prose	prosa
minatory	minatorio	rose	rosa
obligatory*	obbligatorio	saccharose	saccarosio
observatory*	osservatorio	**-OT**	**-OTA**
offertory	offertorio	aliquot	aliquota
oratory	oratorio	compatriot	compatriota
ostensory	ostensorio	Cypriot*	cipriota
peremptory*	perentorio	despot	despota
predatory	predatorio	idiot	idiota
preparatory	preparatorio	patriot	patriota

pilot	pilota	brachycephalous*	brachicefalo
Exceptions:		macrocephalous	macrocefalo
bigot	bigotto	microcephalous	microcefalo
boycott	boicottaggio	**-EOUS**	**-EO**
mascot	mascotte	aculeous	aculeo
parrot	pappagallo	aqueous*	acqueo
polyglot	poliglotta	calcareous	calcareo
-OUS INDEX:		caseous	caseo
-acious		cetaceous	cetaceo
-arious		consanguineous	consanguineo
-cephalous		contemporaneous	contemporaneo
-eous		coriaceous	coriaceo
-ferous		corneous	corneo
-gamous		cretaceous	cretaceo
-ious		cutaneous	cutaneo
-ous		endogenous	endogeno
-parous		erroneous	erroneo
-ulous		extemporaneous*	estemporaneo
-ulous		extraneous*	estraneo
-uous		ferreous	ferreo
-uous		gallinaceous	gallinaceo
-vorous		graminaceous	graminaceo
-ACIOUS	**-ACE**	herbaceous*	erbaceo
audacious	audace	heterogeneous*	eterogeneo
capacious	capace	homogeneous*	omogeneo
efficacious	efficace	igneous	igneo
fallacious	fallace	instantaneous*	istantaneo
inefficacious	inefficace	ligneous	ligneo
loquacious	loquace	miscellaneous	miscellaneo
mendacious	mendace	momentaneous	momentaneo
perspicacious	perspicace	rosaceous	rosaceo
pugnacious	pugnace	saponaceous	saponaceo
rapacious	rapace	simultaneous	simultaneo
sagacious	sagace	spontaneous	spontaneo
tenacious	tenace	subaqueous*	subacqueo
veracious	verace	sulphureous*	sulfureo
vivacious	vivace	terraqueous	terracqueo
voracious	vorace	testaceous	testaceo
-ARIOUS	**-ARIO**	violaceous	violaceo
gregarious	gregario	vitreous	vitreo
nefarious	nefario	*Some exceptions*:	
precarious	precario	argillaceous	argilloso
temerarious	temerario	corteous	cortese
various	vario	courageous	coraggioso
-CEPHALOUS	**-CEFALO**	gaseous	gassoso
acephalous	acefalo	gorgeous (fam.)	stupendo

173

piteous	pietoso	imperious	imperioso
umbrageous	ombroso	industrious	industrioso
-FEROUS	**-FERO**	injurious*	ingiurioso
argentiferous	argentifero	inofficious	inofficioso
auriferous	aurifero	insidious	insidioso
cruciferous*	crocifero	irreligious	irreligioso
fructiferous*	fruttifero	judicious*	giudizioso
herbiferous*	erbifero	laborious	laborioso
lactiferous*	lattifero	licentious*	licenzioso
metalliferous	metallifero	melodious	melodioso
odoriferous	odorifero	minacious*	minaccioso
ossiferous	ossifero	mysterious*	misterioso
pestiferous	pestifero	obsequious*	ossequioso
petroliferous	petrolifero	odious	odioso
somniferous*	sonnifero	officious*	ufficioso
but:		opprobrious	opprobrioso
coniferous	conifera	parsimonious	parsimonioso
-GAMOUS	**-GAMO**	penurious	penurioso
bigamous	bigamo	pernicious	pernicioso
monogamous	monogamo	precious*	prezioso
polygamous*	poligamo	pretentious*	pretenzioso
-IOUS	**-IOSO**	prodigious	prodigioso
-itious		religious	religioso
-ivious		seditious*	sedizioso
-monious		semiprecious*	semiprezioso
-tious		sententious*	sentenzioso
acrimonious	acrimonioso	spacious*	spazioso
ambitious*	ambizioso	specious	specioso
anxious*	ansioso	studious	studioso
capricious*	capriccioso	superstitious*	superstizioso
captious*	capzioso	tedious	tedioso
ceremonious*	cerimonioso	tendentious*	tendenzioso
compendious	compendioso	vainglorious*	vanaglorioso
conscientious*	coscienzioso	victorious*	vittorioso
contagious	contagioso	*Exceptions*:	
copious	copioso	amphibious	anfibio
curious	curioso	atrocious	atroce
delicious*	delizioso	auspicious	auspicale
dubious*	dubbioso	avaricious	avaro
envious	invidioso	carious	cariato
factious*	fazioso	cautious	cauto
furious	furioso	conscious	conscio
glorious	glorioso	delirious	delirante
gracious*	grazioso	fictitious	fittizio
harmonious*	armonioso	hilarious	ilare
ignominious	ignominioso	illustrious	illustre

174

inauspicious	inauspicato	farraginous	farraginoso
incautious	incauto	ferrous	ferroso
infectious	infetto	ferruginous	ferruginoso
ingenious	ingegnoso	fibrous	fibroso
insalubrious	insalubre	gangrenous*	cancrenoso
invidious	spiacevole	gelatinous	gelatinoso
lascivious	lascivo	generous	generoso
lugubrious	lugubre	gibbous	gibboso
malicious	maligno	granulous	granuloso
malleolous	malleolo	impediginous(med.)	impediginoso
meritorious	meritorio	indecorous	indecoroso
nefarious	nefasto	joyous*	gioioso
notorious	notorio	leprous*	lebbroso
nutritious	nutriente	libidinous	libidinoso
oblivious	dimentico	luminous	luminoso
obvious	òvvio	membranous	membranoso
ostentatious	ostentato	miraculous*	miracoloso
perfidious	perfido	monstrous*	mostruoso
precocious	precoce	mountainous*	montuoso
propitious	propizio	mucous	mucoso
rebellious	ribelle	nervous	nervoso
repetitious	ripetitivo	numerous	numeroso
sacrilegious	sacrilego	odorous	odoroso
salubrious	salubre	onerous	oneroso
semiconscious	semicosciente	perilous*	pericoloso
serious	serio	pilous*	peloso
spurious	spurio	ponderous	ponderoso
unconscious	inconscio	porous	poroso
-OUS	**-OSO**	rigorous	rigoroso
-idinous		ruinous*	rovinoso
-iginous		sarcomatous	sarcomatoso
-itous		scandalous	scandaloso
-urous		squamous	squamoso
adventurous*	avventuroso	sulphurous*	solforoso
amorous	amoroso	tenebrous	tenebroso
bulbous	bulboso	timorous	timoroso
calamitous	calamitoso	ulcerous	ulceroso
callous	calloso	valorous	valoroso
cancerous	canceroso	venous	venoso
cavernous	cavernoso	vertiginous	vertiginoso
clamorous	clamoroso	vigorous	vigoroso
decorous	decoroso	villous	villoso
desirous*	desideroso	virtuous	virtuoso
disastrous	disastroso	viscous	viscoso
dolorous	doloroso	voluminous	voluminoso
famous	famoso	*Exceptions*:	

175

ambidextrous	ambidẹstro	**-ULOUS**	**-OLOSO**
amorphous	amọrfo	fabulous*	favolọso
analogous	anạlogo	meticulous	meticolọso
anomalous	anọmalo	miraculous	miracolọso
asynchronous	asịncrono	populous	popolọso
autochthonous	autọctono	scrupulous	scrupolọso
autonomous	autọnomo	**-ULOUS**	**-ULO**
barbarous	bạrbaro	garrulous	gạrrulo
Bosphorous	Bọsforo	granulous	grạnulo
cacophonous	cacọfono	credulous	crẹdulo
credulous	crẹdulo	incredulous	incrẹdulo
dangerous	pericolọso	querulous	quẹrulo
dexterous	destro	tremulous	trẹmulo
diaphanous	diạfano	*Exception*:	
ferocious	ferọce	ridiculous	ridịcolo
fortuitous	fortụito	**-UOUS**	**-UO**
frivolous	frịvolo	ambiguous	ambịguo
gratuitous	gratụito	arduous	ạrduo
homologous	omọlogo	assiduous	assịduo
homonymous	omọnimo	congruous	cọngruo
horrendous	orrẹndo	conspicuous*	cospịcuo
idolatrous	idolạtrico	contiguous	contịguo
indigenous	indịgeno	continuous	contịnuo
infamous	infạme	deciduous	decịduo
iniquitous	inịquo	fatuous	fạtuo
intravenous	endovenọso	incongruous	incọngruo
languorous	lạnguido	inconspicuous*	incospịcuo
magnanimous	magnạnimo	ingenuous	ingẹnuo
necessitous	bisognọso	innocuous	innọcuo
posthumous	pọstumo	mellifluous	mellịfluo
prosperous	prọspero	perspicuous	perspịcuo
pusillanimous	pusillạnime	promiscuous	promịscuo
ridiculous	ridịcolo	strenuous	strẹnuo
sonorous	sonọro	superfluous	supẹrfluo
stupendous	stupẹndo	*Exceptions*:	
synchronous	sịncrono	sensuous	sensuạle
synonymous	sinọnimo	tenuous	tẹnue
terrigenous	terrịgeno	**-UOUS**	**-UOSO**
tremendous	tremẹndo	anfractuous*	anfrattuọso
unanimous	unạnime	flexuous*	flessuọso
zealous	zelạnte	fructuous*	fruttuọso
zoophilous	zoọfilo	impetuous	impetuọso
-PAROUS	**-PARO**	incestuous	incestuọso
multiparous	multịparo	infructuous*	infruttuọso
oviparous	ovịparo	presumptuous*	presuntuọso
viviparous	vivịparo	sinuous	sinuọso

176

sumptuous*	sontuoso	zoophile	zoofilo
tortuous	tortuoso	**-PHILIA**	**-FILIA**
tumultuous	tumultuoso	necrophilia	necrofilia
unctuous*	untuoso	pedophilia	pedofilia
virtuous	virtuoso	zoophilia	zoofilia
voluptuous*	voluttuoso	**-PHOBIA**	**-FOBIA**
Exceptions:		agoraphobia	agorafobia
tempestuous	tempestoso	claustrophobia	claustrofobia
-VOROUS	**-VORO**	hydrophobia*	idrofobia
carnivorous	carnivoro	phobia*	fobia
insectivorous*	insettivoro	xenophobia	xenofobia
granivorous	granivoro	zoophobia	zoofobia
herbivorous*	erbivoro	**-PHOBIC**	**-FOBO**
omnivorous*	onnivoro	agoraphobic*	agorafobo
-PATHY	**-PATIA**	claustrophobic	claustrofobo
apathy	apatia	hydrophobic*	idrofobo
antipathy	antipatia	xenophobic	xenofobo
cardiopathy*	cardiopatia	**-PHONE**	**-FONO**
homeopathy*	omeopatia	dictaphone*	dittafono
osteopathy	osteopatia	gramophone*	grammofono
psychopathy*	psicopatia	interphone	interfono
telepathy	telepatia	megaphone	megafono
but:		microphone	microfono
sympathy	comprensione, condoglianze, cordoglio	saxophone*	sassofono
		telephone	telefono
-PED	**-PEDE**	vibraphone	vibrafono
biped	bipede	xylophone*	silofono
palmiped	palmipede	*but:*	
pinniped	pinnipede	earphone	auricolare
quadruped	quadrupede	**-PHONY**	**-FONIA**
Exception:		aphony	afonia
velocipede	velocipede	antiphony	antifonia
-PEDE	**-PIEDI**	cacophony	cacofonia
centipede*	centopiedi	euphony	eufonia
millepede	millepiedi	polyphony*	polifonia
-PHILE	**-FILO**	stereophony	stereofonia
Americanophile	americanofilo	symphony*	sinfonia
Anglophile	anglofilo	**-PLANE**	**-PLANO**
bibliophile	bibliofilo	aeroplane	aeroplano
Francophile	francofilo	airplane*	aeroplano
Italophile	italofilo	biplane	biplano
necrophile	necrofilo	monoplane	monoplano
pedophile	pedofilo	**-PLE**	**-PLO**
Russophile	russofilo	centuple	centuplo
xenophile	xenofilo	multiple	multiplo
		octuple*	ottuplo

quadruple	quadruplo	monoscope	monoscopio
quintuple	quintuplo	periscope	periscopio
sextuple*	sestuplo	spectroscope*	spettroscopio
triple	triplo	stereoscope	stereoscopio
Exceptions:		stethoscope*	stetoscopio
duple	doppio	telescope	telescopio
simple	semplice	*Exception*:	
-POLIS	**-POLI**	horoscope	oroscopo
acropolis	acropoli	**-SCOPY**	**-SCOPIA**
megalopolis	megalopoli	colonoscopy	colonoscopia
metropolis	metropoli	copy	copia
necropolis	necropoli	hygroscopy*	igroscopia
-PORT	**-PORTO**	microscopy	microscopia
airport*	aeroporto	photocopy*	fotocopia
heliport*	eliporto	spectroscopy*	spettroscopia
passport*	passaporto	stereoscopy	stereoscopia
port	porto	stethoscopy*	stetoscopia
rapport	rapporto	telescopy	telescopia
transport*	trasporto	**-SIS**	**-SI**
Exception:		-asis	
import	importazione	-esis	
-REME	**-REME**	-gnosis	
bireme	bireme	-iasis	
trireme	trireme	-lysis	
quadrireme	quadrireme	-neurosis	
quinquereme	quinquereme	-osis	
-RRHEA	**-RREA**	-phasis	
diarrhea	diarrea	-synthesis	
gonorrhea	gonorrea	-thesis	
logorrhea	logorrea	analysis*	analisi
pyorrhea*	piorrea	anchylosis*	anchilosi
-SAUR/TAUR	**-SAURO/TAURO**	ankylosis*	anchilosi
brontosaur	brontosauro	antithesis*	antitesi
centaur	centauro	apotheosis*	apoteosi
dinosaur	dinosauro	arteriosclerosis	arteriosclerosi
Minotaur	minotauro	arthrosis*	artrosi
-SAURUS	**-SAURO**	biogenesis	biogenesi
brachiosaurus	brachiosauro	biosynthesis	biosintesi
brontosaurus	brontosauro	catalysis*	catalisi
megalosaurus	megalosauro	cataphoresis*	cataforesi
-SCOPE	**-SCOPIO**	catharsis*	catarsi
electroscope*	elettroscopio	chemosynthesis	chemiosintesi
gyroscope*	giroscopio	cirrhosis*	cirrosi
hygroscope*	igroscopio	crisis	crisi
kaleidoscope*	caleidoscopio	diaeresis*	dieresi
miscroscope	miscroscopio	diagnosis	diagnosi

dialysis — dialisi
dieresis* — dieresi
diverticulosis* — diverticolosi
ecchymosis* — ecchimosi
electrolysis* — elettrolisi
elephantiasis* — elefantiasi
ellipsis* — ellissi
embryogenesis* — embriogenesi
emphasis* — enfasi
exegesis* — esegesi
genesis — genesi
halitosis — alitosi
hemoptysis* — emottisi
hydrolisis* — idrolisi
hypnosis* — ipnosi
hypodermoclysis* — ipodermoclisi
hypostasis* — ipostasi
hypothesis* — ipotesi
karyokinesis* — cariocinesi
metamorphosis* — metamorfosi
metastasis — metastasi
metathesis* — metatesi
metempsychosis* — metempsicosi
narcosis — narcosi
Nemesis — nemesi
nephrosis* — nefrosi
neurosis — neurosi
oasis — oasi
osmosis — osmosi
osteoporosis — osteoporosi
osteosclerosis — osteosclerosi
osteosynthesis — osteosintesi
paralysis* — paralisi
parenthesis* — parentesi
periphrasis* — perigfrasi
photosynthesis* — fotosintesi
phthisis* — tisi
prognosis — prognosi
prosthesis* — prostesi
psoriasis — psoriasi
psychoanalysis* — psicanalisi
psychosis* — psicosi
pyrolysis* — pirolisi
sclerosis — sclerosi
scoliosis — scoliosi
sepsis — sepsi

stasis — stasi
symbiosis* — simbiosi
symphysis* — sinfisi
synesis* — sinesi
synopsis* — sinossi
synthesis* — sintesi
thesis* — tesi
thrombosis* — trombosi
trichiasis — trichiasi
tubercolosis — tubercolosi
basis — base

-SOPHY — **-SOFIA**
anthroposophy* — antroposofia
philosophy* — filosofia
theosophy* — teosofia

-SPERM — **-SPERMA**
angiosperm — angiosperma
but:
zoosperm — spermatozoo

-SPHERE — **-SFERA**
atmosphere — atmosfera
hydrosphere* — idrosfera
ionosphere — ionosfera
lithosphere* — litosfera
sphere* — sfera
stratosphere — stratosfera
but:
hemisphere — emisfero
planisphere — planisfero

-STER — **-STRO**
-aster
alabaster — alabastro
baluster* — balaustro
burgomaster* — borgomastro
cloister* — chiostro
disaster — disastro
minister — ministro
monster* — mostro
pilaster — pilastro
pinaster — pinastro
poetaster — poetastro
register — registro
sinister — sinistro
Zoroaster — Zoroastro
Exceptions:
semester — semestre

trimester	trimestre	-UCTION	-UZIONE
-STICE	**-STIZIO**	-UPTION	
armistice	armistizio	-UTION	
interstice	interstizio	**-TION**	**-ZIONE**
solstice	solstizio	*preceded by consonant:*	
-STOLE	**-STOLE**	*The nouns ending in-IZATION change to-*	
diastole	diastole	*IZZAZIONE. See list at end of*	
systole*	sistole	*-ATION*	
-STROPHE	**-STROFE**	*Examples:*	
apostrophe	apostrofe	civilization	civilizzazione
catastrophe	catastrofe	colonization	colonizzazione
epistrophe	epistrofe	**-ACTION**	**-AZIONE**
Exception:		-faction	
strophe	strofa	abstraction*	astrazione
-SYLLABLE	**-SILLABO**	action	azione
hendecasyllable*	endecasillabo	attraction	attrazione
monosyllable	monosillabo	contraction	contrazione
polysyllable*	polisillabo	detraction	detrazione
trisyllable	trisillabo	diffraction	diffrazione
Exception:		distraction	distrazione
syllable*	sillaba	exaction*	esazione
-THERAPY	**-TERAPIA**	extraction*	estrazione
chemotherapy*	chemioterapia	faction	fazione
physiotherapy*	fisioterapia	fraction	frazione
psychotherapy*	psicoterapia	infraction	infrazione
radiotherapy*	radioterapia	liquefaction	liquefazione
therapy*	terapia	petrifaction*	pietrifazione
-THROPY	**-TROPIA**	protraction	protrazione
misanthropy	misantropia	putrefaction	putrefazione
philanthropy*	filantropia	rarefaction	rarefazione
-TION	**-ZIONE**	reaction	reazione

The nouns with desinence in-tion are numerous. They are assimilated as follows:

-ACTION	**-AZIONE**	refraction	rifrazione
-APTION		retraction	ritrazione
-ATION		satisfaction*	soddisfazione
-ECTION	**-EZIONE**	subtraction*	sottrazione
-EPTION		traction	trazione
-ETION		transaction	transazione
-ICTION	**-IZIONE**	tumefaction	tumefazione
-IPTION		vitrifaction*	vetrificazione
-ITION		*but:*	
-OCTION	**-OZIONE**	olfaction	olfatto
-OPTION		**-APTION**	**-AZIONE**
-OTION		*only exceptions*:	
		contraption	aggeggio; congegno strano
		caption	didascalia; sottotitolo

recaption	reintegrazione nel possesso di beni	aspiration	aspirazione
usucaption	usucapione	assignation*	assegnazione
-ATION	**-AZIONE**	assimilation	assimilazione
abbreviation	abbreviazione	association	associazione
abdication	abdicazione	attenuation	attenuazione
aberration	aberrazione	attestation	attestazione
ablation	ablazione	auscultation (med.)	auscultazione
abnegation	abnegazione	authentication*	autenticazione
abomination	abominazione	automation	automazione
abrogation	abrogazione	aviation	aviazione
acceleration	accelerazione	beatification	beatificazione
acclamation	acclamazione	calcination	calcinazione
adaptation*	adattazione	cancellation	cancellazione
adjudication*	aggiudicazione	capitulation*	capitolazione
administration*	amministrazione	carnification	carnificazione
admiration*	ammirazione	cassation	cassazione
adoration	adorazione	castigation	castigazione
adulation	adulazione	castration	castrazione
adulteration	adulterazione	celebration	celebrazione
aeration	aerazione	cessation	cessazione
affectation*	affettazione	circulation*	circolazione
affiliation	affiliazione	citation	citazione
affirmation*	affermazione	clarification*	chiarificazione
agglomeration	agglomerazione	classification	classificazione
aggravation	aggravazione	coagulation	coagulazione
aggregation	aggregazione	codification	codificazione
agitation	agitazione	cogitatation	cogitatazione
alienation	alienazione	cohabitation*	coabitazione
alimentation	alimentazione	collaboration	collaborazione
alteration	alterazione	collation	collazione
altercation	altercazione	collimation	collimazione
alternation	alternazione	collocation	collocazione
amalgamation	amalgamazione	coloration	colorazione
ambulation	ambulazione	combination	combinazione
amplification	amplificazione	commemoration	commemorazione
amputation	amputazione	communication*	comunicazione
animation	animazione	commutation	commutazione
annihilation*	annichilazione	compilation	compilazione
annotation	annotazione	complication	complicazione
annunciation	annunciazione	computation	computazione
anticipation	anticipazione	concatenation	concatenazione
application	applicazione	concentration	concentrazione
appropriation	appropriazione	conciliation	conciliazione
approximation*	approssimazione	condensation	condensazione
arrogation	arrogazione	condonation	condonazione
articulation*	articolazione	confabulation	confabulazione

confederation	confederazione	defalcation	defalcazione
configuration	configurazione	defamation*	diffamazione
confirmation*	confermazione	defecation	defecazione
conflagration	conflagrazione	deflagration	deflagrazione
conformation	conformazione	deflation	deflazione
confutation	confutazione	defloration	deflorazione
congelation	congelazione	deformation	deformazione
congratulation	congratulazione	degeneration	degenerazione
congregation	congregazione	degradation	degradazione
conjugation*	coniugazione	degustation	degustazione
conjuration*	congiurazione	deification	deificazione
connotation	connotazione	delation	delazione
consecration*	consacrazione	delegation	delegazione
conservation	conservazione	deliberation	deliberazione
consideration	considerazione	delineation	delineazione
consolation	consolazione	demonstration*	dimostrazione
consolidation	consolidazione	denomination	denominazione
constellation*	costellazione	denotation	denotazione
consternation*	costernazione	denudation	denudazione
constipation*	costipazione	deodoration	deodorazione
consultation	consultazione	deportation	deportazione
consummation*	consumazione	depravation	depravazione
contamination	contaminazione	depredation	depredazione
contemplation	contemplazione	deprivation	deprivazione
continuation	continuazione	derivation	derivazione
conversation	conversazione	derogation	derogazione
convocation	convocazione	desiccation*	essiccazione
cooperation	cooperazione	designation	designazione
coordination	coordinazione	desolation	desolazione
copulation	copulazione	desperation*	disperazione
coronation	coronazione	destination	destinazione
correlation	correlazione	determination	determinazione
corroboration	corroborazione	detestation	detestazione
creation	creazione	detonation	detonazione
cremation	cremazione	devastation	devastazione
culmination	culminazione	deviation	deviazione
cultivation*	coltivazione	differentiation*	differenziazione
damnation*	dannazione	digitation	digitazione
debilitation	debilitazione	dilapidation	dilapidazione
decalcification	decalcificazione	dilatation	dilatazione
decimation	decimazione	dilation*	dilatazione
declamation	declamazione	discrimination	discriminazione
declaration*	dichiarazione	disinclination	disinclinazione
declination	declinazione	disintegration	disintegrazione
decoration	decorazione	dislocation*	dislogazione
dedication	dedicazione	dispensation	dispensazione

disputation	disputazione	exhumation*	esumazione
dissemination	disseminazione	expiation*	espiazione
dissertation	dissertazione	expiration*	espirazione,
dissimilation	dissimilazione		scadenza
dissipation	dissipazione	explication*	esplicazione
dissociation	dissociazione	exploration*	esplorazione
distillation	distillazione	exportation*	esportazione
divagation	divagazione	expropriation*	espropriazione
divarication	divaricazione	expurgation*	espurgazione
divination	divinazione	exsiccation*	essiccazione
documentation	documentazione	extenuation*	estenuazione
domination	dominazione	extirpation*	estirpazione
donation	donazione	exultation	esultazione
dulcification*	dolcificazione	exultation	esultanzaone
edification	edificazione	fabrication*	fabbricazione
education	educazione,	falsification	falsificazione
	cortesia	fecundation*	fecondazione
ejaculation*	eiaculazione	federation	federazione
elaboration	elaborazione	felicitation	felicitazione
electrification*	elettrificazione	fermentation	fermentazione
elevation	elevazione	figuration	figurazione
elimination	eliminazione	filiation	filiazione
emanation	emanazione	filtration	filtrazione
emancipation	emancipazione	fixation*	fissazione
emigration	emigrazione	flagellation	flagellazione
emulation	emulazione	foliation*	fogliazione
enumeration	enumerazione	formation	formazione
enunciation	enunciazione	formulation	formulazione
epuration	epurazione	fornication	fornicazione
equation	equazione	fortification	fortificazione
equitation	equitazione	foundation*	fondazione
equivocation	equivocazione	frustration	frustrazione
esterification	esterificazione	fumigation	fumigazione
evacuation	evacuazione	gasification*	gas(s)ificazione
evaporation	evaporazione	gelatination	gelatinazione
evocation	evocazione	gemination	geminazione
exaggeration*	esagerazione	gemmation	gemmazione
exaltation*	esaltazione	generation	generazione
examination*	esaminazione	germination	germinazione
exasperation*	esasperazione	gestation	gestazione
execration*	esecrazione	gesticulation*	gesticolazione
excitation*	eccitazione	glorification	glorificazione
exclamation*	esclamazione	gradation	gradazione
excogitation*	escogitazione	gravitation	gravitazione
exhalation*	esalazione	habitation*	abitazione
exhortation*	esortazione	hallucination*	allucinazione

183

hesitation*	esitazione	inoculation	inoculazione
hibernation*	ibernazione	inundation	inondazione
homologation*	omologazione	insinuation	insinuazione
horripilation*	orripilazione	inspiration	inspirazione
humiliation*	umiliazione	installation	installazione
hybridation*	ibridazione	instigation*	istigazione
hydration*	idratazione	insubordination	insubordinazione
hydrogenation*	idrogenazione	integration	integrazione
identification	identificazione	intensification	intensificazione
illation	illazione	interpolation	interpolazione
illumination	illuminazione	interpretation	interpretazione
illustration	illustrazione	interrogation	interrogazione
imagination*	immaginazione	intimation	intimazione
imitation	imitazione	intimidation	intimidazione
immigration	immigrazione	intonation	intonazione
immolation	immolazione	intoxication*	intossicazione
implication	implicazione	inundation*	inondazione
importation	importazione	invalidation	invalidazione
imprecation	imprecazione	investigation	investigazione
impregnation	impregnazione	invitation	invitazione
improvisation*	improvvisazione	invocation	invocazione
imputation	imputazione	irradiation	irradiazione
inauguration	inaugurazione	irrigation	irrigazione
incarceration	incarcerazione	irritation	irritazione
incarnation	incarnazione	isolation	isolazione
inclination	inclinazione	justification*	giustificazione
inconsideration	inconsiderazione	laceration	lacerazione
incoordination	incoordinazione	lachrymation*	lacrimazione
incorporation	incorporazione	lactation*	lattazione
incrimination	incriminazione	lamentation	lamentazione
incrustation*	incrostazione	lamination	laminazione
incubation	incubazione	legation	legazione
inculcation	inculcazione	legislation	legislazione
indetermination	indeterminazione	legitimation*	legittimazione
indication	indicazione	levitation	levitazione
indignation	indignazione	liberation	liberazione
infatuation	infatuazione	limitation	limitazione
infiltration	infiltrazione	liquidation	liquidazione
inflammation*	infiammazione	lubrication	lubricazione
inflation	inflazione	lunation	lunazione
information	informazione	luxation*	lussazione
inhabitation*	abitazione	maceration	macerazione
inhalation*	inalazione	machination*	macchinazione
initiation*	iniziazione	malformation	malformazione
innervation	innervazione	malversation	malversazione
innovation	innovazione	manifestation	manifestazione

manipulation*	manipolazione	oxygenation*	ossigenazione
mastication	masticazione	pacification	pacificazione
masturbation	masturbazione	palpation	palpazione
matriculation*	immatricolazione	palpitation	palpitazione
maturation	maturazione	panification	panificazione
mediation	mediazione	participation*	partecipazione
medication	medicazione	penetration	penetrazione
meditation	meditazione	peregrination	peregrinazione
menstruation*	mestruazione	perforation	perforazione
migration	migrazione	permutation	permutazione
mitigation	mitigazione	peroration	perorazione
moderation	moderazione	perpetration	perpetrazione
modification	modificazione	personification	personificazione
modulation	modulazione	petrification*	pietrificazione
mortification	mortificazione	phonation*	fonazione
motivation	motivazione	population*	popolazione
multiplication*	moltiplicazione	precipitation	precipitazione
mutilation	mutilazione	predestination	predestinazione
mystification*	mistificazione	prefiguration	prefigurazione
narration	narrazione	premeditation	premeditazione
nation	nazione	preoccupation	preoccupazione
navigation	navigazione	preparation	preparazione
negation	negazione	presentation	presentazione
negotiation*	negoziazione	preservation	preservazione
nidification	nidificazione	privation	privazione
nomination	nominazione	proclamation	proclamazione
notation	notazione	procrastination	procrastinazione
notification	notificazione	procreation	procreazione
nullification	nullificazione	profanation	profanazione
numeration	numerazione	proliferation	proliferazione
oblation	oblazione	promulgation	promulgazione
obligation*	obbligazione	propagation	propagazione
observation*	osservazione	propitiation*	propiziazione
obstination*	ostinazione	prostration	prostrazione
occupation	occupazione	provocation	provocazione
operation	operazione	publication*	pubblicazione
oration	orazione	pullulation	pullulazione
orchestration	orchestrazione	pulsation	pulsazione
ordination	ordinazione	purification	purificazione
ornamentation	ornamentazione	qualification	qualificazione
oscillation	oscillazione	quotation	quotazione
ossification	ossificazione	radiation	radiazione
ostentation	ostentazione	ramification	ramificazione
ovation	ovazione	ratification	ratificazione
ovulation	ovulazione	ration	razione
oxidation*	ossidazione	reciprocation	reciprocazione

recitation	recitazione	sporation* (bot.)	sporulazione
recommendation*	raccomandazione	stagnation	stagnazione
reconciliation*	riconciliazione	station	stazione
recreation*	ricreazione	stimulation*	stimolazione
recrimination	recriminazione	stipulation	stipulazione
rectification*	rettificazione	stratification	stratificazione
recuperation*	ricuperazione	subjugation*	soggiogazione
refrigeration	refrigerazione	subordination	subordinazione
regeneration*	rigenerazione	suffocation*	soffocazione
registration	registrazione	sulphuration*	solforazione
rehabilitation*	riabilitazione	suppuration	suppurazione
reincarnation*	reincarnaazione	syllabification*	sillabazione
relation	relazione	taxation*	tassazione
remuneration*	rimunerazione	temptation*	tentazione
renovation*	rinnovazione	tergiversation	tergiversazione
reparation*	riparazione	termination	terminazione
representation*	rappresentazione	transfiguration*	trasfigurazione
reputation	reputazione	transformation*	trasformazione
respiration	respirazione	transmigration*	trasmigrazione
restoration*	ristaurazione	transmutation*	trasmutazione
resuscitation*	risuscitazione	transportation*	trasportazione
retrogradation	retrogradazione	transubstantiation*	transustanziazione
revelation*	rivelazione	trepidation	trepidazione
revendication*	rivendicazione	triangulation*	triangolazione
revivification*	rivivificazione	tribulation*	tribolazione
revocation	revocazione	triplication	triplicazione
rotation	rotazione	ulceration	ulcerazione
rumination	ruminazione	unification	unificazione
salivation	salivazione	usurpation	usurpazione
salvation	salvazione	vaccination	vaccinazione
sanctification*	santificazione	vacillation	vacillazione
saponification	saponificazione	validation*	convalidazione
saturation	saturazione	valuation*	valutazione
scintillation	scintillazione	variation	variazione
sedimentation	sedimentazione	vegetation	vegetazione
segmentation	segmentazione	veneration	venerazione
segregation	segregazione	ventilation	ventilazione
sensation	sensazione	versification	versificazione
separation	separazione	vexation*	vessazione
simulation	simulazione	vibration	vibrazione
situation	situazione	vindication*	rivendicazione
solicitation*	sollecitazione	violation	violazione
solidification	solidificazione	vitrification*	vetrificazione
sophistication*	sofisticazione	vituperation	vituperazione
specification	specificazione	vivification	vivificazione
speculation	speculazione	vocation	vocazione

186

vociferation	vociferazione	reverberation	riverbero
Exceptions:		revocation	revoca
abjuration	abiura	ruination	rovina
absorption	assorbimento	salutation	saluto
annexation	annessione	salvation	salvezza
arbitration	arbitrato	satiation	sazietà
asphyxiation	asfissia	scintillation	scintillio
assassination	assassino	semination	semina
calculation	calcolo	sequestration	sequestro
condemnation	condanna	signification	significato
confiscation	confisca	striation	striatura
counterreformation	controriforma	summation	somma
dictation	dettato	toleration	tolleranza
dispensation	dispensa	translation	traduzione
duration	durata	ululation	ululato
effemination	effeminatezza	vacation	vacanza
exoneration	esonero	vaporization	evaporazione
expatriation	espatrio	verification	verifica
extermination	sterminio	visitation	visita
exultation	esultanza	**-IZATION**	**-IZZAZIONE**
fascination	fascino	actualization*	attualizzazione
imperturbation	imperturbabilità	aromatization	aromatizzazione
incapacitation	incapacita'	atomization	atomizzazione
induration	indurimento	authorization*	autorizzazione
interpellation	interpellanza	canonization	canonizzazione
invitation	invito	carbonization	carbonizzazione
jubilation	giubilo	civilization	civilizzazione
libation	libagione	colonization	colonizzazione
molestation	molestia	crystallization*	cristallizzazione
origination	origine	decentralization	decentralizzazione
pagination	paginatura	demilitarization	demilitarizzazione
perspiration	sudore	demoralization	demoralizzazione
plantation	piantagione	disorganization	disorganizzazione
prognostication	pronostico	evangelization	evangelizzazione
pronunciation	pronuncia	fertilization	fertilizzazione
prorogation	proroga	fossilization	fossilizzazione
punctuation	punteggiatura	fraternization	fraternizzazione
ratification	ratifica	generalization	generalizzazione
ratiocination	raziocinio	hospitalization*	ospedalizzazione
reformation	riforma	humanization*	umanizzazione
regurgitation	rigurgito	idealization	idealizzazione
repatriation	rimpatrio	immobilization	immobilizzazione
repudiation	ripudio	immunization	immunizzazione
reservation	prenotazione	individualization	individualizzazione
retardation	ritardo	industrialization	industrializzazione
retrogradation	regressione		

internationalization*	
	internazionalizzaziọne
ionization	ionizzaziọne
legalization	legalizzaziọne
magnetization	magnetizzaziọne
mesmerization	mesmerizzaziọne
monetization	monetizzaziọne
moralization	moralizzaziọne
nasalization	nasalizzaziọne
nationalization*	nazionalizzaziọne
naturalization	naturalizzaziọne
neutralization	neutralizzaziọne
organization	organizzaziọne
pasteurization*	pastorizzaziọne
polarization	polarizzaziọne
polymerization*	polimerizzaziọne
popularization*	popolarizzaziọne
pulverization*	polverizzaziọne
rationalization*	razionalizzaziọne
realization	realizzaziọne
reorganization*	riorganizzaziọne
specialization	specializzaziọne
spiritualization	spiritualizzaziọne
stabilization	stabilizzaziọne
standardization	standardizzaziọne
sterilization	sterilizzaziọne
stylization*	stilizzaziọne
synchronization*	sincronizzaziọne
urbanization	urbanizzaziọne
vocalization	vocalizzaziọne
vulcanization	vulcanizzaziọne
vulgarization*	volgarizzaziọne
Exceptions:	
demobilization*	smobilitaziọne
mobilization	mobilitaziọne
systematization*	sistemaziọne
-ATION	**-AMENTO**
accumulation	accumulamẹnto
alleviation	alleviamẹnto
annihilation*	annichilamẹnto
corrugation	corrugamẹnto
decentralization*	decentramẹnto
depopulation*	spopolamẹnto
deterioration	deterioramẹnto.
discoloration	discoloramẹnto
incatenation	incatenamẹnto

incineration*	icenerimento
incitation	incitamẹnto
indoctrination*	indottrinamẹnto
mutation	mutamẹnto
obscuration*	oscuramẹnto
occultation	occultamẹnto
orientation	orientamẹnto
pernoctation*	pernottamẹnto
prolongation*	prolungamẹnto
recalcitration*	ricalcitramẹnto
regulation*	regolamẹnto
relaxation*	rilassamẹnto
renovation*	rinnovamẹnto
resuscitation*	risuscitamẹnto
strangulation*	strangolamẹnto
temporization*	temporeggiamẹnto
titillation	titillamẹnto
-ECTION	**-EZIONE**
abjection*	abieziọne
affection	affeziọne
collection	colleziọne
confection	confeziọne
convection	conveziọne
correction	correziọne
defection	defeziọne
direction	direziọne
election	eleziọne
erection	ereziọne
imperfection	imperfeziọne
infection	infeziọne
injection*	inieziọne
inspection*	ispeziọne
insurrection	insurreziọne
interjection*	interieziọne
intersection*	intersecazione
introspection	introspeziọne
objection*	obieziọne
perfection	perfeziọne
projection*	proieziọne
protection	proteziọne
refection	refeziọne
resurrection*	risurreziọne
section	seziọne
selection	seleziọne
vivisection	viviseziọne
but:	

188

English	Italian	English	Italian
connection	connessione	addition	addizione
-ECTION	**-ESSIONE**	admonition*	ammonizione
(-flection)		ambition	ambizione
flection	flessione	ammunition*	munizione
genuflection	genuflessione	apparition	apparizione
inflection	inflessione	apposition	apposizione
reflection*	riflessione	audition	audizione
-EPTION	**-EZIONE**	coalition	coalizione
conception	concezione	cognition	cognizione
exception*	eccezione	competition	competizione
perception	percezione	composition	composizione
reception*	ricezione	condition	condizione
Some *Exceptions*:		contraposition*	contrapposizione
interception	intercettamento	contrition	contrizione
preconception	preconcetto	decomposition	decomposizione
-ETION	**-EZIONE**	definition	definizione
discretion	discrezione	demolition	demolizione
excretion*	escrezione	deposition	deposizione
indiscretion	indiscrezione	disposition	disposizione
secretion	secrezione	disquisition	disquisizione
-ICTION	**-IZIONE**	ebullition*	ebollizione
affliction	afflizione	edition	edizione
benediction	benedizione	erudition	erudizione
constriction*	costrizione	exhibition*	esibizione
contradiction*	contraddizione	exposition*	esposizione
diction	dizione	extradition*	estradizione
dereliction	derelizione	ignition	ignizione
eviction	evizione	imposition	imposizione
friction	frizione	inanition	inanizione
infliction	inflizione	indisposition	indisposizione
interdiction	interdizione	inhibition*	inibizione
jurisdiction*	giurisdizione	inquisition	inquisizione
malediction	maledizione	interposition	interposizione
prediction	predizione	intuition	intuizione
restriction	restrizione	malnutrition	malnutrizione
-IPTION	**-IZIONE**	nutrition	nutrizione
circumscription*	circoscrizione	opposition	opposizione
description	descrizione	perdition	perdizione
inscription*	iscrizione	petition	petizione
prescription	prescrizione	position	posizione
proscription	proscrizione	precognition	precognizione
transcription*	trascrizione	predisposition	predisposizione
-ITION	**-IZIONE**	premonition	premonizione
-position		preposition	preposizione
abolition	abolizione	presupposition	presupposizione
acquisition	acquisizione	prohibition*	proibizione

proposition	proposizione
proposition	proposa
repartition*	ripartizione
recomposition*	ricomposizione
repetition*	ripetizione
requisition	requisizione
sedition	sedizione
superstition	superstizione
supposition	supposizione
tradition	tradizione
transition	transizione
transposition*	trasposizione
Some exceptions:	
coition	coito
munition	munizione
recognition	riconoscimento
requisition	richiesta
volition	volontà
-OCTION	**-OZIONE**
decotion	decozione
-OPTION	**-ZIONE**
adoption*	adozione
Exception:	
option	opzione
-OTION	**-OZIONE**
devotion	devozione
emotion	emozione
lotion	lozione
locomotion	locomozione
motion	mozione
notion	nozione
potion	pozione
promotion	promozione
-UCTION	**-UZIONE**
adduction	adduzione
conduction	conduzione
construction*	costruzione
deduction	deduzione
destruction*	distruzione
instruction*	istruzione
introduction	introduzione
obstruction*	ostruzione
production	produzione
reconstruction*	ricostruzione
reduction*	riduzione
reproduction*	riproduzione
seduction	seduzione
but:	
auction	asta
-UPTION	**-UZIONE**
corruption	corruzione
eruption	eruzione
interruption	interruzione
irruption	irruzione
-UTION	**-UZIONE**
ablution	abluzione
absolution*	assoluzione
allocution	allocuzione
attribution	attribuzione
caution	cauzione
circumlocution*	circonlocuzione
constitution*	costituzione
contribution	contribuzione
counter-revolution*	controrivoluzione
destitution	destituzione
devolution	devoluzione
diminution	diminuzione
dissolution	dissoluzione
distribution	distribuzione
elocution	elocuzione
evolution	evoluzione
execution*	esecuzione
institution*	istituzione
interlocution	interlocuzione
involution	involuzione
irresolution	irresoluzione
locution	locuzione
persecution	persecuzione
precaution	precauzione
prosecution	prosecuzione
prostitution	prostituzione
restitution	restituzione
retribution	retribuzione
revolution*	rivoluzione
solution	soluzione
substitution*	sostituzione
Exception:	
prosecution	processo
-TION	**-ZIONE**
Preceded by consonant	Preceduta da consonante
abstention*	astenzione

English	Italian	English	Italian
assertion	asserzione	dichotomy*	dicotomia
assumption*	assunzione	ebryotomy*	embriotomia
attention	attenzione	laparotomy	laparotomia
contention	contenzione	lobotomy	lobotomia
contravention*	contravvenzione	phlebotomy*	flebotomia
convention	convenzione	trichotomy*	tricotomia
desertion*	diserzione	**-TRESS**	**-TRICE**
detention	detenzione	-ress	
disjunction*	disgiunzione	actress*	attrice
distinction*	distinzione	authoress*	autrice
exemption*	esenzione	directress*	direttrice
expunction*	espunzione	editress	editrice
extinction*	estinzione	empress*	imperatrice
fiction*	finzione	huntress*	cacciatrice
function*	funzione	protectress*	protettrice
injunction*	ingiunzione	sculptress*	scultrice
insertion	inserzione	traitress*	traditrice
intention	intenzione	**-TRIX**	**-TRICE**
invention	invenzione	-rix	
mention	menzione	administratrix*	amministratrice
portion	porzione	aviatrix	aviatrice
presumption*	presunzione	Beatrix	Beatrice
prevention	prevenzione	bisectrix*	bisettrice
proportion	proporzione	directrix*	direttrice
redemption*	redenzione	executrix*	esecutrice
retention*	ritenzione	matrix	matrice
sanction*	sanzione	mediatrix	mediatrice
Some exceptions:		testatrix	testatrice
abortion	aborto	**-TUDE**	**-TUDINE**
absorption	assorbimento	-itude	
bastion	bastione	-etude	
combustion	combustione	altitude	altitudine
congestion	congestione	amplitude	amplitudine
consumption	consumo	aptitude *	attitudine
contortion	contorsione	attitude	attitudine
digestion	digestione	beatitude	beatitudine
contention	disputa	consuetude	consuetudine
distortion	distorsione	fortitude	fortitudine
exhaustion	esaurimento	gratitude	gratitudine
extortion*	estorsione	habitude*	abitudine
indigestion	indigestione	inaptitude*	inattitudine
intervention	intervento	ineptitude*	inettitudine
question	questione	ingratitude	ingratitudine
suggestion	suggestione	inquietitude	inquietitudine
-TOMY	**-TOMIA**	latitude	latitudine
anatomy	anatomia	longitude	longitudine

magnitude	magnitųdine
mansuetude	mansuetųdine
multitude*	moltitųdine
pulchritude*	pulcritųdine
quietude*	quietitųdine
rectitude*	rettitųdine
similitude	similitųdine
solicitude*	sollecitųdine
solitude	solitųdine
turpitude	turpitųdine
vicissitude	vicissitųdine

Note:

decrepitude	decrepitęzza
lassitude	stanchęzza
verisimilitude	verosimigliạnza

-TY   **-TÀ**

Note: stress on the final "à"

-acity
-ality
-aneity
-arity
-bility
-city
-eity
-ety
-icity
-idity
-ility
-ity

ability	abilità
abnormality*	anormalità
abnormity*	anormità
absurdity*	assurdità
acerbity	acerbità
acidity	acidità
activity*	attività
acuity	acuità
adiposity	adiposità
adaptability*	adattabilità
adoptability*	adottabilità
adversity*	avversità
affability	affabilità
affinity	affinità
agility	agilità
alacrity	alacrità
ambiguity	ambiguità

amenity	amenità
animosity	animosità
anonymity*	anonimità
antiquity*	antichità
anxiety*	ansietà
aridity	aridità
asperity	asperità
assiduity	assiduità
atomicity	atomicità
atrocity	atrocità
austerity	austerità
authenticity*	autenticità
authority*	autorità
avidity	avidità
banality	banalità
benignity	benignità
bestiality	bestialità
brevity	brevità
brutality	brutalità
caducity	caducità
calamity	calamità
callosity	callosità
capability*	capacità
capacity	capacità
captivity*	cattività
carnality	carnalità
casuality	casualità
catholicity*	cattolicità
causality	causalità
cavity	cavità
celebrity	celebrità
celerity	celerità
centrality	centralità
charity*	carità
chastity*	castità
Christianity*	Cristianità
city*	città
civility	civiltà
community*	comunità
commutability	commutabilità
compatibility	compatibilità
complicity	complicità
conductibility*	conducibilità
conformity	conformità
confraternity	confraternità
congeniality	congenialità

congruity	congruità	fallibility	fallibilità
consanguinity*	consanguineità	falsity	falsità
consubstantiality*	consustanzialità	familiarity	familiarità
contiguity	contiguità	fatality	fatalità
continuity	continuità	fecundity*	fecondità
convexity*	convessità	felicity	felicità
cordiality	cordialità	femineity*	femmininità
corporality*	corporeità	femininity*	femmininità
corporeity*	corporalità	fertility	fertilità
credibility	credibilità	festivity	festività
credulity	credulità	fidelity*	fedeltà
criminality	criminalità	finality	finalità
cruelty*	crudeltà	flexibility*	flessibilità
cupidity	cupidità	fluidity	fluidità
curiosity	curiosità	formality	formalità
debility	debilità	fragility	fragilità
declivity	declività	fraternity	fraternità
deformity	deformità	friability	friabilità
deity	deità	frigidity	frigidità
density	densità	frugality	frugalità
dexterity*	desterità	futility	futilità
difficulty*	difficoltà	garrulity	garrulità
dignity	dignità	generality	generalità
dishonesty*	disonestà	generosity	generosità
disparity	disparità	globosity	globosità
dissimilarity	dissimilarità	grandiosity	grandiosità
dissolubility	dissolubilità	gravity	gravità
diversity	diversità	heredity*	ereditarietà
divinity	divinità	heterogeneity*	eterogeneità
docility	docilità	historicity*	storicità
ductility*	duttilità	homogeneity*	omogeneità
duplicity	duplicità	homosexuality*	omosessualità
durability	durabilità	honesty*	onestà
eccentricity	eccentricità	hospitality*	ospitalità
elasticity	elasticità	hostility*	ostilità
electricity*	elettricità	humanity*	umanità
entity	entità	humidity*	umidità
equanimity	equanimità	humility*	umiltà
equity	equità	identity	identità
eternity	eternità	illegality	illegalità
eventuality	eventualità	illegibility*	illeggibilità
exiguity*	esiguità	imbecility*	imbecillità
exteriority*	esteriorità	immobility	immobilità
extremity*	estremità	immorality	immoralità
facility	facilità	immortality	immortalità
faculty*	facoltà	immunity	immunità

immutability	immutabilità	ineligibility*	ineleggibilità
impartiality*	imparzialità	inequality*	inequalità
impassibility	impassibilità	inequity*	iniquità
impeccability	impeccabilità	inevitability	inevitabilità
impenetrability	impenetrabilità	inexhaustibility*	inesauribilità
impermeability	impermeabilità	inexorability*	inesorabilità
impetuosity	impetuosità	inexplicability*	inesplicabilità
implacability	implacabilità	infallibility	infallibilità
imponderability	imponderabilità	infelicity	infelicità
impossibility	impossibilità	inferiority	inferiorità
impracticability*	impraticabilità	infertility	infertilità
impressionability	impressionabilità	infidelity*	infedeltà
improbability	improbabilità	infinity	infinità
impropriety	improprietà	infirmity*	infermità
impunity	impunità	inflexibility*	inflessibilità
impurity	impurità	ingenuity	ingenuità
inability	inabilità	inhospitality*	inospitalità
inaccessibility	inaccessibilità	inhumanity*	inumanità
inadaptability*	inadattabilità	iniquity	iniquità
inadmissibility*	inammissibilità	inscrutability	inscrutabilità
inalienability	inalienabilità	insensibility	insensibilità
inanity	inanità	inseparability	inseparabilità
inapplicability	inapplicabilità	insincerity	insincerità
incalculability*	incalcolabilità	insipidity	insipidità
incapacity	incapacità	insolubility	insolubilità
incivility*	inciviltà	instability	instabilità
incombustibility	incombustibilità	insuperability	insuperabilità
incommensurability	incommensurabilità	insurmountability*	insormontabilità
incommunicability*	incomunicabilità	intangibility	intangibilità
incomparability	incomparabilità	integrality	integralità
incompatibility	incompatibilità	integrity	integrità
incomprehensibility*	incomprensibilità	intellectuality*	intellettualità
incongruity	incongruità	intelligibility	intelligibilità
inconvertibility	inconvertibilità	intensity	intensità
incorporeality*	incorporeità	intimity	intimità
incorporeity	incorporeità	intrepidity	intrepidità
incorrigibility*	incorreggibilità	inutility	inutilità
incorruptibility*	incorruttibilità	invalidity	invalidità
incredibility	incredibilità	invariability	invariabilità
incredulity	incredulità	invincibility	invincibilità
incurability	incurabilità	invisibility	invisibilità
indemnity*	indennità	invulnerability	invulnerabilità
indestructibility*	indistruttibilità	irascibility	irascibilità
indigestibility*	indigeribilità	irrationality*	irrazionalità
indispensability	indispensabilità	irregularity*	irregolarità
individuality	individualità	irresponsibility*	irresponsabilità
indivisibility	indivisibilità		

irreversibility	irreversibilità	nodosity	nodosità
irrevocability	irrevocabilità	normality	normalità
irritability	irritabilità	notoriety	notorietà
jocundity*	giocondità	novelty*	novità
joviality*	giovialità	nudity	nudità
Latinity	latinità	nullity	nullità
legality	legalità	obesity	obesità
liability*	responsabilità	objectivity*	oggettività
liberality	liberalità	obscenity*	oscenità
liberty	libertà	obscurity*	oscurità
limpidity	limpidità	opacity	opacità
locality	località	opportunity	opportunità
longevity	longevità	originality	originalità
loquacity	loquacità	parity	parità
loyalty*	lealtà	partiality*	parzialità
lucidity	lucidità	particularity*	particolarità
luminosity	luminosità	passivity	passività
magnanimity	magnanimità	paternity	paternità
majesty*	maestà	peculiarity	peculiarità
malignity	malignità	penalty*	penalità
malleability	malleabilità	perpetuity	perpetuità
masculinity*	mascolinità	perplexity*	perplessità
maternity	maternità	perceptibility*	percettibilità
maturity	maturità	personality	personalità
mediocrity	mediocrità	perspicacity	perspicacità
mendacity	mendacità	perspicuity	perspicuità
mendicity	mendicità	pity*	pietà
mentality	mentalità	pilosity*	pelosità
minority	minorità	placidity	placidità
mobility	mobilità	plasticity	plasticità
modality	modalità	plausibility	plausibilità
modernity	modernità	plurality	pluralità
monstrosity*	mostrosità	polarity	polarità
morality	moralità	ponderability	ponderabilità
mortality	mortalità	popularity*	popolarità
municipality	municipalità	porosity	porosità
musicality	musicalità	possibility	possibilità
mutability	mutabilità	posteriority	posteriorità
natality	natalità	potentiality*	potenzialità
nationality*	nazionalità	poverty	povertà
nativity	natività	practicability*	praticabilità
navigability	navigabilità	practicality*	praticalità
nebulosity	nebulosità	preciosity*	preziosità
necessity	necessità	priority	priorità
neutrality	neutralità	probability	probabilità
nobility*	nobiltà	probity	probità

proclivity	proclività	serenity	serenità
productivity*	produttività	serosity*	sierosità
profanity	profanità	servility	servilità
profundity*	profondità	severity	severità
promiscuity	promiscuità	sexuality*	sessualità
propinquity	propinquità	similarity	similarità
propriety	proprietà	simplicity*	semplicità
prosperity	prosperità	sincerity	sincerità
proximity*	prossimità	singularity*	singolarità
puberty	pubertà	sinuosity	sinuosità
publicity*	pubblicità	sobriety	sobrietà
puerility	puerilità	sociality*	sociabilità
punctuality*	puntualità	society	società
purity	purità	solemnity*	solennità
pusillanimity	pusillanimità	solidarity*	solidarietà
putridity	putridità	solidity	solidità
quality	qualità	solubility	solubilità
quantity	quantità	sonority	sonorità
radioactivity*	radioattività	sovereignty*	sovranità
rancidity	rancidità	specialty*	specialità
rapacity	rapacità	speciality	specialità
rapidity	rapidità	specificity	specificità
rarity	rarità	spontaneity	spontaneità
rationality*	razionalità	stability	stabilità
reactivity*	reattività	sterility	sterilità
reality*	realtà	stupidity	stupidità
reciprocity	reciprocità	substantiality*	sostanzialità
regality	regalità	suggestibility*	suggestionabilità
regularity*	regolarità	superficiality	superficialità
relativity	relatività	superiority	superiorità
religiosity	religiosità	susceptibility*	suscettibilità
respectability*	rispettabilità	tangibility	tangibilità
responsibility*	responsabilità	taxability*	tassabilità
rotundity*	rotondità	temerity	temerità
rusticity	rusticità	tenacity	tenacità
salacity	salacità	tenuity	tenuità
salinity	salinità	theatricality*	teatralità
salubrity	salubrità	timidity	timidità
sanctity*	santità	tonality	tonalità
sanity	sanità	tortuosity	tortuosità
scurrility	scullilità	totality	totalità
senility	senilità	toxicity*	tossicità
sensibility	sensibilità	tractability*	trattabilità
sensivity	sensività	tranquillity	tranquillità
sensuality	sensualità	trinity	trinità
separability	separabilità	turbidity*	torbidità

ubiquity	ubiquità	certainty	certẹzza
unanimity	unanimità	clarity	chiarẹzza
unity	unità	crudity	crudẹzza
uniformity	uniformità	culpability	colpevolẹzza
universality	universalità	ebriety	ebbrẹzza
university	università	frivolity	frivolẹzza
unpopularity*	impopolarità	insecurity*	insicurẹzza
unreality*	irrealtà	lividity	lividẹzza
urbanity	urbanità	scarcity	scarsẹzza
utility	utilità	security*	sicurẹzza
validity	validità	sociability	socievolẹzza
vanity	vanità	timidity	timidẹzza
variability	variabilità	turgidity	turgidẹzza
varicosity	varicosità	uncertainty	incertẹzza
variety	varietà	*Exceptions*:	
vascularity*	vascolarità	admiralty	ammiraglịato
vastity	vastità	amity	amicịzia
velleity	velleità	amnesty	amnistịa
velocity	velocità	audacity	audạcia
venality	venalità	barbarity	barbạrie
venerability	venerabilità	classicality	classicịsmo
veniality	venialità	county	contẹa
veracity	veracità	depravity	depravazịone
verbosity	verbosità	deputy	deputạto
verity	verità	dynasty	dinastịa
versatility	versatilità	ferocity	ferọcia
verticality	verticalità	immodesty	immodẹstia
viability	viabilità	majority	maggiorạnza
vicinity	vicinità	modesty	modẹstia
virginity*	verginità	party	partịto
virility	virilità	principality	principạto
virtuosity	virtuosità	pudicity	pudicịzia
viscosity	viscosità	sacristy	sagrestịa
visibility	visibilità	sentimentality	sentimentalịsmo
vitality	vitalità	sodality	sodalịzio
vitreosity*	vetrosità	synonymity	sinonimịa
vivacity	vivacità	technicality	tecnicịsmo
voluminosity	voluminosità	treaty	trattạto
vulgarity*	volgarità	volcanicity	vulcanịsmo
vulnerability	vulnerabilità	**-TYPE**	**-TIPO**
but:		archetype	archẹtipo
mendacity (also)	mendạcia	daguerreotype*	dagherrọtipo
seniority	anzianità	monotype	monotịpo
sympathy	comprensione	prototype	protọtipo
-TY	**-EZZA**	stereotype	stereọtipo
beauty	bellẹzza	type	tipo

Note:

linotype	linotipista
-ULE	**-ULO**
-cule	
globule	globulo
tubule	tubulo
but:	
animalcule	microbio
molecule	molecola
vestibule	vestibolo
-ULT	**-ULTO**

(From Latin *tumultus, adultus*, etc.)
English dropped the "us".

adult	adulto
consult	consulto
cult	culto
insult	insulto
occult	occulto
tumult	tumulto
Exceptions:	
catapult	catapulta
result	risultato
-UM	**-O**
-arium	
-cranium	
-ellum	
-ennium	
-ium	
-orium	
-podium	
-sternum	
aluminum*	alluminio
aquarium*	acquario
asylum*	asilo
athenaeum*	ateneo
auditorium	auditorio
bacterium*	batterio
barium	bario
Belgium	Belgio
beryllium*	berillio
biennium	biennio
Byzantium*	Bisanzio
caecum*	cieco
calcium	calcio
candelabrum	candelabro
cerebellum*	cervelletto
chromium*	cromo
chrysanthemum*	crisantemo
ciborium	ciborio
coagulum	coagulo
Colosseum	Colosseo
columbarium*	colombario
compendium	compendio
condominium	condominio
consortium*	consorzio
cranium	cranio
decennium	decennio
decorum	decoro
deuterium	deuterio
dictum*	detto
duodenum	duodeno
effluvium	effluvio
emporium	emporio
epigrastrium	epigastrio
epithelium*	epitelio
equilibrium	equilibrio
exordium*	esordio
flagellum	flagello
forum	foro
fulcrum	fulcro
geranium	geranio
gypsum*	gesso
helium*	elio
herbarium*	erbario
honorarium*	onorario
insectarium*	insettario
interregnum	interregno
iridium	iridio
Ischium	ischio
Janiculum*	Gianicolo
laburnum	laburno
laudanum	laudano
leprosarium*	lebbrosario
magnesium	magnesio
mausoleum	mausoleo
maximum*	massimo
medium	medio
millennium	millennio
minimum	minimo
minium	minio
molybdenum*	molibdeno

moratorium	moratorio	vivarium*	vivaio
museum	museo	*Exceptions*:	
nasturtium*	nasturzio	harmonium	armonium
odium	odio	referendum	referendum
opium*	oppio	**-UND**	**-ONDO**
opprobrium	opprobrio	-bund	
ostensorium	ostensorio	-cund	
ovum*	uovo	fecund	fecondo
pandemonium	pandemonio	furibund	furibondo
pendulum*	pendolo	iracund	iracondo
petroleum*	petrolio	jocund*	giocondo
planetarium	planetario	moribund	moribondo
platinum	platino	profound*	profondo
plutonium	plutonio	rotund	rotondo
podium	podio	rubicund	rubicondo
potassium	potassio	*Exception*:	
premium	premio	gerund	gerundio
quinquennium	quinquennio	**-UNE**	**-UNA**
radium	radio	dune	duna
rectum*	retto	fortune	fortuna
rostrum	rostro	rune	runa
sanatorium	sanatorio	tribune	tribuna
scrotum	scroto	**-UNE**	**-UNO**
sensorium	sensorio	importune	importuno
serum*	siero	inopportune	inopportuno
sistrum	sistro	Neptune*	Nettuno
sodium	sodio	opportune	opportuno
solarium	solario	tribune	tribuno
spectrum*	spettro	**-URE**	**-URA**
speculum* (med.)	specolo	-ature	
sputum	sputo	-cure	
stadium	stadio	-facture	
sternum	sterno	-ture	
stratum	strato	adventure*	avventura
strontium*	stronzio	agriculture*	agricoltura
substratum*	sostrato	aperture	apertura
sudarium	sudario	apiculture	apicultura
symposium*	simposio	aquiculture*	acquicoltura
titanium	titanio	arboriculture*	arboricoltura
trapezium	trapezio	architecture*	architettura
triennium	triennio	armature	armatura
trivium	trivio	aviculture*	avicoltura
tympanum*	timpano	candidature	candidatura
uranium	uranio	capture*	cattura
velum	velo	caricature	caricatura
viaticum	viatico	censure	censura

cincture*	cintura	mature	maturo
conjecture*	congettura	obscure*	oscuro
coverture*	copertura	premature	prematuro
creature	creatura	pure	puro
culture	cultura	*Exceptions*:	
cure	cura	denture	dentiera
figure	figura	epicure	epicureo
filature	filatura	manicure	manicure
fissure*	fessura	pedicure	pedicure
floriculture	floricultura	pleasure	piacere
fracture*	frattura	pressure	pressione
horticulture*	orticoltura	signature	firma
infrastructure*	infrastruttura	sinecure	sinecura
investiture	investitura	treasure*	tesoro
juncture*	giuntura	**-URN**	**-URNO**
legislature	legislatura	nocturn*	notturno
literature*	letteratura	taciturn	taciturno
manufacture*	manifattura	*but:*	
measure*	misura	urn	urna
miniature	miniatura	churn	bidone
musculature*	muscolatura	**-US**	**-O**
nature	natura	abacus*	abaco
nomenclature	nomenclatura	acanthus*	acanto
pisciculture*	piscicoltura	Aeolus*	Eolo
prefecture*	prefettura	alumnus*	alunno
primogeniture	primogenitura	alveolus	alveolo
procedure	procedura	anus	ano
puncture*	puntura	apparatus	apparato
quadrature	quadratura	asparagus	asparago
rupture*	rottura	Aurelius	Aurelio
sculpture*	scultura	Bacchus*	Bacco
sericulture*	sericoltura	bacillus	bacillo
sinecure	sinecura	bronchus*	bronco
stature	statura	calamus	calmo
structure*	struttura	calculus*	calcolo
suture	sutura	callus	callo
temperature	temperatura	calycanthus*	calicanto
tonsure	tonsura	carpus	carpo
torture	tortura	Catullus	Catullo
venture*	avventura	census	censo
verdure	verdura	Cerberus	Cerbero
viniculture*	vinicoltura	chorus*	coro
viticulture*	viticoltura	circus	circo
-URE	**-URO**	coccus	cocco
immature	immaturo	coitus	coito
insecure	insicuro	colossus	colosso

200

Confucius	Confucio	nucleus	nucleo
consensus	consenso	oesophagus*	esofago
corpus	corpo	Olympus*	Olimpo
cothurnus*	coturno	Orpheus*	Orfeo
crocus	croco	papyrus*	papiro
cumulus	cumulo	Parnassus*	Parnaso
Cyprus*	Cipro	Phaedrus*	Fedro
Daedalus*	Dedalo	Phoebus*	Febo
Damascus	Damasco	phosphorus*	fosforo
Darius	Dario	Piraeus*	Pireo
detritus	detrito	plexus*	plesso
Dionysus*	Dionisio	Polonius	Polonio
discus	disco	polypus*	polipo
esophagus*	esofago	Prometheus*	Prometeo
exodus*	esodo	prospectus*	prospetto
fetus	feto	pruritus	prurito
focus*	fuoco	pylorus*	piloro
foetus*	feto	radius	radio
fungus	fungo	Remus	Remo
funiculus*	funicolo	rhesus* (zool.)	reso
genius	genio	rhombus*	rombo
gladiolus	gladiolo	Sagittarius	Sagittario
gymnotus*	gimnoto	sarcophagus*	sarcofago
Herodotus*	Erodoto	sexus* (1)	sesso
hibiscus*	ibisco	sinus* (anat.)	seno
hippocampus*	ippocampo	Sirius	Sirio
hippopotamus*	ippopotamo	status	stato
impetus	impeto	stimulus*	stimolo
incubus	incubo	Stradivarius	Stradivario
Indus	Indo	stratocumulus	stratocumulo
isthmus*	istmo	stratus (metereol.)	strato
Janus*	Giano	streptococcus	streptococco
Julius*	Giulio	stylus*	stilo
lapillus	lapillo	syllabus	sillabo
Lazarus*	Lazzaro	tarsus	tarso
locus*	luogo	Tartarus	Tartaro
lotus	loto	Taurus	Tauro
Lycurgus*	Licurgo	tetanus	tetano
meniscus	menisco	Titus	Tito
metacarpus	metacarpo	tonus	tono
metatarsus	metatarso	tumulus	tumulo
minus*	meno	typhus*	tifo
mucus	muco	Uranus	Urano
narcissus*	narciso	uterus	utero
nautilus	nautilo	vagus	vago
nimbus*	nembo	Vesuvius	Vesuvio

villus	villo

Some exceptions:

ignoramus	ignorantone
Jesus	Gesù
octopus	polpo
onus	onere
pus	pus
Venus	Venere

Exception:

syllabus	programma
-USE	**-USA**
cause	causa
hypotenuse*	ipotenusa
menopause	menopausa
Muse	Musa
pause	pausa
Syracuse*	Siracusa
-USE	**-USO**
abstruse*	astruso
abuse	abuso
applause	applauso
diffuse	diffuso
disuse	disuso
obtuse*	ottuso
profuse	profuso
recluse	recluso
use	uso
-UTE	**-UTO**
absolute*	assoluto
acute	acuto
astute	astuto
attribute	attributo
brute	bruto
destitute	destituto
dissolute	dissoluto
institute*	istituto
involute	involuto
irresolute	irresoluto
minute	minuto
mute	muto
prostitute	prostituto/a
resolute*	risoluto
salute	saluto
statute	statuto
substitute*	sostituto
tribute	tributo

Some exceptions:

parachute	paracadute
prostitute	prostituta
repute	riputazione
-VORE	**-VORO**
carnivore	carnivoro
herbivore*	erbivoro
insectivore*	insettivoro
-VOROUS	**-VORO**
carnivorous	carnivoro
insectivorous*	insettivoro
granivorous	granivoro
herbivorous*	erbivoro
omnivorous*	onnivoro
-Y	**-IA**
academy*	accademia
agony	agonia
allegory	allegoria
allergy	allergia
amnesty*	amnistia
apostasy	apostasia
armoury*	armeria
artery	arteria
artillery*	artiglieria
atony	atonia
autopsy	autopsia
battery	batteria
buffoonery*	buffoneria
carpentry	carpenteria
cavalry*	cavalleria
ceremony*	cerimonia
chancellery*	cancelleria
chivalry*	cortesia
chivalry* (mil.)	cavalleria
colony	colonia
comedy*	commedia
controversy	controversia
cosmogony	cosmogonia
courtesy*	cortesia
custody	custodia
cutlery*	coltelleria
devilry*	diavoleria
distillery	distilleria
dramaturgy*	drammaturgia
dynasty*	dinastia
economy	economia

elegy	elegia	pedantry	pedanteria
embryogeny*	embriogenia	penury	penuria
energy	energia	peony	peonia
epilepsy*	epilessia	perfidy	perfidia
Epiphany*	Epifania	perfumery*	profumeria
euphony*	eufonia	phantasy*	fantasia
falconry	falconeria	philanthropy*	filantropia
fantasy	fantasia	philately*	filatelia
foundry*	fonderia	phlebotomy*	flebotomia
fury	furia	poetry*	poesia
gallantry*	galanteria	polyandry*	poliandria
geodesy	geodesia	prophecy	profezia
geometry	geometria	prosody	prosodia
Germany	Germania	psalmody*	salmodia
heresy*	eresia	psychiatry*	psichiatria
history*	storia	rhapsody*	rapsodia
homily*	omelia	siderurgy	siderurgia
hydropsy*	idropisia	sodomy	sodomia
hypocrisy*	ipocrisia	story	storia
hypothermy*	ipotermia	strategy	strategia
idolatry	idolatria	taxidermy*	tassidermia
ignominy	ignominia	thaumaturgy*	taumaturgia
industry	industria	tragedy	tragedia
infamy	infamia	tragicomedy*	tragicommedia
injury*	ingiuria	*Exceptions:*	
irony	ironia	century	secolo
Italy	Italia	clergy	clero
jealousy*	gelosia	drudgery	lavoro faticoso
jewelry*	gioielleria	ecstasy	estasi
jury*	giuria	leprosy	lebbra
liturgy	liturgia	lethargy*	letargo
Lombardy	Lombardia	mercury	mercurio
lottery	lotteria	palsy	paralisi
Mary	Maria	pleurisy	pleurite
melody	melodia	pleasantry	scherzo
metallurgy	metallurgia	prodigy	prodigio
misanthropy*	misantropia	progeny	progenie
misery	miseria	Ptolemy*	Tolomeo
monody	monodia	remedy	rimedio
mummy	mummia	study	studio
Normandy	Normandia	subsidy	sussidio
orgy	orgia	surgery	chirurgia
otary	otaria	trigonometry	trigonometria
parody	parodia		
pedagogy	pedagogia		

Exercises

Exercise 1. Given the pattern that English adjectives ending in "able" normally change the ending to "abile," provide the Italian equivalent for the following words:

1. affable, curable, formidable, inevitable, imitable, inseparable, irritable, portable, separable, comparable, impermeable, inviolable, irrecoverable.

Exercise 2. Some of the adjectives in Exercise 1 can be changed into their antonyms (opposite meaning) by adding a prefix or removing it. Form as many antonyms as you can and give their English meanings.

Exercise 3. Given that nouns ending in "age" in English change to "aggio" in Italian, replace the English word(s) in parenthesis with the Italian equivalent:

1. Un uomo ha bisogno di _____ per fare la guerra. (courage)
2. Il _____ non arrivò al _____ . (message, village).
3. Nel deserto videro un _____ (mirage).
4. Il _____ dei Medici fu importante per lo sviluppo delle arti. (patronage)
5. I terroristi presero degli _____ . (hostages*)
6. Questo è un _____ alla natura. (outrage*)
7. Avevo proprio bisogno di un _____ alla gamba. (massage)
8. Bisogna difendersi dallo _____ facendo. _____ (espionage* , counterespionage*)
9. Il _____ durò tre mesi. (voyage*)
10. Il _____ non era sufficiente. (voltage)

Exercise 4. Italian nouns ending in "enza" generally change the ending to "ence" in English. In the following sentences change the underlined word into English keeping in mind the rules of root assimilation:

1. Ho sentito molto la sua assenza.* _____
2. Ho passato la mia adolescenza in Italia. _____
3. Ho una certa ambivalenza per questo argomento. _____
4. Che simpatica coincidenza! _____
5. Il signore non aveva la coscienza* pulita. _____
6. Il professore ha parlato con grande eloquenza. _____
7. La sua esistenza* fu negata da tutti. _____
8. La differenza era notevole. _____
9. La mia pazienza* era al limite. _____
10. La prudenza*, la sapienza* e l'ubbidienza* sono virtù poco praticate oggi. _____ _____ _____

*denotes root change.

Exercise 5. English adjectives and nouns ending in "ic" generally change to "ico" in Italian. Convert the English adjective to the Italian equivalent, keeping in mind the possibility of a root change. To verify you work check the Root converter on p. 100.

1. L'anno _____ stava per terminare. (academic*)
2. Il segnale _____ del telefono non c'era. (acoustic*)
3. Vanzetti era un _____. (anarchic)
4. Certe modelle sono veramente _____. (anorexic*)
5. L'acido _____ è buono per lavare gli occhi. (boric)
6. Il signor Jones è un _____ d'arte. (critic)
7. Robin Williams non è un _____. (comic classic)
8. Giovanni è un _____ del calcio. (fanatic)
9. L'incontro tra Mohammed Ali e Joe Frazier è stata una lotta _____.(epic)
10. Cè stato un terremoto _____ in India. (catastrophic*)

Exercise 6. Given that English nouns ending in "ion" change to "ione" in Italian, form Italian nouns from the following English nouns: for example region= regione
1. Admission*   _____
2. Aggression   _____
3. Champion*   _____
4. Confusion   _____
5. Illusion   _____
6. Explosion*   _____
7. Expansion   _____
8. Precision   _____
9. Prevision   _____
10. Scorpion   _____

Exercise 7. English nouns that end in "ist" or "yst" change in Italian to "ista". Remember that these nouns can be masculine or feminine and change to *i* and *e* in the plural. Convert the English word in parenthesis into its Italian equivalent.

1. Per l'_____ americano la situazione era grave. (analyst)
2. Botticelli fu un grande _____ del Rinascimento. (artist)
3. A Wall Street lavora chi è _____.(capitalist)
4. Il mio _____ ha la mano leggera e non fa mai male. (dentist)
5. Hai visto il film L'_____? (exorcist*)
6. Sono andato in un colonia di _____ ed ho incontrato mio zio. (nudists)
7. I _____ _____ _____ hanno idee simili sull'economia. (Communists*, Socialists and Marxists*)
8. Io sono un _____ Non sono un _____. (optimist,* fatalist)
9. Bisogna essere _____ nella vita, non _____.(altruists, egoists)
10. Il _____ della banda era un _____. (guitarist,* terrorist)

* denotes root change.

205

Exercise 8. English nouns ending in "or" change in Italian to "ore". Convert the words in the parenthesis into their Italian equivalent.

1. Richard Geere è un bravo _____(actor*).
2. L'_____del *Decameron* è Giovanni Boccaccio. (author*)
3. Nel Medioevo bisognava amare il _____ non la creatura. (Creator)
4. Recentemente ho visto un bel film sui Romani intitolato Il _____.(Gladiator)
5. Ho fatto un grosso _____. Ho parlato con troppo _____. *(*error, candor)
6. L'_____ della radio fu Guglielmo Marconi. (inventor)
7. Quel libro ha fatto _____ e l'_____ha guadagnato molto denaro. (furor, editor)
8. Saddam Hussein è un _____. Gli_____ non hanno scoperto le sue armi nucleari. (dictator, inspectors*)
9. Il _____ era un grande _____ dell'ambiente. (professor, protector*)
10. L'_____ dell'azienda ricevette una salario _____a quello del padrone. (administrator,* inferior)

Exercise 9. Replace the English words in parenthesis with the Italian equivalent.
Example: Mario è dotato di una _____(incredible)_____ (intelligence).
Mario è dotato di una incredibile (incredible) intelligenza (intelligence).

1. La _____non significa_____. (liberty, licence)
2. La frazione è composta di un _____ ed un _____.(numerator, denominator)
3. Il _____ della nostra_____ è molto_____. (president, society, eloquent)
4. La sua _____ è _____. (presence, indispensable)
5. Lo_____ ha commesso un grave _____. (student, error)
6. Il prezzo del _____è molto_____.(motor, convenient)
7. La tua idea è di _____ _____.(incredible importance)
8. Il senator fu _____ alla_____. (present, conference)
9. La moglie del_____ è una signora molto_____. (doctor, intelligent)
10. L'_____ è la maestra della vita. (experience)
11. Il vino è _____ ed il ferro è _____. (liquid, solid)
12. Mio fratello è molto _____. (affable)
14. La tua _____ è _____. (eloquence, impeccable)

Exercise 10. Convert the following words into Italian. Example: affable, *affabile*

1. adorable, alienable, applicable, applicable, impeccable, probable.

2. assistance, ambulance, elegance, anniversary, beneficiary, contrary, diary.

3. invisible, impossible, invincible, irresistible, credible, compatible, incredible.

4. cellular, nuclear, ocular, familiar, lunar, solar, polar, linear, anular.

5. affliction, affection, selection, correction, exception, friction, perfection.

Chapter V
THE ADVERB CONVERTER

Much like English that forms its adverbs by adding "ly" (meaning "in the manner of, or like") to the adjective, Italian adverbs are formed following the pattern that existed in Latin. When the Romans wanted to say that something was done "honestly," they would say "honesta mente," that is, "with an honest mind". The word "mente," originally a noun, which could be translated as "mind," "inclination," "manner," became in time a suffix that indicated the manner in which something was done. Thus, in Italian adverbs are formed by adding the suffix " mente" to the adjective.

If an adjective ends in "o" the ending is changed to the feminine and "mente" is added, for example, "vero" (true) changes to "veramente" (truly), "umano" (human) becomes "umanamente" (humanly). Adjectives that end in "e" simply add "mente" as in "felice" (happy) "felicemente" (happily). However, adjectives that end in "le" "ore" or "are" drop the final "e" before adding "mente" as in "gentile" "gentilmente," "popolare," "popolarmente," "inferiore," "inferiormente". Italian also has many adverbs that are formed differently like "bene" "male" "subito" "presto" etc... These adverbs are not included here.

The following table shows how adverbs are formed:

Adjective	adverb	English
Alto	altamente	highly
Giusto	giustamente	justly
Precedente	precedentemente	precedingly
Gentile	gentilmente	kindly
Amorevole	amorevolmente	lovingly
Regolare	regolarmente	regularly
Anteriore	anteriormente	before

In this section we list Italian adverbs formed with "mente" with their English equivalents arranged in alphabetical order by the endings of the adjective, immediately followed by the adverbial endings. Thus, if you wanted to know how to say "essentially" in Italian, you would look for the adjective-adverb ending in "al-ALLY" which becomes "ale-ALMENTE" and you would find "essenzialmente" arranged alphabetically. Here is another example: To look up "affably" you would find the adjective-adverb ending in "able-ABLY" which in Italian becomes "abile-ABILMENTE" and you would find the adverb "affabilmente".

-able-ABLY	See-ble	dictatorially	dittatorialmente
		dorsally	dorsalmente
-act-ACTLY	-atto-ATTAMENTE	essentially	essenzialmente
abstractly	astrattamente	eventually	eventualmente
exactly	esattamente	exceptionally	eccezionalmente
inexactly	inesattamente	existentially	esistenzialmente
		fatally	fatalmente
-al-ALLY	-ale-ALMENTE	filially	filialmente
abnormally	anormalmente	finally	finalmente
accidentally	accidentalmente	formally	formalmente
adjectivally	aggettivalmente	frontally	frontalmente
annually	annualmente	fundamentally	fondamentalmente
artificially	artificialmente	generally	generalmente
asexually	asessualmente	glacially	glacialmente
autumnally	autunnalmente	gradually	gradualmente
banally	banalmente	gutturally	gutturalmente
bestially	bestialmente	habitually	abitualmente
bilaterally	bilateralmente	horizontally	orizzontalmente
brutally	brutalmente	ideally	idealmente
carnally	carnalmente	illegally	illegalmente
casually	casualmente	immaterially	immaterialmente
causally	causalmente	immorally	immoralmente
celestially	celestialmente	immortally	immortalmente
centrally	centralmente	impartially	imparzialmente
cerebrally	cerebralmente	impersonally	impersonalmente
collaterally	collateralmente	incidentally	incidentalmente
colloquially	colloquialmente	individually	individualmente
colossally	colossalmente	industrially	industrialmente
commercially	commercialmente	infernally	infernalmente
conceptually	concettualmente	initially	inizialmente
conditionally	condizionalmente	integrally	integralmente
confidentially	confidenzialmente	intellectually	intellettualmente
conjugally	coniugalmente	intentionally	intenzionalmente
constitutionally	costituzionalmente	internationally	internazionalmente
contextually	contestualmente	irrationally	irrazionalmente
contractually	contrattualmente	judicially	giudizialmente
conventionally	convenzionalmente	legally	legalmente
cordially	cordialmente	lexically	lessicalmente
criminally	criminalmente	literally	letteralmente
crucially	crucialmente	manually	manualmente
culturally	culturalmente	marginally	marginalmente
diagonally	diagonalmente	martially	marzialmente
dialectally	dialettalmente	materially	materialmente

mentally	mentalmente	unnaturally	innaturalmente
morally	moralmente	usually	usualmente
mortally	mortalmente	visually	visualmente
mutually	mutualmente	vitally	vitalmente
naturally	naturalmente	vocally	vocalmente
neutrally	neutralmente	*Some exceptions*.	
normally	normalmente	equivocally	equivocamente
officially	ufficialmente	financially	finanziariamente
optionally	opzionalmente	perennially	perennemente
orally	oralmente	perpetually	perpetuamente
originally	originalmente	reciprocally	reciprocamente
partially	parzialmente		
potentially	potenzialmente	-ant-ANTLY	-ante-ANTEMENTE
prejudicially	pregiudizialmente	arrogantly	arrogantemente
primordially	primordialmente	brilliantly	brillantemente
principally	principalmente	constantly	costantemente
professionally	professionalmente	elegantly	elegantemente
professorially	professoralmente	exorbitantly	esorbitantemente
proportionally	proporzionalmente	exuberantly	esuberantemente
proverbially	proverbialmente	flagrantly	flagrantemente
providentially	provvidenzialmente	ignorantly	ignorantemente
provincially	provincialmente	importantly	importantemente
punctually	puntualmente	incessantly	incessantemente
rationally	razionalmente	inconstantly	inconstantemente
really	realmente	inelegantly	inelegantemente
regally	regalmente	intolerantly	intollerantemente
ritually	ritualmente	redundantly	ridondantemente
sentimentally	sentimentalmente	repugnantly	ripugnantemente
sexually	sessualmente	vigilantly	vigilantemente
socially	socialmente	*Some exceptions*.	
specially	specialmente	benignantly	benignamente
structurally	strutturalmente	instantly	istantaneamente
substantially	sostanzialmente	malignantly	malignamente
superficially	superficialmente	valiantly	valorosamente
supernaturally	soprannaturalmente		
temporally	temporalmente	-ar-ARLY	-are-ARMENTE
territorially	territorialmente	angularly	angolarmente
textually	testualmente	circularly	circolarmente
totally	totalmente	familiarly	familiarmente
traditionally	tradizionalmente	irregularly	irregolarmente
triumphantly	trionfalmente	linearly	linearmente
unequally	inegualmente	muscularly	muscolarmente
unilaterally	unilateralmente	particularly	particolarmente
universally	universalmente	peculiarly	peculiarmente

perpendicularly — perpendicolarmente
popularly — popolarmente
regularly — regolarmente
singularly — singolarmente
unpopularly — impopolarmente
vulgarly — volgarmente
Exceptions:
similarly — similmente
spectacularly — spettacolosamente

-ary-ARILY — -ario-ARIAMENTE
arbitrarily — arbitrariamente
involuntarily — involontariamente
necessarily — necessariamente
ordinarily — ordinariamente
primarily — primariamente
secondarily — secondariamente
summarily — sommariamente
voluntarily — volontariamente
Some exceptions:
militarily — militarmente
temporarily — temporaneamente

-ate-ATELY — -ato-ATAMENTE
accurately — accuratamente
adequately — adeguatamente
affectionately — affezionatamente
alternately — alternatamente
appropriately — appropriatamente
considerately — consideratamente
delicately — delicatamente
desolately — desolatamente
desperately — disperatamente
disparately — disparatamente
elaborately — elaboratamente
exaggeratedly — esageratamente
fortunately — fortunatamente
immaculately — immacolatamente
immediately — immediatamente
inadequately — inadeguatamente
inarticulately — inarticolatamente
inconsiderately — inconsideratamente
indelicately — indelicatamente
indeterminately — indeterminatamente

indiscriminately — indiscriminatamente
insubordinately — insubordinatamente
intricately — intricatamente
inviolately — inviolatamente
irately — iratamente
moderately — moderatamente
privately — privatamente
proportionately — proporzionatamente
separately — separatamente
subordinately — subordinatamente
Some exceptions:
approximately — approssimativamente
illegitimately — illegittimamente
intimately — intimamente

-BLE preceded by "a, i, o, u" change as follows:

-able-ABLY — abilmente-
ABILMENTE
-ible-IBLY — ibilmente-
IBILMENTE
-oble-OBLY — obilmente-
OBILMENTE
-uble-UBLY — ubilmente-
UBILMENTE

-able-ABLY — -abile-ABILMENTE
ably — abilmente
affably — affabilmente
amiably — amabilmente
comfortably — confortabilmente
comparably — comparabilmente
considerably — considerabilmente
desirably — desiderabilmente
formidably — formidabilmente
honorably — onorabilmente
imaginably — immaginabilmente
impeccably — impeccabilmente
impenetrably — impenetrabilmente
imperturbably — imperturbabilmente
implacably — implacabilmente
improbably — improbabilmente
incalculably — incalcolabilmente
incommensurably — incommensurabilmente

incomparably	incomparabilmente	indefinably	indefinibilmente
inconsolably	inconsolabilmente	indescribably	indescrivibilmente
incontestably	incontestabilmente	indistinguishably	indistinguibilmente
incurably	incurabilmente	inequitably	inegualmente
indeterminably	indeterminabilmente	irremovably	irremovibilmente
indispensably	indispensabilmente	laudably	lodevolmente
indisputably	indisputabilmente	preferably	preferibilmente
indomitably	indomabilmente	recognizably	riconoscibilmente
ineffably	ineffabilmente	sociably	socievolmente
ineluctably	ineluttabilmente		
inestimably	inestimabilmente	-ible-IBLY	-ibile-IBILMENTE
inevitably	inevitabilmente	compatibly	compatibilmente
inexorably	inesorabilmente	comprehensibly	comprensibilmente
inexpiably	inespiabilmente	credibly	credibilmente
inexplicably	inesplicabilmente	divisibly	divisibilmente
innumerably	innumerabilmente	flexibly	flessibilmente
insatiably	insaziabilmente	horribly	orribilmente
inscrutably	inscrutabilmente	impassibly	impassibilmente
inseparably	inseparabilmente	impossibly	impossibilmente
insuperably	insuperabilmente	inaccessibly	inaccessibilmente
interminably	interminabilmente	incomprehensibly	incomprensibilmente
intolerably	intollerabilmente	incorrigibly	incorregibilmente
invariably	invariabilmente	incorruptibly	incorruttibilmente
inviolably	inviolabilmente	incredibly	incredibilmente
irreconcilably	irreconciliabilmente	indestructibly	indistruttibilmente
irrecoverably	irrecuperabilmente	indivisibly	indivisibilmente
irrefutably	irrefutabilmente	inexpressibly	inesprimibilmente
irremediably	irrimediabilmente	infallibly	infallibilmente
irreparably	irreparabilmente	inflexibly	inflessibilmente
irrevocably	irrevocabilmente	insensibly	insensibilmente
memorably	memorabilmente	intelligibly	intelligibilmente
miserably	miserabilmente	invincibly	invincibilmente
probably	probabilmente	invisibly	invisibilmente
stably	stabilmente	irresistibly	irresistibilmente
supportably	sopportabilmente	legibly	leggibilmente
tolerably	tollerabilmente	ostensibly	ostensibilmente
unstably	instabilmente	plausibly	plausibilmente
venerably	venerabilmente	possibly	possibilmente
Some exceptions.		reversibly	reversibilmente
amicably	amichevolmente	sensibly	sensibilmente
charitably	caritàtevolmente	tangibly	tangibilmente
conformably	conformemente	terribly	terribilmente
favorably	favorevolmente	visibly	visibilmente
inconceivably	inconcepibilmente	*Some exceptions.*	

indelibly	indelebilmente	evidently	evidentemente
irresponsibly	irresponsabilmente	excellently	eccellentemente
responsibly	responsabilmente	fervently	ferventemente
		fraudulently	fraudolentemente
-oble-OBLY	-obile-OBILMENTE	frequently	frequentemente
ignobly	ignobilmente	impatiently	impazientemente
nobly	nobilmente	imprudently	imprudentemente
		impudently	impudentemente
-uble-UBLY	-ubile-UBILMENTE	incoherently	incoerentemente
insolubly	insolubilmente	inconsequently	inconseguentemente
		inconveniently	inconvenientemente
END OF "BLE" LISTING		indecently	indecentemente
		independently	indipendentemente
-ect-ECTLY	-etto-ETTAMENTE	indifferently	indifferentemente
correctly	correttamente	indulgently	indulgentemente
directly	direttamente	infrequently	infrequentemente
imperfectly	imperfettamente	inherently	inerentemente
incorrectly	incorrettamente	innocently	innocentemente
indirectly	indirettamente	insistently	insistentemente
perfectly	perfettamente	insolently	insolentemente
		insufficiently	insufficientemente
-ense-ENSELY	-enso-ENSAMENTE	intelligently	intelligentemente
densely	densamente	intermittently	intermittentemente
immensely	immensamente	irreverently	irriverentemente
intensely	intensamente	negligently	negligentemente
		omnipotently	onnipotentemente
-ent-ENTLY	-ente-ENTEMENTE	patiently	pazientemente
apparently	apparentemente	permanently	permanentemente
ardently	ardentemente	persistently	persistentemente
coherently	coerentemente	presently	presentemente
congruently	congruentemente	prevalently	prevalentemente
consequently	conseguentemente	prudently	prudentemente
contingently	contingentemente	recently	recentemente
conveniently	convenientemente	reverently	riverentemente
correspondently	corrispondentemente	sapiently	sapientemente
currently	correntemente	sufficiently	sufficientemente
decently	decentemente	urgently	urgentemente
dependently	dipendentemente	vehemently	veementemente
differently	differentemente	violently	violentemente
diffidently	diffidentemente	*Some exceptions:*	
diligently	diligentemente	benevolently	benevolmente
eloquently	eloquentemente	magnificently	magnificamente
eminently	eminentemente	malevolently	malevolmente
equivalently	equivalentemente	silently	silenziosamente

English	Italian
ible-IBLY	See-ble
-ic/ical-ICALLY	-icale-ICAMENTE
academically	accademicamente
acoustically	acusticamente
acrobatically	acrobaticamente
aerodynamically	aerodinamicamente
aesthetically	esteticamente
agonistically	agonisticamente
algebraically	algebricamente
allegorically	allegoricamente
allergically	allergicamente
alphabetically	alfabeticamente
altruistically	altruisticamente
analytically	analiticamente
anarchically	anarchicamente
anatomically	anatomicamente
apathetically	apaticamente
apostolically	apostolicamente
archaeologically	archeologicamente
archaically	arcaicamente
architectonically	architettonicamente
aristocratically	aristocraticamente
arithmetically	aritmeticamente
artistically	artisticamente
astrologically	astrologicamente
astronomically	astronomicamente
asymmetrically	asimmetricamente
athletically	atleticamente
atmospherically	atmosfericamente
atomically	atomicamente
authentically	autenticamente
autobiographically	autobiograficamente
automatically	automaticamente
axiomatically	assiomaticamente
bacteriologically	batteriologicamente
biblically	biblicamente
bibliographically	bibliograficamente
biographically	biograficamente
biologically	biologicamente
bucolically	bucolicamente
bureaucratically	burocraticamente
canonically	canonicamente
capitalistically	capitalisticamente
catastrophically	catastroficamente
categorically	categoricamente
caustically	causticamente
chaotically	caoticamente
chemically	chimicamente
chronically	cronicamente
chronologically	cronologicamente
civically	civicamente
classically	classicamente
climatically	climaticamente
clinically	clinicamente
comically	comicamente
concentrically	concentricamente
cosmically	cosmicamente
critically	criticamente
cyclically	ciclicamente
cylindrically	cilindricamente
cynically	cinicamente
demagogically	demagogicamente
demographically	demograficamente
despotically	dispoticamente
diabolically	diabolicamente
diagnostically	diagnosticamente
dialectically	dialetticamente
dialogically	dialogicamente
didactically	didatticamente
diplomatically	diplomaticamente
dogmatically	dogmaticamente
domestically	domesticamente
dramatically	drammaticamente
drastically	drasticamente
dynamically	dinamicamente
dynastically	dinasticamente
eccentrically	eccentricamente
ecclesiastically	ecclesiasticamente
eclectically	ecletticamente
ecologically	ecologicamente
economically	economicamente
ecstatically	estaticamente
ecumenically	ecumenicamente
elastically	elasticamente
electrically	elettricamente
electronically	elettronicamente
emblematically	emblematicamente

emphatically	enfaticamente	hygienically	igienicamente
empirically	empiricamente	hyperbolically	iperbolicamente
endemically	endemicamente	hypostatically	ipostaticamente
energetically	energicamente	hypothetically	ipoteticamente
enthusiastically	entusiasticamente	hysterically	istericamente
epidemically	epidemicamente	iconographically	iconograficamente
epigraphically	epigraficamente	idealistically	idealisticamente
episodically	episodicamente	identically	identicamente
erotically	eroticamente	ideologically	ideologicamente
esoterically	esotericamente	idiomatically	idiomaticamente
ethically	eticamente	idyllically	idillicamente
ethnically	etnicamente	individualistically	individualisticamente
ethnographically	etnograficamente	inorganically	inorganicamente
ethnologically	etnologicamente	ironically	ironicamente
etymologically	etimologicamente	juridically	giuridicamente
euphemistically	eufemisticamente	laconically	laconicamente
euphonically	eufonicamente	laically	laicamente
euphuistically	eufuisticamente	lethargically	letargicamente
evangelically	evangelicamente	lexicographically	lessicograficamente
exegetically	esegeticamente	linguistically	linguisticamente
exotically	esoticamente	liturgically	liturgicamente
fanatically	fanaticamente	logically	logicamente
frenetically	freneticamente	logistically	logisticamente
gastronomically	gastronomicamente	luetically	lueticamente
genealogically	genealogicamente	lyrically	liricamente
generically	genericamente	magically	magicamente
genetically	geneticamente	magnetically	magneticamente
geographically	geograficamente	manneristically	manieristicamente
geologically	geologicamente	mathematically	matematicamente
geometrically	geometricamente	mechanically	meccanicamente
graphically	graficamente	medically	medicamente
graphologically	grafologicamente	melancholically	malinconicamente
gynecologically	ginecologicamente	melodically	melodicamente
hedonistically	edonisticamente	metaphorically	metaforicamente
heretically	ereticamente	metaphysically	metafisicamente
hermetically	ermeticamente	meteorologically	meteorologicamente
heroically	eroicamente	methodically	metodicamente
hierarchically	gerarchicamente	metrically	metricamente
historically	storicamente	microscopically	microscopicamente
histrionically	istrionicamente	mimetically	mimeticamente
honorifically	onirificamente	mnemonically	mnemonicamente
humoristically	umoristicamente	monastically	monasticamente
hydraulically	idraulicamente	moralistically	moralisticamente
hydrographically	idrograficamente	morphologically	morfologicamente

mystically	misticamente	satirically	satiricamente
mythically	miticamente	skeptically	scetticamente
mythologically	mitologicamente	scientifically	scientificamente
nostalgically	nostalgicamente	skeptically	scetticamente
numerically	numericamente	socialistically	socialisticamente
oligarchically	oligarchicamente	sociologically	sociologicamente
organically	organicamente	spasmodically	spasmodicamente
pacifically	pacificamente	specifically	specificamente
panoramically	panoramicamente	spherically	sfericamente
pathologically	patologicamente	sporadically	sporadicamente
patriotically	patriotticamente	statistically	statisticamente
pedagogically	pedagogicamente	stoically	stoicamente
periodically	periodicamente	strategically	strategicamente
peripherically	pefericamente	stylistically	stilisticamente
philanthropically	filantropicamente	syllogistically	sillogisticamente
philologically	filologicamente	symbolically	simbolicamente
philosophically	filosoficamente	symmetrically	simmetricamente
phlegmatically	flemmaticamente	symptomatically	sintomaticamente
phonetically	foneticamente	synoptically	sinotticamente
photographically	fotograficamente	syntactically	sintatticamente
physically	fisicamente	systematically	sistematicamente
physiologically	fisiologicamente	technically	tecnicamente
platonically	platonicamente	telegraphically	telegraficamente
pleonastically	pleonasticamente	telephonically	telefonicamente
plutocratically	plutocraticamente	theoretically	teoricamente
poetically	poeticamente	topographically	topograficamente
polemically	polemicamente	tragically	tragicamente
politically	politicamente	trigonometrically	trigonometricamente
pornographically	pornograficamente	typically	tipicamente
practically	praticamente	tyrannically	tirannicamente
pragmatically	pragmaticamente	*Exceptions.*	
prehistorically	preistoricamente	diametrically	diametralmente
problematically	problematicamente	extrinsically	estrinsecamente
prophetically	profeticamente	hypocritically	ipocritamente
prosaically	prosaicamente	intrinsically	intrinsecamente
psychiatrically	psichiatricamente	majestically	maestosamente
psychically	psichicamente	pedantically	pedantamente
psychologically	psicologicamente		
rhetorically	retoricamente	-ical-ICALLY	-ale-ALMENTE
rhythmically	ritmicamente	paradoxically	paradossalmente
romantically	romanticamente	theatrically	teatralmente
rustically	rusticamente		
sarcastically	sarcasticamente	-ical-ICALLY	-icale-ICALMENTE
sardonically	sardonicamente	clerically	clericalmente

grammatically	grammaticalmente	tacitly	tacitamente
musically	musicalmente		
pontifically	pontificalmente	-ite-ITELY	-ito-ITAMENTE
radically	radicalmente	eruditely	eruditamente
vertically	verticalmente	infinitely	infinitamente
-id-IDLY	-IDO-idamente	-ive-IVELY	-ivo-IVAMENTE
aridly	aridamente	abusively	abusivamente
avidly	avidamente	actively	attivamente
candidly	candidamente	affirmatively	affermativamente
fervidly	fervidamente	aggressively	aggressivamente
fetidly	fetidamente	alternatively	alternativamente
floridly	floridamente	apprehensively	apprensivamente
fluidly	fluidamente	assertively	assertivamente
gelidly	gelidamente	attractively	attrattivamente
horridly	orridamente	coercively	coercitivamente
intrepidly	intrepidamente	collectively	collettivamente
invalidly	invalidamente	comparatively	comparativamente
languidly	languidamente	competitively	competitivamente
limpidly	limpidamente	conclusively	conclusivamente
lucidly	lucidamente	consecutively	consecutivamente
placidly	placidamente	constructively	costruttivamente
rapidly	rapidamente	contemplatively	contemplativamente
rigidly	rigidamente	copulatively	copulativamente
solidly	solidamente	correlatively	correlativamente
stupidly	stupidamente	decisively	decisivamente
timidly	timidamente	defensively	difensivamente
torpidly	torpidamente	definitively	definitivamente
tumidly	tumidamente	demonstratively	dimostrativamente
turbidly	torbidamente	emotively	emotivamente
turgidly	turgidamente	evasively	evasivamente
validly	validamente	excessively	eccessivamente
vividly	vividamente	exclusively	esclusivamente
		expressively	espressivamente
-ine-INELY	-ino-INAMENTE	extensively	estensivamente
clandestinely	clandestinamente	figuratively	figurativamente
divinely	divinamente	furtively	furtivamente
genuinely	genuinamente	imperatively	imperativamente
		impulsively	impulsivamente
-it-ITLY	-ito-ITAMENTE	incisively	incisivamente
explicitly	esplicitamente	inclusively	inclusivamente
illicitly	illecitamente	inexpressively	inespressivamente
implicitly	implicitamente	insinuatively	insinuativamente
licitly	lecitamente	instinctively	istintivamente

intensively	intensivamente	falsely	falsamente
intransitively	intransitivamente	finely	finemente
intuitively	intuitivamente	firmly	fermamente
inventively	inventivamente	gently	gentilmente
meditatively	meditativamente	graphically	graficamente
negatively	negativamente	gravely	gravemente
objectively	oggettivamente	grotesquely	grottescamente
offensively	offensivamente	honestly	onestamente
passively	passivamente	inhumanly	inumanamente
pejoratively	peggiorativamente	justly	giustamente
persuasively	persuasivamente	largely	largamente
positively	positivamente	precisely	precisamente
primitively	primitivamente	presumably	presumibilmente
productively	produttivamente	profoundly	profondamente
progressively	progressivamente	promptly	prontamente
prohibitively	proibitivamente	properly	propriamente
qualitatively	qualitativamente	repeatedly	ripetutamente
reflectively	riflessivamente	secretly	segretamente
reflexively	riflessivamente	severely	severamente
relatively	relativamente	simply	semplicemente
respectively	rispettivamente	sincerely	sinceramente
sensitively	sensitivamente	solely	solamente
significatively	significativamente	succinctly	succintamente
speculatively	speculativamente	unexpectedly	inaspettatamente
successively	successivamente	uniformly	uniformemente
superlatively	superlativamente	vastly	vastamente
transitively	transitivamente	-nal-NALLY	-no-NAMENTE
vindictively	vendicativamente	eternally	eternamente
Some exceptions:		externally	esternamente
attentively	attentamente	fraternally	fraternamente
derisively	derisoriamente	internally	internamente
insensitively	insensibilmente	maternally	maternamente
pensively	pensosamente	paternally	paternamente

-ly (miscellaneous)	-mente (vari)	-oble-OBLY	See-ble
		The adverbs ending in-ously are assimilated as follows:	
alternatingly	alternatamente	-acious-aciously	-ace-acemente
amply	ampiamente	-arious-ariously	-ario-ariamente
beastly	bestialmente	-eous-eously	-eo-eamente
bravely	bravamente	-ious-iously	-ioso-iosamente
caressingly	carezzevolmente	-itious-itiously	-izio-iziamente
concisely	concisamente	-onymous--ously	-onimo-onimamente
continually	continuamente	-orious-oriously	-orio-oriamente
expressly	espressamente		

-ous-ously — -oso-osamente
-ulous-ulously — -oloso-olosamente
-uous-uously — -uo-uamente

-acious-ACIOUSLY — -ace-acemente
audaciously — audacemente
efficaciously — efficacemente
fallaciously — fallacemente
inefficaciously — inefficacemente
loquaciously — loquacemente
perspicaciously — perspicacemente
pugnaciously — pugnacemente
rapaciously — rapacemente
sagaciously — sagacemente
tenaciously — tenacemente
veraciously — veracemente
vivaciously — vivacemente
voraciously — voracemente

-arious-ARIOUSLY — -ario-ARIAMENTE
nefariously — nefariamente
precariously — precariamente
temerariously — temerariamente
variously — variamente
-eous-EOUSLY — -eo-EAMENTE
erroneously — erroneamente
extemporaneously — estemporaneamente
extraneously — estraneamente
homogeneously — omogeneamente
instantaneously — istantaneamente
simultaneously — simultaneamente
spontaneously — spontaneamente

Exceptions:
courteously — cortesemente
courageously — coraggiosamente

-ious-IOUSLY — -ioso-IOSAMENTE
ambitiously — ambiziosamente
anxiously — ansiosamente
capriciously — capricciosamente
ceremoniously — cerimoniosamente
compendiously — compendiosamente
conscientiously — coscienziosamente

contagiously — contagiosamente
copiously — copiosamente
curiously — curiosamente
deliciously — deliziosamente
dubiously — dubbiosamente
furiously — furiosamente
gloriously — gloriosamente
harmoniously — armoniosamente
ignominiously — ignominiosamente
imperiously — imperiosamente
industriously — industriosamente
injuriously — ingiuriosamente
insidiously — insidiosamente
irreligiously — irreligiosamente
judiciously — giudiziosamente
laboriously — laboriosamente
mysteriously — misteriosamente
obsequiously — ossequiosamente
odiously — odiosamente
officiously — ufficiosamente
parsimoniously — parsimoniosamente
perniciously — perniciosamente
preciously — preziosamente
pretentiously — pretenziosamente
prodigiously — prodigiosamente
religiously — religiosamente
seditiously — sediziosamente
studiously — studiosamente
superstitiously — superstiziosamente
tendentiously — tendenziosamente
vaingloriously — vanagloriosamente
victoriously — vittoriosamente
Exceptions:
atrociously — atrocemente
cautiously — cautamente
ferociously — ferocemente
inauspiciously — inauspicatamente
incautiously — incautamente
ingeniously — ingegnosamente
lasciviously — lascivamente
lugubriously — lugubremente
maliciously — malignamente
notoriously — notoriamente
obviously — ovviamente

218

ostentatiously	ostentatamente
perfidiously	perfidamente
precociously	precocemente
propitiously	propiziamente
seriously	seriamente
-itious-ITIOUSLY	-izio-IZIAMENTE
fictitiously	fittiziamente
propitiously	propiziamente
-onymous—OUSLY	-onimo-ONIMAMENTE
anonymously	anonimamente
homonymously	omonimamente
synonymously	sinonimamente
-orious-ORIOUSLY	-orio-ORIAMENTE
meritoriously	meritoriamente
notoriously	notoriamente
-ous-OUSLY	-oso-OSAMENTE
adventurously	avventurosamente
amorously	amorosamente
calamitously	calamitosamente
clamorously	clamorosamente
desirously	desiderosamente
disastrously	disastrosamente
fabulously	favolosamente
flexuously	flessuosamente
fructuously	fruttuosamente
generously	generosamente
impetuously	impetuosamente
indecorously	indecorosamente
libidinously	libidinosamente
meticulously	meticolosamente
miraculously	miracolosamente
monstrously	mostruosamente
nebulously	nebulosamente
numerously	numerosamente
onerously	onerosamente
perilously	pericolosamente
ponderously	ponderosamente
precipitously (1)	precipitosamente
presumptuously	presuntuosamente
rigorously	rigorosamente
scandalously	scandalosamente

scrupulously	scrupolosamente
sinuously	sinuosamente
sumptuously	sontuosamente
tempestuously	tempestosamente
timorously	timorosamente
tumultuously	tumultuosamente
valorously	valorosamente
vertiginously	vertiginosamente
vigorously	vigorosamente
virtuously	virtuosamente
voluptuously	voluttuosamente
zealously	zelosamente

Some exceptions:

infamously	infamemente

(1) also: precipitevolissimevolmente

-ulous-ULOUSLY	-oloso-OLOSAMENTE
meticulously	meticolosamente
miraculously	miracolosamente
scrupulously	scrupolosamente
-uous-UOUSLY	-uo-UAMENTE
ambiguously	ambiguamente
arduously	arduamente
assiduously	assiduamente
congruously	congruamente
conspicuously	cospicuamente
contiguously	contiguamente
continuously	continuamente
fatuously	fatuamente
incongruously	incongruamente
inconspicuously	incospicuamente
ingenuously	ingenuamente
innocuously	innocuamente
mellifluously	mellifluamente
perspicuously	perspicuamente
promiscuously	promiscuamente
strenuously	strenuamente
superfluously	superfluamente
-uble-UBLY	-See-ble
-ure-URELY	-uro-URAMENTE
immaturely	immaturamente

insecurely	insicuramente
maturely	maturamente
obscurely	oscuramente
prematurely	prematuramente
purely	puramente
-use-USELY	-uso-USAMENTE
abstrusely	astrusamente
diffusely	diffusamente
profusely	profusamente
-ute-UTELY	-uto-UTAMENTE
absolutely	assolutamente
acutely	acutamente
astutely	astutamente
dissolutely	dissolutamente
irresolutely	irresolutamente
minutely	minutamente
resolutely	risolutamente

Exercises

Exercise 1. Given that adverbs are formed by adding *mente* to the adjective, complete the following sentences by forming an adverb from the underlined adjective.

1. Il signor Jones è un uomo <u>elegante</u>. Si veste sempre _____
2. La signora Bianchi era <u>grave</u>. Era stata _____ferita in un incidente stradale.
3. Il professore era molto <u>conciso</u> e <u>preciso</u> nelle sue spiegazioni. Spiegava le regole _____ e _____
4. Il presidente fu molto <u>eloquente</u>. Parlò_____ma non convinse nessuno.
5. L'economia del paese attraversava un periodo <u>lento</u>. Si muoveva _____.
6. Era <u>raro</u> che lui venisse a scuola. Veniva a scuola_____
7. Fu un incidente <u>orribile</u>. Molte persone furono ferite_____.
8. La tavola era stata preparata con cibi <u>abbondanti</u> e <u>deliziosi</u>. Gli invitati avrebbero mangiato _____ e _____.
9. Ti proibisco di parlare in maniera <u>assoluta</u>. Ti proibisco_____di parlare.
10. Era un tipo <u>arrogante</u> e <u>maleducato</u>. Trattava tutti _____ e_____.

Exercise 2. Given the adverbial form, provide the adjective from which it was derived. See the beginning of this section for the general rules.
Example: Fatalmente= fatale

1. Oralmente _____
2. Mentalmente _____
3. Popolarmente _____
4. Regolarmente _____
5. Veramente _____
6. Disperatamente _____
7. Gloriosamente _____
8. Gioiosamente _____
9. Gentilmente _____
10. Comicamente _____

Exercise 3. Give the Italian adjective and the adverb for the following English adverbs: example: positively   <u>positivo</u>   <u>positivamente</u>

1. Victoriously _____ _____
2. Fabulously _____ _____
3. Attractively _____ _____
4. Typically _____ _____
5. Stupidly _____ _____
6. Alternatively _____ _____
7. Horribly _____ _____
8. Considerably _____ _____
9. Solidly _____ _____

10. Partially   _____   _____

Exercise 4. Give the English equivalent of the underlined adverbs.

1. Parlò <u>estemporaneamente.</u>
2. Il ragazzo era <u>relativamente</u> contento dei voti ricevuti.
3. Mario era <u>completamente</u> negato per la matematica.
4. <u>Sfortunatamente</u>, i ragazzi non erano preparati per l'esame.
5. Trattava tutti <u>affabilmente</u> e <u>cortesemente</u>.

Exercise 5. Give the equivalent of the phrases by using an adverb. Example: in maniera delicata. *delicatamente.*

1. In maniera assoluta.   _____
2. In maniera crudele.   _____
3. In maniera gioiosa.   _____
4. In maniera pignola   _____
5. In maniera regolare   _____
6. In maniera intelligente   _____
7. In maniera folle   _____
8. In maniera ridicola   _____
9. In maniera caparbia   _____
10. In maniera dittatoriale   _____

Exercise 5. Paying attention to the root changes, rewrite the following adverbs in Italian. Each adverb contains at least one root change:
Example: symptomatically= *sintomaticamente*

1. peripherically   _____
2. philologically   _____
3. theoretically   _____
4. phonetically   _____
5. spherically   _____
6. skeptically   _____
7. photographically   _____
8. prehistorically   _____
9. psychically   _____
10. rhetorically   _____

APPENDIX A
LATIN WORDS AND PHRASES

ab initio	from the beginning.
ab origine	from the beginning.
ad hoc	for this only.
ad infinitum	to infinity; without limit; endlessly.
ad interim	in the meantime.
ad libitum	to the desire; at one's pleasure.
ad nauseam	to a sickening or disgusting degree.
ad verbum	to the word; verbatim.
Alma Mater	dear mother; a school at which a person has studied.
alter ego	a second self; another exactly the same.
angina pectoris	chest pain.
ante meridiem	before noon.
ars longa, vita brevis	art is long, life is short.
bona fide	in good faith.
carta manet, verba volant	documents remain, words fly away
casus belli	an event or occurrence that brings a declaration of war.
caveat emptor	let the buyer beware.
cogito ergo sum	I think, therefore I am.
corpus delicti	the basic element of a crime
cum laude	with honors.
curriculum vitae	a brief biographic résumé of one's carrier.
de facto	in fact; really.
de jure	according to the law; by right.
de novo	again; anew; from the beginning.
dulcis in fundo	the sweetest at the end.
errando discitur	you learn by mistakes
homo sapiens	the modern man.
humanum est errare	to err is human.
in absentia	in absence.
in aeternum	to eternity, forever.
in flagrante delicto	in the act of committing the offense, crime.
in memoriam	in memory.
in medio stat virtus	moderation is a virtue.
in vino veritas	He who drinks tells the truth.
intelligenti pauca	A word to the wise.
justitia omnibus	justice for all.
lapsus linguae	a slip of the tongue.
lex loci	the law of a place.
lex non scripta	unwritten law; common law.
lex scripta	statute law; written law.
mea culpa	my fault.
memento mori	remember that you must die.

mens sana in corpore sano	a sound mind in a sound body.
modus operandi	mode of operation.
modus vivendi	manner of living.
multum in parvo	much in little.
nemo propheta in patria sua	no one is a prophet in his own country
nolens volens	whether willing or not; willy-nilly.
Noli me tangere	person or thing not to be touched.
nolo contendere	a defendant pleading he did not admit guilt but subjects him to be punished as if he did.
ora pro nobis	pray for us.
pater familias	head of the household or family.
pater patriae	father of his country.
per annum	by the year; yearly.
persona non grata	an unacceptable or unwelcome person.
post bellum	after the war.
post mortem	occurring or pertaining after death
post partum	after birth.
pro bono publico	for the public good.
pro forma	according to form; as a matter of form.
pro rata	in proportion.
qui gladio ferit gladio perit	he who lives by the sword, dies by the sword
quid pro quo	a thing in return for another.
requiescat in pace	may he (she) rest in peace.
risus abundat in ore stultorum	laughter abounds in the mouths of fools
schola cantorum	a school of singer; a choir school.
semper fidelis	always faithful.
sic transit gloria mundi	thus passes away the glory of this world.
sine die	without fixing a future action or day.
sine prole	without descendants, children, etc.
sine qua non	without which not.
si vis pacem para bellum	If you want peace, prepare for war.
status quo	the existing state or condition.
summa cum laude	with highest honor.
tabula rasa	clean slate; to start from the beginning.
talis pater qualis filius	like father like son.
tempus fugit	time flies.
veni, vidi, vici	I came, I saw, I conquered.
verbatim et literatim	word for word and letter by letter.

APPENDIX B
ROME, CRADLE OF LATIN

Latin is the cradle of Italian. Italian is a direct descendant of Latin. There are many word in Latin and Italian that mean the same thing and did not change at all. What follows is a list of a number of these words where no assimilation occurred.

Latin/Italian nouns: English: (identical)

ala	wing	meta	object
amor	love	modestia	modesty
anima	soul	multa	fine
aquila	eagle	nota	note
barba	beard	patria	motherland
bestia	beast	penuria	shortage
campana	bell	perfidia	perfidy
carta	paper	poeta	poet
cella	cell	porta	door
cera	wax	rana	frog
corona	crown	regina	queen
cura	cure	rosa	rose
custodia	custody	scala	ladder
disciplina	discipline	serva	servant
fama	fame	spina	thorn
formica	ant	sporta	basket
gratis	free	terra	land
ignominia	ignominy	tutela	guardianship
invidia	envy	vena	vein
lacrima	tear	vespa	bee
lana	wool	vita	life
lingua	tongue		

In its evolution, Italian usually derived its present form from either the nominative or accusative case of the Latin form. For example: pacem, peace becomes pace; argentum, silver, became argento. What follows is a list of Latin words and their Italian derivatives.

LATIN:	ITALIAN: (derivation)	ENGLISH:
altus	alto	tall, high
calvus	calvo	bald
collum	collo	neck
damnum	danno	damage
difficilis	difficile	difficult

225

Latin	Italian	English
dignus	degno	worthy, deserving
doctus	dotto	learned, erudite
dolor	dolore	pain
dubium	dubbio	doubt
dulcis	dolce	sweat
fungus	fungo	mushroom
gigas, gigantis	gigante	giant
gula	gola	throat
inutilis	inutile	useless
latus	lato	side
liber, libri	libro	book
lupus	lupo	wolf
manus	mano	hand
mas, maris	mare	sea
mentum	mento	chin
musca	mosca	fly
nix, nives	neve	snow
panis	pane	bread
partus	parto	childbirth
petra	pietra	stone
piscis	pesce	fish
pons, pontis	ponte	bridge
pulvis, pulveris	polvere	dust
rex, regis	re	king
risus	riso	laugh
salus, salutis	salute	health
sanguis	sangue	blood
sol, solis	sole	sun
sudor, sudoris	sudore	sweat
tempestas	tempesta	storm
tempus	tempo	time
terrae motus	terremoto	earthquake
titulus	titolo	title
velocitas	velocità	speed
veritas	verità	truth
vinum	vino	wine

VERBS THAT ARE IDENTICAL IN LATIN AND ITALIAN:

Latin/Italian	English	Latin/Italian	English
agitare	to shake	dare	to give
amare	to love	discernere	to discern
cantare	to sing	distinguere	to distinguish
credere	to believe	dividere	to divide

dormire	to sleep	persuadere	to persuade
dubitare	to doubt	ponderare	to ponder
fumare	to smoke	portare	to bring
invadere	to invade	ridere	to laugh
lavare	to wash	sentire	to hear
mordere	to bite	sperare	to hope
navigare	to sail	stabilire	to establish
negare	to deny	superare	to surpass
nominare	to name	vendere	to sell
offendere	to offend	venire	to come
opprimere	to oppress	vincere	to win
peccare	to sin	vivere	to live
pensare	to think	volare	to fly
perire	to perish		

English preserves the Anglo-Saxon noun form, while borrowing the Latin adjectival form

LATIN	ITALIAN NOUN	ENGLISH	ENGLISH	ITALIAN ADJECTIVE
amicus	amico	friend	amicable	amichevole
annus	anno	year	annual	annuale
asinus	asino	donkey	asinine	asinino
bene	bene	well	benevolent	benevolente
bestia	bestia	beast	bestial	bestiale
bos, bovis	bove, bue	ox	bovine	bovino
callum	callo	corn	callous	calloso
canis	cane	dog	canine	canino
capillus	capello	hair	capillary	capillare
caro, carnis	carne	meat	carnal	carnale
centum	cento	hundred	centennial	centennale
coelum	cielo	sky	celestial	celestiale
crux, crucis	croce	cross	cruciferous	crocifero
cutis	cute, pelle	skin	cutaneous	cutaneo
dolor	dolore	pain	dolorous	doloroso
ferrum	ferro	iron	ferrous	ferreo
filius	figlio	son	filial	filiale
finis	fine	end	final	finale
herba	erba	grass	herbaceous	erbaceo
insula	isola	island	insular	insulare
incendium	incendio	fire	incendiary	incendiario
lac, lactis	latte	milk	lactose	lattoso
latus	lato	side	lateral	laterale
male	male	bad	malevolent	malevolente
manus	mano	hand	manual	manuale

227

mas, maris	mare	sea	marine	marino
mater	madre	mother	maternal	materno
matrimonium	matrimonio	marriage	matrimonial	matrimoniale
mundus	mondo	world	mundane	mondano
nasus	naso	nose	nasal	nasale
navis	nave	ship	naval	navale
nox, noctis	notte	night	nocturnal	notturno
os, ossis	osso	bone	osseous	osseo
ovum	uovo	egg	oval	ovale
pater	padre	father	paternal	paterno
pax, pacis	pace	peace	pacific	pacifico
ren, renis	rene	kidney	renal	renale
sol, solis	sole	sun	solar	solare
solus	solo	alone	solitary	solitario
somnus	sonno	sleep	somnolent	sonnolento
ventus	vento	wind	ventilator	ventilatore
vitrum	vetro	glass	vitreous	vitreo
voluntas	volontà	will	voluntary	volontario
vox, vocis	voce	voice	vocal	vocale

Note:

sex	sei	six	sextuple	sestuplo
sexus	sesso	sex	sexual	sessuale

Samples of Derivation and Borrowing:

LATIN (ITALIAN) (verbs)	ENGLISH:	ITALIAN: (derivation)	ENGLISH: (borrowing)
amare (amare)	-to love	amabile	amiable
legere (leggere)	-to read	leggibile	legible
vincere (vincere)	-to win	invincibile	invincible
credere (credere)	-to believe	credibile	credible
portare (portare)	-to bring	portabile	portable
posse (potere)	-can	possibile	possible
videre (vedere)	-to see	visibile	visible
tangere (toccare)	-to touch	tangibile	tangible
mutare (mutare)	-to change	immutabile	immutable
navigare (navigare)	-to sail	navigabile	navigable

The following examples show the common adjectival, verbal and adverbial form. The noun and verbal form remain Anglo-Saxon:

LATIN:	ITALIAN:	ENGLISH:
AQUA	**ACQUA**	**water**

aquatic (acquatico); aqueduct (acquedotto); aqueous (acqueo); aquarium (acquario); aquiculture (acquicoltura); etc.

| CREDERE | CREDERE | to believe |

credible (credìbile); incredible (incredìbile); credo (credo); credibly (credibilmęnte); incredulous (incrędulo); credibility (credibilità); credence (credęnza), etc.

| CULPA | COLPA | fault, to fault |

culpable (colpęvole); culpability (colpevolęzza); culprit (colpęvole); to inculpate (incolpąre); to exculpate (discolpąre); etc.

| DORMIRE | DORMIRE | to sleep |

dormitory (dormitǫrio); dormant, (dormięnte); dormancy (dormięnza), etc.

| FINIS | FINE | end |

final (finąle); to finish (finįre); infinite (infinįto); finalist (finalįsta); semifinalist (semifinalįsta); finally (finalmęnte); indefinitely (indefinitamęnte) etc.

| INITIUM | INIZIO | beginning |

initial (iniziąle); initiative (iniziatįva); to initiate (iniziąre); initiation (iniziazįǫne, inįzio); initially (inizialmęnte) etc.

| LEGERE | LEGGERE | to read |

legible (leggįbile); legibility (leggibilità); illegible (illeggįbile); legend (leggęnda), etc.

| LEX, LEGIS | LEGGE | law |

legal (legąle); legality (legalità); to legalize (legalizząre);
legislation (legislazįǫne); legislator (legislatǫre); legislative (legislatįvo), etc.

| LINGUA | LINGUA | tongue |

lingual (linguąle); linguist (linguįsta); linguistic (linguįstico); linguistics (linguįstica); bilingual (bilįngue) etc.

| LUNA | LUNA | moon |

lunar (lunąre); lunatic (lunątico); lunation (lunazįǫne); lunate (lunąto); lunacy (pazzįa), etc.

| LUX, LUCIS | LUCE | light |

lucent (lucęnte); lucidity (lucidità) ; lucid (lųcido); Lucifer (Lucįfero); lucency (lucentęzza), etc.

| MENS, | MENTIS MENTE | mind |

mental (mentąle); mentality (mentalità); mentally (mentalmęnte) etc.

| MORS, | MORTIS MORTE | death |

mortal (mortąle); mortality (mortalità); mortuary (mortuąrio); to immortalize (immortaląre), moribund (moribǫndo, moręnte), etc.

| MULTUS | MOLTO/MULTI | much, many |

multiply (moltiplicąre); multiplication (moltiplicazįǫne); multitude (moltitųdine); (multiple (mųltiplo); multiplicity (molteplicità); multiform (multifǫrme); multimillionaire (multimillionąrio); multilateral (multilaterąle) etc.

| NATUS | NATO | born |

natal (natąle); nativity (natività); native (natįvo); neonatal (neonatąle), etc.

| OCULUS | OCCHIO | eye |

ocular (oculąre); oculist (oculįsta); oculistic (oculįstico) etc.

| PECCATUM | PECCATO | sin |

peccable (peccąbile); impeccable (impeccąbile); peccability (peccabilità); peccancy (peccąto), etc.

| PECTUS | PETTO | chest |

pectic (pęttico); pectoral (pettorąle); parapet (parapętto), etc.

PES, PEDIS	**PIEDE**	**foot**

pedal (pedạle); pedestrian (pedọne, pedẹstre); pedicụre (pedicure); to pedal (pedalạre); pedestal (piedistạllo) etc.

TERRA	**TERRA**	**earth**

terrestrial (terrẹstre); territory (territọrio); terracotta (terracọtta); terraqueous (terrạcqueo); terrafirma (terrafẹrma) etc.

VITA	**VITA**	**life**

vitality (vitalità); vital (vitạle); vitamin (vitamịna); vitals (ọrgani vịtali); to vitaminize (vitaminizzạre); longevity (longevità), etc.

APPENDIX C:
LOAN WORDS

The following words are common to both English and Italian. In some cases, where the words were derived from Latin they will be the same in three languages. Naturally, the rules of pronunciation governing each language will apply. Thus, the word "incognito" will have the "gn" sound in English while in Italian the "gn" sound will be pronounced like the Spanish ñ in "mañana". In addition, the stress will fall on the first "o" while in English the stress falls on the second "i". There are some exceptions, however. If the word is of American or English derivation, it will be pronounced as it is in the original language. Thus, "baby sitter" will be the same in both languages. If the word is an Italian musical term such as "allegro" "con brio" or "andante" it will be pronounced as it would be in Italian. For the rest, American speakers will pronounce Italian words following the rules of their language. This sometimes results in sounds that are quite different and at times have little resemblance to the original, such as in "tutti-frutti" or "Bologna". The American pronunciation of the consonant "t" makes it close to an Italian "r". Thus, in Italian the sound of these two words would be written as "turi fruri" and "baloni".

a cappella (mus.)
a tempo (mus.)
a tergo
abracadabra
abulia (med.)
acacia
acetone
acme
acne
acre
acridine
adagio (mus.)
addax
addendum
adenoma (med.)
aerosol
affettuoso (mus.)
afro
agave
agenda
agile
agora
aids
airedale terrier
Alamo
albino
album
albuminuria
alfa
alga
algebra
alias
alibi
Alice
alla breve (mus.)
allargando (mus.)
allegretto (mus.)
allegro (mus.)
alleluia
alligator
aloe
alpaca
altissimo (mus.)
alto (mus.)
ambrosia
amen

ametropia
amnesia
amorino
ampere
analgesia
anasarca (path.)
andante (mus.)
androsterone (biol.)
anemia
anemone
angelus
angina
angioma (med.)
angora
angostura
anosmia (pathol.)
antenna
antimissile
antipasto
antitrust
antonomasia
aorta
aplasia (pathol.)
apnea
apologia
arapaima
araucaria
architrave
area
arena
aria (Mus.)
arietta (mus.)
arioso (mus.)
arista
armadillo
arnica
aroma
arpeggio (mus.)
ars poetica
art director
artemisia
aspidistra
aster
atelier
audio
auditing

aura
aureola
aurora
autobus
autoclave
automobile
avocado
azalea
azotemia
babà
baby
baby sitter
baby-doll
baccarat
bacon
baguette
bambino
banana
banana split
banderol(e)
bantu
bar
barbecue
barracuda
base
baseball
basilica
basso (mus.)
bassorilievo
bauxite
bazar
bazooka
beat
begonia
belcanto
Beluga
benzene
beta
bibliomania
bile
bireme
blitz
bluff
bob (sport)
bolero
bonsai

bonus
boogie woogie
boom
boomerang
booster
boss
bossa nova
bouquet
boy-scout
bravo
buffet
bulimia
bulldog
bulldozer
bunker
by-pass
byte
cabaret
cacao
camorra
camper
cappuccino
carcinoma (pathol.)
carillon
carotene (chem.)
cash and carry
cassia
cast
cavatina (mus.)
caveat
cavetto (archit.)
cella (archit.)
champagne
chance
chaperon
charleston
chassis
check up
chewing gum
chintz
ciao
cicerone
cicisbeo
cinema
clan
clergyman

climax
clip
clone
clown
club
cobra
coke
coma
computer
condor
consommé
cornea (anat.)
cornucopia
cortisone
credo
cupola
curriculum
decade
deficit
Delta
dessert
detective
diastole (med.)
diesel
dilemma
diploma
diva
docile
dogma
dolce vita
dose
duo
duplex
Eden
ego
enigma
era
erotomania
errata
Esperanto
facsimile
factotum
Fatima
fauna
fertile
fiasco

fibula (anat.)
film
floppy disk
flora
formica (plastic)
formula
forum
gabardine
garage
gardenia
gas
ghetto
gigolo
glaucoma
gondola
gong
gorilla
gratis
habitat
habitué
hamburger
hangar
hard core
harem
harmonium
hashish
high fidelity
hit
hobby
hockey (sport)
hooligan
hot dog
hotel
humus
idea
igloo
immune
imprimatur
in memoriam
in vitro
inane
incognito
infantile
inferno
influenza
interim

iota
jazz
jazz-band
jeans
jeep
jet
jet-set
jet-society
jockey
jogging
judo
jujitsu
juke-box
jumbo jet
kamikaze
kapok
kaputt
karate
kayak
Kenia
ketchup
killer
kleenex
knock-out
larva
lasagna
lasso
lava
leadership
leucite
leucoma
libido
Libra
lira
loggia
logos
long playing
macula (anat.)
Madonna
maestro
magenta
magma
magnate
magnesia
magnolia
majorette

malaria
Maltese
mambo
mamma
manganese
mango
mania
manicure
manicure
manna
mantissa (math.)
mascara
matador
Mecca
mediocre
medusa
meeting
megalomania
memento
memorandum
menu
mercantile
meteorite
miasma
micron
mimosa
missile
mohair
monomania
motel
mozzarella
mulatto
nadir
nausea
neon
night-club
nostalgia
nylon
oboe
ocelot
ode
odontalgia
ok
omega
opera
orchestra

organza
Oscar
overdose
P.S.
pagoda
panacea
pancreas
panda
panorama
paranoia
part time
partner
partnership
pasta
patina
pedicure
petunia
photo finish
piano
Pinocchio
pizza
pizzeria
placenta
plasma
platina
pleura (anat.)
poker
polo (sport)
pompon
pony

pro forma
propaganda
pro-rata
prosciutto
quorum
radio
radon
referendum
retina
robot
rodeo
roulette
rugby
rum
rumba
safari
saga
saliva
salmonella
samba
sarcoma (med.)
sari
satellite
satin
sauna
sciatica
scintilla
self-service
senile
shampoo

Siamese
sigma
soprano
SOS
sottovoce
souvenir
sport
standard
stereo
sterile
stress
sublime
tandem
tango
tapioca
TB
tennis
terracotta
testosterone
tiara
tibia (anat.)
toga
transistor
trauma
traveler's cheque
trio
trireme
trombone
tunnel
tuttifrutti

UFO
ulna
ultimatum
USA
utopia
vademecum
vagina
velocipede
veranda
versatile
veto
vile
villa
virile
virus
vodka
volatile
volume
vulva (anat.)
week-end
yacht
yen
yoga
yucca
zebra
zero
Zulu

Exercises

Exercise 1. In the following sentences, identify the words that are identical in Italian and English by underlining them.

1. La terra era molto fertile perché anticamente vi era passata la lava.
2. Non sono bravo in algebra e nemmeno in Esperanto, ma sono bravo a fare la pizza.
3. A Roma la gente fa la dolce vita andando da un night-club all'altro.
4. Un film di Fellini parla di una diva dell'opera.
5. Quel leader è un enigma. Il suo curriculum offre un panorama sulla politica italiana.
6. Il manifesto dei giovani musicisti ha creato un dilemma per i virtuosi del jazz.
7. Preferisco un cappuccino al bar.
8. Con l'età non sono più agile come prima. Ora preferisco l'automobile allo scooter.
9. Il boom edilistico dell'ultima stagione da un'idea della mania di costruire palazzi sempre più grandi.
10. I signori Lanza ci hanno invitati a un barbecue insieme al loro partner.

Exercise 2. Read the description and provide a word common to English and Italian that fits best: example: la musica di Verdi è straordinariamente bella, è veramente <u>sublime.</u> Check your answers on page 240.

1. Una proposta definitiva e perentoria a cui bisogna rispondere entro un limite di tempo. _ _ _ _ _ _ _ _ _(sette lettere)
2. La coppia non poteva avere bambini perché il marito era _ _ _ _ _ _ _ (7 lettere).
3. Era un uomo molto abile e _ _ _ _ _ _ _ _ _. Sapeva fare tanti mestieri (9 lettere).
4. Il signor Jones era molto anziano ma aveva tutte le sue facoltà mentali. Non era affatto _ _ _ _ _ _ (6 lettere).
5. Ci sono ormai varie dozzine di _ _ _ _ _ _ _ _ _ (9 lettere) che girano attorno alla terra.
6. Hanno indetto un _ _ _ _ _ _ _ _ _ _ (10 lettere) per sapere che legalizzare il divorzio.
7. Dio è l'Alfa e l'_ _ _ _ _ (5 lettere) l'inizio e la fine di tutto.
8. La signora non si sentiva bene ogni mattina. Le veniva un po' di _ _ _ _ _ _(6 lettere).
9. Vado a vedere un film ogni sera. Mi piace il _ _ _ _ _ _(6 lettere) italiano.
10. A giugno i ragazzi della scuola media hanno finito la scuola e hanno ricevuto il loro _ _ _ _ _ _ _ (7 lettere).

APPENDIX D
GREEK BORROWING
* denotes root change.

-ITIS	-ITE	-GRAPHY	-GRAFÌA
appendicitis	appendicite	choreography*	coreografia
arthritis*	artrite	ethnography*	etnografia
encephalitis*	encefalite	geography	geografia
hepatitis*	epatite	-CRACY	-CRAZIA
-LOGY	-LOGIA	bureaucracy*	burocrazia
archaeology*	archeologia	plutocracy	plutocrazia
bacteriology*	batteriologia	-EM	-EMA
cardiology	cardiologia	apothem*	apotema
-SIS	-SI	poem	poema
analysis*	analisi	theorem*	teorema
apotheosis*	apoteosi	-ECTOMY	-ETOMIA/ECTOMIA
crisis	crisi	appendectomy*	appendicetomia
-PATHY	-PATIA	mastectomy	mastectomia
apathy	apatia	tonsillectomy	tonsillectomia
homeopathy*	omeopatia	-ARCHY	-ARCHIA
psychopathy*	psicopatia	anarchy	anarchia
-PHOBIA	-FOBIA	hierarchy*	gerarchia
agoraphobia	agorafobia	oligarchy	oligarchia
hydrophobia*	idrofobia	-ICIAN	-ICO
xenophobia	xenofobia	academician*	accademico
obstetrician*	ostetrico	metaphysician*	metafisico
agronomy	agronomia		
astronomy	astronomia		
autonomy	autonomia		
gastronomy	gastronomia		
physiognomy*	fisionomia		

As an aid to the student the following is a short list of the meaning of some Latin and Greek suffixes and prefixes and combining forms.

Abbreviation: s.a. = See also.

Lat.	altus/ altitudo	height	altezza	altitude	altitudine
Lat.	annus	year	anno	annual	annuale
Gr.	anthropos	man	uomo	anthropology	antropologia
Lat.	aqua	water	acqua	aquatic	acquatico
Gr.	arch	first, chief	primo	archangel	arcangelo
Gr.	archy	rule, government	comando, capo	monarchy	monarchia

236

Lat.	astro	star	stella	astrology	astrologia
Gr.	auto	self	stesso	autobiography	autobiografia
Lat.	bellum	war	guerra	bellicose	bellicoso
Lat.	bene	good; well	bene	benefactor	benefattore
Gr.	bi	life	vita	biology	biologia
Lat.	bi, bin-	two, twice	due	bilingual	bilingue
Gr.	cardio	heart	cuore	cardiology	cardiologia
Lat.	carn	meat	carne	carnal	carnale
Lat.	centi	hundred	cento	centimeter	centimetro
Gr.	cephalous	brain	cervello	cephalic	cefalico
Lat.	cide	kill	uccidere	matricide	matricidio
Lat.	circum	around	intorno	circumference	circonferenza
Gr.	cracy	rule, government	dominio, potere	democracy	democrazia
Gr.	crat	one who advocates rule	chi patrocinia	autocrat	autocrate
Lat.	decem	ten	dieci	decennium	decennio
Gr.	demo	people	popolo	democracy	democrazia
Lat.	dentem (s.a.odonto]	tooth	dente	dentist	dentista
Gr.	derm(at)	skin	pelle	dermatology	dermatologia
Lat.	deus (s.a. theo)	God	Dio	deification	deificazione
Lat.	dico, dicto	say	dire	verdict	verdetto
Gr.	drome	run, course	corsa	hyppodrome	ippodromo
Gr.	ectomy	surgical removal of	asportazione	appendectomy	appendicectomia
Lat.	ego	I	io	egoism	egoismo
Lat.- Gr.	etymo	meaning	significato	etymology	etimologia
Gr.	eu	well, good	bene	euphonic	eufonico
Lat.	florem	flower	fiore	floriculture	fioricultura
Lat.	frater	brother	fratello	fraternal	fraterno
Lat.	fratri	brother	fratello	fratricide	fratricida
Gr.	ge	earth	terra	geology	geologia
Lat.- Gr.	gen, gene	born	nascere, genere	generation	generazione
Gr.	glossa	tongue, language	lingua	glossary	glossario
Gr.	gon	angle	angolo	polygon	poligono
Gr.	graphy	writing	scrivere	biography	biografia
Lat.	grat	pleasing, grateful	grato	gratitude	gratitudine
		half	metà	hemisphere	emisfero

Gr.	hipp	horse	cavallo	hippopotamus	ippopotamo
Gr.	hydro	water	acqua	hydraulic	idraulico
Gr.	hyper	over, above	sopra	hypertension	ipertensione
Gr.	iasis	diseased condition	malattia	psoriasis	psoriasi
Gr.	ic	pertaining to	che riguarda	biologic	biologico
Gr.	ician	specialist in	specialista in	technician	tecnico
Gr.	ics	science, art or study of	scienza, studio	linguistics	linguistica
Lat.	infans, infantis	infant, child	infante	infantile	infantile
Gr.	ism	belief in	dottrina, teoria	idealism	idealismo
Gr.	ist	the one who believes in	chi crede in	romanticism	romanticismo
Gr.	itis	inflammation	infiammazione	appendicites	appendicite
Gr.	kilo	thousand	mille	kilogram	chilogrammo
Gr.	klepto	thief	ladro	kleptomaniac	cleptomane
Lat.	lactem	milk	latte	lacteous	latteo
Lat.	librum (s.a.biblion)	book	libro	library	libreria
Lat.-Gr.	logy	study, science	studio	geology	geologia
Lat.	lucem	light	luce	lucid	lucido
Lat.	luna	moon	luna	lunatic	lunatico
Lat.	male, mal	ill, bad, evil	male, cattivo	malediction	maledizione
Lat.	manus	hand	mano	manual	manuale
Lat.	mare	sea	mare	marina	marina
Lat.	mater	mother	madre	maternal	materno
Lat.	matri	mother	madre	matricide	matricidio
Lat.	memoria	memory	memoria	memorable	memorabile
Lat.	mentem	mind	mente	mental	mentale
Gr.	metre	mother	madre	metropolis	metropoli
Gr.	micro	small	piccolo	microphone	microfono
Lat.-	mille (s.a.kilo)	thousand	mille	millimeter	millimetro
Gr.	mono (s.a.uni)	single	singolo	monocle	monocolo
Gr.	morpho	form, shape	forma	morphology	morfologia
Lat.	mortem	death	morte	mortal	mortale
Gr.	mytho	myth	mito	mythology	mitologia
Lat.	nasus	nose	naso	nasal	nasale
Gr.	nauticus	navigator	navigatore	astronaut	astronauta
Lat.-Gr.	neo	new, recent	nuovo, recente	neoclassicism	neoclassicismo
Lat.	noctem	night	notte	nocturn	notturno
Lat.	novem	nine	nove	november	novembre
Lat.	novus	new	nuovo	novelty	novità

Lat.	nudus	naked	nudo	nudity	nudità
Lat.	octo	eight	otto	october	ottobre
Lat.	oculus	eye	occhio	oculist	oculista
Gr.	odont	tooth	dente	orthodontic	ortodontico
Gr.	oma	tumor	tumore	osteoma	osteoma
Lat.	omnis	all	tutto	omnipotent	onnipotente
Gr.	opto	sight	vista	optometry	optometria
Gr.	ortho	straight, right, correct	corretto, esatto	orthography	ortografia
Gr.	osis	diseased condition	condizione, malattia	osteoporosis	osteoporosi
Gr.	osteo	bone	osso	osteopathy	osteopatia
Lat.	ovum	egg	uovo	oval	ovale
Lat.	pater	father	padre	paternity	paternità
Gr.	pathy	decease, suffering	malattia, sofferenza	osteopathy	osteopatia
Gr.	pathy	feeling,	sentimento	antipathy	antipatia
Lat.	patri	father	padre	patricide	patricidio
Lat.	pectus	chest	petto	pectoral	pettorale
Lat.	pedem	foot	piede	pedestrian	pedone, pedestre
Gr.	penta	five	cinque	pentagon	pentagono
Lat.	petra	stone	pietra	petrify, v.	pietrificare
Gr.	philo	lover	amante	philology	filologia
Gr.	phobia	fear, hatred of	paura	hydrophobia	idrofobia
Gr.	phono	sound	suono	telephone	telefono
Lat.	piscis	fish	pesce	piscatory	piscatorio
Gr.	polis	city	città	metropolis	metropoli
Gr.	poly	much, many	molti	polygamy	poligamia
Lat.	primus	first	primo	primary	primario
Lat.	profundus	deep	profondo	profundity	profondità
Gr.	pseudo	false	falso	pseudonym	pseudonimo
Gr.	psycho	mind	mente	psychology	psicologia
Lat.	quadr-quadri	four	quattro	quadruplicate	quadruplicare, v.
Lat.	quinque	five	cinque	quinquennial	quinquenniale
Lat.	radix	root	radice	radical	radicale
Lat.	rect	straight	retto	rectilinear	rettilineo
Lat.	sanguinem	blood	sangue	sanguineous	sanguigno, sanguineo
Lat.	scriptum	written	scritto	scriptural	scritturale
Lat.	senilis	old	vecchio	senility	senilità
Lat.	septem	seven	sette	september	settembre
Lat.	sex	six	sei	sextet	sestetto
Lat.	sexus	sex	sesso	sexuality	sessualità

Gr.	sis	act of	azione	analysis	analisi
Gr.	sophy	wisdom	saggezza	philosophy	filosofia
Gr.	tele	distance, far	distanza	television	televisione
Lat.	terra	earth	terra	terrene	terreno
Gr.	theo (s.a.deus) God		Dio	Theology	Teologia
Gr.	therapy	treatment	cura	psychotherapy	psicoterapia
Gr.	therm	heat	calore	thermostat	termostato
Gr.	tic	pertaining to	che riguarda	poetic	poetico
Gr.	tics	science, art or study of	scienza, studio	mathematics	matematica
Gr.	tomy	See ectomy			
Gr.	topo (1)	place	luogo	topography	topografia
Lat.-Gr.	tri	three	tre	triangle	triangolo
Lat.	uni- (s.a.mono)	one	one	unification	unificazione
Lat.	uxor [ussor]	wife	moglie	uxoricide	uxoricida, ussoricida
Lat.	ventus	wind	vento	ventilation	ventilazione
Lat.	video	see	vedere	evident	evidente
Lat.	vita	life	vita	vital	vitale
Lat.	vocem	voice	voce	vocalize, v.	vocalizzare

(1) Note: Topo in Italian means mouse.

Answers to exercise 2, p. 235.

1. ultimatum
2. sterile
3. versatile
4. senile
5. satellite
6. referendum
7. omega
8. nausea
9. cinema
10. diploma

APPENDIX E
ENGLISH BORROWINGS FROM LATIN

Italian and English share an extensive common vocabulary, by virtue of their *derivation* and *borrowing* from Latin.

In order to simplify conversion, each word will be divided to show its ROOT and a DESINENCE.

English borrowed many Latin words in their entirety. Italian follows very closely the Latin model, but changes the endings as shown:

LATIN:	ENGLISH:	ITALIAN:
	Latin and English invariable:	Assimilation of desinence only:
EX	EX	ICE
apex	apex	apice
vortex	vortex	vortice
index	index	indice
IX/YX	IX/YX	ICE
appendix	appendix	appendice
cervix	cervix	cervice
onyx	onyx	onice
OR	OR	ORE
orator	orator	oratore
senator	senator	senatore
professor	professor	professore
UM	UM	O
decorum	decorum	decoro
forum	forum	foro
stadium	stadium	stadio
US	US	O
apparatus	apparatus	apparato
colossus	colossus	colosso
genius	genius	genio
nucleus	nucleus	nucleo
US		O

Usually Latin adjectives ending in (id)*us* drop the *us* in English:

fluidus	fluid	fluido
liquidus	liquid	liquido
solidus	solid	solido

Note:

LATIN:	ENGLISH:	ITALIAN:
Latin and Italian invariable	Root and desinence	Desinence assimilation only
root	assimilation	
caritas	charity	carità
castitas	chastity	castità

but the following shows root and desinence assimilation for both languages:

| iurisprudentia | jurisprudence | giurisprudẹnza |
| iusticia | justice | giustịzia |

Examples in which the only thing that changes is the desinence

LATIN:	ENGLISH:	ITALIAN:
impeccabilis	impeccable	impeccạbile
implacabilis	implacable	implacạbile
distantia	distance	distạnza
elegantia	elegance	elegạnza
destinatio	destination	destinaziọne
deliberatio	deliberation	deliberaziọne
convocatio	convocation	convocaziọne
sapiens	sapient	sapiẹnte
prudens	prudent	prudẹnte
intelligens	intelligent	ntelligẹnte
intelligentia	intelligence	intelligẹnza
innocentia	innocence	innocẹnza
eloquentia	eloquence	eloquẹnza
incredibilis	incredible	incredịbile
credibilis	credible	credịbile
possibilis	possible	possịbile
confessio	confession	confessiọne
missio	mission	missiọne
digestio	digestion	digestiọne
tranquillitas	tranquillity	tranquillità
divinitas	divinity	divinità
libertas	liberty	libertà
pubertas	puberty	pubertà

Examples of English borrowing from Latin without assimilation:

LATIN/ENGLISH:	ITALIAN:	LATIN/ENGLISH:	ITALIAN:
-or	**-ore**	**-us**	**-o**
clamor	clamọre	asparagus	asparago
color	colọre	census	censo
educator	educatọre	corpus	corpo
fervor	fervọre	discus	disco
furor	furọre	fetus	feto
gladiator	gladiatọre	fungus	fungo
inventor	inventọre	impetus	ịmpeto
liberator	liberatọre	minor	minọre
motor	motọre	radius	radio
		uterus	ụtero

MEMBRE DE SCABRINI MEDIA

Québec, Canada
2003